THE DANCE
OF Legislation

Eric Redman

SIMON AND SCHUSTER   NEW YORK

For My Parents,
Marj and Mac Redman

CONTENTS

FOREWORD 11

PREFACE 15

I FIRST STIRRINGS 25

II BEGINNER'S LESSONS 39

III GETTING SERIOUS 53

IV A FRESH START 73

V S. 4106: BORN OR STILLBORN? 98

VI A SENATE HEARING 114

VII DECISION IN THE SENATE 138

VIII LOOSE ENDS 163

IX INTERLUDE 187

X DOCTORS IN THE HOUSE 216

XI A WAR OF NERVES 233

XII A NEW YEAR'S RESOLUTION 260

EPILOGUE 286

APPENDIX 297

LIST OF ABBREVIATIONS 309

INDEX 311

Once begin the dance of legislation, and you must struggle through its mazes as best you can to the breathless end—if any end there be.

—Woodrow Wilson,
Congressional Government

FOREWORD

Imagine yourself fresh from college, a Rhodes scholarship ahead of you, temporarily in Washington as junior staffer for a senior Senator and given scope by him to try to put a bill through Congress: a good bill—a health bill—a bill you care about. Imagine that, and you are in Ric Redman's shoes at the start of this book.

The book is a delight.

From there, it takes you on Ric's way precisely as *he* went —first-person, present tense—racing and stumbling, sometimes fumbling, in pursuit of action on his bill until its fate is sealed. I shall not reveal the result. That would be as unfair as unveiling the denouement of a murder mystery. For this is a thriller too, and part of the pleasure lies in letting it happen to you as it did to him.

Trying to make something happen on Capitol Hill can be absorbing, exhausting, exciting, dull, frustrating in turn, and also great fun. These feelings are conveyed with an immediacy as engaging as it is unusual. I know no other book that so evokes the spirit of the thing, including the fun.

There is a certain magic about having youth and scope and a perceived good cause in that last refuge of free enterprise, the United States Senate. Redman makes this manifest. It is one with the magic that in other times touched other parts of Washington. His enjoyment has a lot in common with the zest of civil rights-ers in the sixties, Marshall Planners, young New Dealers, or still earlier, T.R.'s Progressives.

With the same immediacy Redman conjures up the spirit of the legislative process in Washington—each bill an Eliza crossing the ice, a Pauline in perpetual peril. And not alone the spirit: this book offers also, in the nicest way, a rich array of facts about Congressional procedures, personalities, and points of view—nicest because interwoven with the story, integral to it, emerging from it; not in the least textbookish, yet informative on many scores beyond the reach of textbooks.

Redman does not purport to "tell all" about Congress. He tells what he found as he chased one bill (and that a relatively small one). The chase does not happen to have traversed bedrooms, or triggered psychoses, or trailed through the lairs of the corporate lobbies. Redman reads neither like Alan Drury nor like a Nader report.

Neither does he read like the account his Senator or a cosponsor or a House sponsor or any of their senior staffs might offer. This book is intensely personal, hence unavoidably—and quite avowedly—parochial. It concentrates upon the things that Redman did and saw, and on his own associates—above all, "his" Senator. As befits a Senate staffer, Redman is intensely loyal. His affectionate view of his boss is part of the charm of the book.

Because Redman's story is both vivid and concrete, his book illuminates a lot of the terrain on which contemporary issues of Congressional reform will be fought out. The bill owed its beginnings to the privileged access of a Senator's constituent—the *causeur* in this case—in combination with the Senator's seniority, hence status, and staff. Access, seniority, staff; to these add cooperative colleagues, assiduous effort, and happy accident. The bill is kept alive by their interaction. Enmity downtown at departmental levels turns out in this instance to be functional, as good as friendship, possibly better.

None of this need have been so. None of it is guaranteed to any cause, however meritorious. Much of it, indeed, is almost guaranteed *against,* absent the link of access to seniority. For those who care about Congressional reform, the way this cuts depends upon the causes they espouse. Redman's story suggests the connections.

Redman has a classic Capitol Hill reaction to the "bureaucrats" downtown. It is mildly paranoid—sometimes not so mildly. They probably returned his feelings. The bill his Senator sought happened, coincidentally, to threaten a reorganization plan maturing at the upper levels of the Nixon Administration. A twenty-one-year-old, astride a Senator's seniority, barring the way to management reform may have been no less galling to his adversaries than they to him.

Mutual paranoia is not the only form of interaction between staffs on the Hill and staffs downtown. Another is mutual assistance. This too is classic in its widespread character, although it naturally does not affect the same staffs at the same time. Redman's story gives a glimpse of this as well. The bureau chief with most to gain from the bill and most to lose from the reorganization had relations as warm with Senators and staff as theirs were cold with the reorganizers.

I stress these aspects of the Redman story—which themselves are incidental in its telling—because they underscore the most ironic thing about a bill like this: its indeterminacy in ensuring a real-world result. If the bill should pass, there will be need for bureaucratic counterparts of Redman's Senator and associates, even perhaps of Redman, moving things along from printed statute to delivered services. Otherwise, nothing may happen. These new men may be far removed from the initial team—removed not only in location but in spirit. So unwanted things may happen.

Thus the ultimate hazards in the legislative process are administrative: not on Capitol Hill but off it, down the Avenue. Redman is aware of this—witness his Epilogue, an important part of the book. But he rightly keeps *his* story-telling focused on the Hill. Those ultimate hazards become someone else's story.

Never mind; one story at a time. The Congressional story has never been better told. I can think of no happier way to gain an introduction to the legislative process.

More than a delight, the book enlightens.

RICHARD E. NEUSTADT

Cambridge, Massachusetts
February, 1973

PREFACE

What is this book about? That's a peculiar question for the author to ask, I know; like John Alden, the book should speak for itself. I hope it does—but frankly, the manuscript created some confusion among those who read it in its first draft form.

What I *hope* this book is about is "the dance of legislation," particularly in the U.S. Senate, and I hope it imparts some of the fascination that Woodrow Wilson and thousands of people since have felt for the conditions of life and work on Capitol Hill. The book did not grow out of (nor, I hope, into) a presumption that I could adequately capture the intricacies and rhythm of the Senate, but rather out of the frustration that no one else had really done so either. I first felt this frustration shortly after I became a Senate staff man, long before the events described here took place, and it became acute when I was simultaneously working in the Senate and trying to complete my undergraduate thesis. The thesis concerned certain aspects of the Senate and how it functions, and I based my argument primarily on my own observations. To pass academic inspection, however, the thesis needed to demonstrate what scholars call "a familiarity with the literature" on the Senate, and as my deadline drew near, I spent many nights in the Congressional Reading Room of the Library of Congress. The disconcerting result of this last-minute research was that the books I read seemed to describe a wholly different institution from the one I worked in and had come to know, if only imperfectly, a block away. The more I read, the more difficult it became to reconcile these dry academic analyses with the excitement and diversity I had found in the Senate, and I began to wonder if a demonstration of "familiarity with the literature" could be incorporated successfully into a thesis purporting to demonstrate a familiarity with the Senate itself.

Perhaps the academic literature on the Senate was never so deficient as I then imagined (except in the thesis, I've never pretended to be a thorough scholar), and no doubt a number of worthwhile studies have appeared since. But I *believed* the literature to be inadequate, and that belief—in someone accustomed to placing great faith in academic writing—helps explain the origins and purpose of this book.

I found in the literature two major misconceptions. The first was that the President had eclipsed the Senate, and Congress as a whole, in the performance of the legislative function. One professor I had respected in college expressed this view most starkly when he wrote that Congress had become merely a place to "amend and delay." The Executive Branch, he went on, had become the "aggressive spirit" in the American legislative process, and Congress was now little more than a vestigial legislative body, capable of "asserting its power or passing laws—but not both." Such pronouncements were surprising, to say the least, when I read them in early 1970. Congress was then bursting with legislative initiative; if anything, the President and his subalterns lived by the creed of "amend and delay." It seemed the scholars had been a bit hasty in driving the last nails into Congress' coffin: Congress was not yet dead as a legislative force, and seemed in fact to be enjoying a hearty rejuvenation, despite the post–New Deal growth of Presidential power that evidently dazzled the scholars so. Perhaps the literature was too simplistic (is power, to use the academic jargon, really a "zero-sum game," or can the President increase his without diminishing Capitol Hill's?). Perhaps, too, the academics—like so many reporters—had simply swallowed too many White House press releases without the requisite grains of salt. This is not to say that the power to pass laws and the power to control public policy necessarily go hand in hand; if nothing else, the Nixon era has taught us how little a law can mean. But it is one thing to say the President dominates policy-making, especially in foreign affairs, and quite another to assume he dominates the legislative process as well.

The second shortcoming of the literature related directly to the first, I felt. It lay in the implicit assumption that the Senate as an institution is made up solely of the one hundred men and women who are Senators. In the postwar era, however, the Senate staff has grown to approximately 3,000 individuals—a fact the literature rarely noted, and less often examined. It was as if the academic community had looked at the glamorous and highly visible tip of an iceberg and declared that tip to *be* the iceberg; the other 97 percent of the individuals who draw their pay from the Senate Disbursing Office, and who support that tip, were simply left in the murky depths. Any self-respecting staff member would inevitably take umbrage at such a slight; but more important, anyone who knew the Senate would know that to ignore the role of staff is to ignore not only Senate reality but the key reason why the Senate is still capable of vying with the President for legislative leadership (the same could be said, of course, for the House of Representatives). The point is worth stating more bluntly: Congress is *not* dependent on the Executive Branch for legislative inspiration and guidance, because Congress has resources of its own—and the key resource is an extensive staff system.* Yet the best-known academic works on the Senate mention staff only in passing, if at all. One writer, for example, considered staffs significant only because they provide psychological clues to Senators themselves; how a Senator selects and utilizes his staff is a sort of "political Rorschach test," he wrote, and then blithely moved on to another topic without analyzing even this proposition. Most other books or articles on the Senate dismiss the role of staff with a hackneyed academic judgment: "further study is needed in this area."

How can an outsider acquire a "feel" for the Senate (much less contemplate working there) if he is told that the President commands the legislative heights, and if only a small—albeit important—portion of the Senate community is described to him? The answer, I think, is that he can't. And this is a major failing of most academic writing on the subject: it suggests little of the drama, the purposefulness, or the fun of the "dance of legislation" because it describes little of the inventiveness and diversity of the Senate, and Senate life.

I suppose the shortcomings of scholarly studies would have rankled me less had the other forms of Senate literature—fiction and journalism—not been misleading in their own ways. I enjoyed novels about the Senate (particularly *Advise and Consent, The Senator,* and *Washington,*

---

* Staff is not the only resource, of course. "Outside" experts now advise Congress as frequently as they do the Executive Branch. In 1969, for example, a number of scientists opposed to the anti–ballistic missile (ABM) provided Congress with detailed technical and strategic arguments against the proposed weapon. When the Senate nonetheless approved the ABM, by a single vote, I spoke with one of these scientists, who I thought would be discouraged. Instead, he was optimistic. "Don't you realize," he said, "that this is the first time Senators have sought advice on weapons from scientists and technicians who don't work for the Pentagon?"

D.C.), but after a few weeks on a Senate staff I discovered what my colleagues already knew: these books exploit the dramatic potential of the institution without making an attempt to render realistically its day-to-day routine and flavor. Journalism, on the other hand, suffers from the need to make stories succinct and dramatic; the journalist (as Stimson Bullitt wrote of politicians) "is left with the dilemma: to speak at length and not be heard, or to speak briefly and either mislead or be misunderstood."* Moreover, the men and women who work in the Senate treat the journalist even more circumspectly than they do novelists or scholars; the information he obtains, except in rare instances, is therefore almost exclusively information that someone *wants* him to obtain. Information deemed inimical to the Senate's interests—notably that Senators are not wholly self-sufficient people—is unlikely to be revealed. Astute reporters know, of course, that the interaction of Senators and their staffs is important, but the topic is hardly dramatic enough to risk angering Senators or compromising friendly staff members, and thus jeopardizing the reporter's access to juicier material. So when a journalistic account appears, purporting to "expose" the inner workings and invisible power of Senate staffs, it invariably centers on an atypical individual—usually an independent committee clerk or counsel—and not on the system as a whole, which is interesting but not sensational.

These considerations prompted me to write this book, but I realize that the book cannot succeed entirely where other forms of literature on the Senate fail. At best, it can supplement academic analysis, fiction, and journalism—it cannot, and should not, supplant them. It is only one man's "truth," after all, and the truth of a man who happened to be young when he wrote it and even younger when he experienced it. What emerges from this "inside" account, I

* *To Be a Politician* (Garden City, 1959), page 72.

hope, is not some definitive statement about the "dance of legislation," but rather some suggestion of the continuing legislative potency of Congress and an impression of how Senators and their staffs work together in the legislative process. If it makes the legislative milieu a bit more real, a bit less dry and formalistic (or a bit less cynical and racy, depending on what one reads), then it will have made as great a contribution as I could hope for.

But did this purpose require me to write the book in the first person? I suppose I could offer an elaborate rationalization that it did, and of course I hope this style of narrative will have its virtues, but in fact I wrote it in the first person only because I couldn't write it any other way. I actually began in the conventional third-person style, but I found I was neither an investigative reporter (since I was no longer on the scene) nor an "omniscient observer" (since I was far from omniscient). Even though I had worked on this legislation for nearly a year, too much information was unavailable to me, locked away in Executive files, lost in unrecorded House conversations, or grown dim in the minds of individual Senators and staff men. All I knew with certainty about this legislation were the things that had crossed my desk or my thoughts as a young Senate staff man, and eventually I realized that the most honest and perhaps the most revealing account would be one written frankly and explicitly from my own perspective. In a sense, then, this book is a legislative variation of an experiment one television network tried several years ago when it wired a microphone to Sam Huff during a football game—except that I make no pretense of having been the Sam Huff of the legislative process. I was only a minor aide in the Senate, and it need hardly be said that any one of the other 3,000 men and women who serve the Senate could have done the same thing.

As for the legislation itself, I should emphasize that the National Health Service Corps is the vehicle, not the object, of this narrative. It is a good vehicle, I think, because the bill had an eventful and dramatic (although somewhat atypical) legislative history, and as a result it illuminates more than another bill might the sequential steps and personalities in the "dance of legislation." But the book is not designed to present a case for Senator Magnuson's bill; that case may be found in the relevant documents of the House and Senate, in the testimony presented to Congressional committees, and in the writings of many experts. While it would be gratifying if the book created a greater public awareness of this program and the health needs of the poor, critics of the program would be foolish to think that in pointing out errors or oversimplifications in this narrative they can in any way detract from the program itself. For me to have attempted a thorough justification of the National Health Service Corps, or to have reargued the voluminous debates of Congress and the Executive Branch, would have been both irrelevant and extremely pretentious.

People familiar with the events described will undoubtedly detect mistakes and misjudgments on my part. None is intentional, although obviously I had to simplify many aspects of the narrative to make it less unwieldy and more interesting for a general audience. I would be grateful to learn of any outright errors of fact or misleading generalizations, and to correct them for any future editions (if I'm so lucky).

I have a great number of people to thank for their assistance in the preparation of this book. Senator Magnuson and his staff obviously made the book possible, but I should take this opportunity not to implicate them in the book itself, with which they had no connection. Jerry Brazda, Richard C. Ernst, Jim and Debbie Fallows, Mike Gorman, Lester Hyman, Richard Larsen, Jeff Rudman, and Kenneth Tite all read the manuscript in one form or another and made possible whatever improvement this version shows over earlier drafts. Richard Paisner offered critical advice

and helped with the proofreading; Stimson Bullitt generously gave permission to quote from his book, *To Be a
Politician*, in this preface.

The quote from Woodrow Wilson that I have taken as
my title and epigraph was not something I found in reading
Congressional Government; I first read it in Sidney Bald-
win's excellent book, *Poverty and Politics*. My parents and
the Jerome Farris family deserve my thanks and my wife's
for giving us a place to live and write the first draft of this
book in the summer of 1971.

Dan Green of Simon and Schuster patiently guided me for
many months and across a distance of many thousands of
miles. Other writers who have worked with him will understand my debt; the reader should know that without him
there would have been no book.

Professor Richard E. Neustadt of Harvard, despite an
exceptionally busy schedule, graciously assisted me in the
early stages of my writing; I hope I have not repaid his
kindness by misquoting him. Philip M. Williams of Nuffield
College, Oxford, encouraged me constantly throughout—in
fact, without his efforts this book might never have been
completed—and he also managed to teach me a great deal
about American politics at the same time. Abe Bergman,
whom the reader will meet, and my wife, Anne, are the two
people who created this book with me, although they would
deny the fact, either out of characteristic modesty or because
they know better than anyone else the book's shortcomings.
For these I am solely responsible, but in no other respect is
this book mine alone.

Seattle, 1971
Oxford, 1972

ERIC REDMAN

THE DANCE
OF Legislation

I

FIRST STIRRINGS

My parents met and fell in love as lower-echelon New Dealers in Washington, D.C., and when they moved to Seattle ten years later, they brought with them a persistent faith in the Democratic Party. I must have disappointed them at first: in 1952, at age four, I became an Eisenhower "man," making life miserable for everyone, especially with my gleeful postelection taunts. By 1956, however, I had realized my mistake, and even tried to redeem myself somewhat by starting a few fistfights for Stevenson on the playground at John Muir Elementary School. I began to collect campaign buttons, pinning them to cloths tacked to my bookshelf, and to make my partisan loyalties clear, I hung the Democratic buttons two shelves above the Republican ones.

I arranged the campaign buttons hierarchically, with Presidential ones at the top of each cloth and with sheriff's gold-star badges along the bottom margin. Directly beneath my ADLAI AND ESTES button on the Democratic cloth, there-

fore, I affixed the various campaign pins of Senator Warren
G. Magnuson, Washington's senior Senator. Even before I
was born, Magnuson had become the most powerful Democratic politician in the state. When he ran for a third term
in 1956 and a fourth in 1962, I proudly lent my I'M STRONG
FOR MAGNUSON buttons to my parents whenever they went
out for the evening, but by the time he ran again in 1968, I
was twenty years old and eager to contribute more substantially to his campaign. The Senator's campaign manager
and Administrative Assistant, Jerry Grinstein, listened patiently to my request and finally hired me as a speech writer.
In June 1968, I went to work.

During the campaign I wrote speeches, shadowed Magnuson's opponent (an obscure State Senator named Jack
Metcalf), supervised a mass mailing, and spent as much
time as I could with the Senator himself. Although he was
three times my age, and occasionally gruff with "outsiders,"
Magnuson and his staff treated me considerately and helped
me feel that I was one of them. My boyhood admiration for
the Senator, based solely on his position and party, soon
grew into a mature respect based on what I learned on his
record and what I came to see in him as a man. When he
won with 65 percent of the vote in the general election, I
viewed the result—as a New York newspaper had once
viewed McKinley's defeat of Bryan—as evidence that God
was just (and that, like me, He had changed parties).

After the election, Magnuson and his staff returned to
Washington, D.C., and the business of government. Grinstein, knowing I had three months free before the college
term began in January, invited me to come along too. The
legislative process, he said, had little in common with electoral campaigning, and I could learn something in addition
to being useful around the office. To cover the higher cost of
living in the Capital, Grinstein magnanimously raised my
salary by $25 per month, and in mid-November I became
the youngest "legislative assistant" in the U.S. Senate.

My new tasks were hardly momentous, but they were educational and fun. I tried, for example, to get the District of Columbia law changed to require cars to stop behind school buses as they unloaded (a motorist had struck Grinstein's son one afternoon). Equally unsuccessfully, I tried to persuade the U.S. Fish and Wildlife Service to transplant lobsters experimentally into Puget Sound. I also failed to interest the Magnuson office in legislation to minimize earthquake damage, a project I conceived after reading in *Esquire* that Seattle as well as San Francisco lies near the San Andreas Fault. Much of my work involved drafting replies and doing research for a portion of the 700 letters Magnuson received daily from his constituents. The entire experience fascinated me, and most rewarding of all was watching proudly from the Senate gallery as Magnuson took his oath of office on January 3, 1969, the day the 91st Congress convened.

I came back to Magnuson's staff the next summer, after an impatient term at college, but although I knew better how to perform legislative duties, the summer ended before I had time to complete any of the projects I worked on. In September, I started my final term as an undergraduate, and by January of 1970 I was in Washington again, this time with nearly a whole year ahead of me. I looked forward to the satisfaction of finishing, instead of merely beginning, the tasks that Grinstein or the Senator would assign me. Grinstein, however, had decided by this time to leave the Senate and return to a Seattle law practice. Since he would no longer be able to guide and direct my work, he took the time to introduce me to several people with whom he thought I might be dealing in the coming months. One man I met this way was Dr. Abraham B. Bergman.

Abe Bergman, a Seattle pediatrician, was a political activist as well as a doctor (or, as some of his colleagues complained, a doctor as well as a political activist). Besides running the outpatient clinic of the Children's Orthopedic

Hospital and teaching at the University of Washington Medical School, Bergman served as an unofficial adviser to Senator Magnuson, whom he had met through Grinstein. In 1965, for example, Bergman had mentioned to Magnuson that power lawn mowers caused 100,000 injuries per year in America; he showed the Senator an X ray of one victim's skull, embedded with shrapnel-like fragments of metal. Disturbed, Magnuson investigated, and found injuries from poorly designed household products (not just lawn mowers) so widespread that he promptly introduced and pushed to passage a bill creating a National Product Safety Commission. Later, at Bergman's instigation, Magnuson visited a burn ward at Children's Hospital and then wrote a new law requiring fireproofing of children's clothing. Soon the Senator began to write one consumer-safety measure after another, and converted the Senate Commerce Committee (of which he was Chairman) from the businessman's representative to a new role as the "consumer's panel" on Capitol Hill. As a result, the theme of Magnuson's 1968 campaign became his demonstrable work in behalf of America's consuming public (MAGNUSON'S LAW FORCES DETROIT TO BUILD CARS SAFER, proclaimed a typical billboard, with typical billboard syntax).

Magnuson's successes convinced Bergman, in his words, that "politicians can save more lives than doctors," and consumer safety alone did not exhaust the possibilities. When, in 1969, Magnuson became Chairman of the Senate Appropriations Subcommittee for the Department of Labor, the Department of Health, Education and Welfare, and related agencies, Bergman had visionary (some would say unrealistic) dreams about what Magnuson could accomplish through his new hold on the purse strings of the Health, Education and Welfare Department (HEW). He organized for Magnuson a loose and unofficial consortium of "health advisers," floating legislative proposals to them by mail and occasionally convening the group in Washington, D.C., for special "skull sessions." To the amusement and sometimes the ire of the Subcommittee staff, Bergman flew to Washington repeatedly to "help" in preparing the HEW Appropriation bill, to lobby for worthwhile programs, and to "carve out a role" (as he put it) for Magnuson in health affairs. When asked why Dr. Bergman spent so much time in Washington instead of at his hospital back home, the Senator's staff had a standard reply: "It's simple—he can't stand the sight of blood."

Magnuson, in fact, already had respectable credentials in the health field, but they dated mainly from his early years on Capitol Hill. As a freshman Congressman in 1937, for example, he had introduced the bill establishing the National Cancer Institute, the first of the National Institutes of Health, and in his first Senate term he produced the National Science Foundation Act. Both the Senator and his staff agreed, however, that he should use his new chairmanship of the HEW Appropriations Subcommittee to increase his health role, and they received Bergman's numerous proposals good-naturedly. But by the time Grinstein left, Bergman's role in the Magnuson organization had become somewhat unclear: the Commerce Committee staff and the Subcommittee staff were fully capable of writing their own consumer-safety legislation and the HEW Appropriation bill. No thirty-seven-year-old activist—conscious of the power Magnuson wielded, and flushed with recent successes—could endure the uncertainties that now confronted Bergman. Aware of his friend's uneasiness, Grinstein felt the doctor needed additional contacts in Magnuson's office, and with a more or less straight face, he nominated me.

My initial introduction to Dr. Bergman did not, however, result in any immediate follow-up when I rejoined the staff in 1970. Bergman did not call, and the Senator's new Administrative Assistant, Stan Barer, immediately delegated to me several pet legislative projects of his own. Stan exempted me from "mail duty" to concentrate on two Magnuson bills, the "National Transportation Act" and the "World Environmental Institute Resolution." The first was to reorganize American transportation policies and systems on a regional basis, fostering the development of balanced, "intermodal" transportation networks more efficient (and more sound environmentally) than the existing "nonsystem," heavily dominated by the Highway Lobby. The second, a proposal for joint international research and information-sharing on pollution and other global environmental problems, was designed as a major initiative in the then burgeoning area of ecology. Both measures intrigued me, particularly because Magnuson himself was "hawkish" about them.

I had almost forgotten Bergman, therefore, when he came to see me on March 11. His sudden appearance disturbed me, for I knew it meant more work, and I felt overburdened already. I had to write speeches for Magnuson on both the bills I'd been assigned, find witnesses for five days of planned hearings on the National Transportation Act, and draft the World Environmental Institute Resolution itself—a difficult task, for I knew almost nothing of international environmental affairs, and the proposal was so novel that there were not even "experts" with whom to consult. Moreover, I was using all my "spare time after hours" (i.e., after 8 or 9 at night) to complete belatedly my undergraduate thesis, which had to be in the mail to the college authorities by the end of March. When I catalogued these obligations to Bergman, however, he showed very little sympathy; problems of the national transportation system and the global environment did not interest him, and he considered my college thesis wholly irrelevant. What mattered was health legislation, and since (as he told me) he had just gotten Magnuson's consent to have me start work on a new health project, he expected me to listen carefully while he outlined his proposal: the National Health Service Corps.

Bergman sat down and began to explain. In addition to their other problems, poverty areas in the United States suffered from a shortage of doctors he said. So did small rural communities, even prosperous ones. The question was how to get more doctors into urban ghettos and isolated towns. The answer was the National Health Service Corps.

The National Health Service Corps (NHSC), Bergman continued, would consist of idealistic young doctors and other health workers—men and women who would serve voluntarily for two years or so in a "doctor deficient" area, such as a slum or a remote farming community. The Federal government would pay their salaries and exempt the men from military service. The purpose of the program, however, would not be to make poor people medically dependent on the government; the ultimate aim would be to encourage NHSC doctors to establish their own practices in needy communities. Bergman believed strongly that at least some of the NHSC doctors would become "sensitized" to the health needs of the poor, and that after their tours of duty in the Corps were complete, these doctors would choose the psychic satisfaction of treating the needy over the financial rewards of practicing in more affluent communities. The NHSC would therefore be something of a "marriage bureau" for doctors and needy areas: volunteers would be paid by the government during a trial period in the Corps, and then they and the community could decide whether to make the arrangement permanent, either through the establishment of a standard private practice or through the creation of a "health care delivery team" composed of socially motivated health professionals.

The National Health Service Corps, as Bergman envisioned it, was thus an experiment rather than a panacea. If it succeeded in transplanting doctors into "medically underserved areas," then it would markedly strengthen America's health-care system. And even if the NHSC "failed"—if the doctors simply served their time and then fled back to the traditional Cadillacs and country clubs of the medical profession—at least needy people would have received better health care in the interim.

Bergman's idea seemed to make sense, although until he explained it I had never really thought about the well-known "doctor shortage" except in terms of absolute numbers. I knew America needed more doctors; I had never stopped to think that the distribution of existing doctors might be an even more urgent problem. Now Bergman pointed out why doctors tend to shun needy areas: why should they risk the financial hazards of a rural community or the added physical hazards of a ghetto when a middle-class practice can produce an income of thirty or fifty or even a hundred thousand dollars a year? Even were a doctor willing to ignore the compelling economics of the situation, poor communities rarely furnish the social life, recreational facilities, or good schools that a professional person looks for in deciding where to live and raise a family. The "pull" of middle-class communities is as natural as it is powerful, and consequently the maldistribution of doctors grows worse as rural areas become more depopulated and as the central cities continue to deteriorate.

The "doctor distribution" problem, Bergman added, had prompted many proposals besides a National Health Service Corps. Some of these other proposals were good, but none provided the ultimate answer and most would be difficult, if not impossible, to achieve. National health insurance, for example, could eliminate the financial disadvantage of practice in poverty areas, for the government would then pay the doctor, whose income would no longer depend on that of his patients. But national health insurance (which of course had other features to recommend it) would take years to become law, involving as it did a wholesale reorganization of American medicine. Less radical proposals, such as paying for a doctor's medical education in exchange for his promise to serve for a period of years in a poverty area, had been tried in a number of states without success.

As a result, Bergman said, National Health Service Corps schemes were discussed increasingly in medical circles, both because such a Corps was "realistic" and because it could draw on the social commitment of young medical-school graduates. The President's Commission on Rural Poverty, for example, had recommended a "National Doctor Corps" in its 1967 report, and in fact Huey Long had made a similar suggestion as long ago as the 1930's. But so far, nothing had been done.

The explanation for this inaction lay in an immediate and seemingly insurmountable obstacle facing any NHSC scheme: the so-called "doctor draft." Unlike the bulk of the male population—of whom only a small percentage ever serve in the military, even in wartime—the Selective Service Act obligates almost all male doctors and dentists to enter the armed forces. Although a doctor can defer this service for some years while pursuing his medical education, ultimately the draft is a fact of life for health professionals with a certainty that no other group must face. Once a doctor has completed his military service, moreover, he is usually anxious to begin earning a living (especially since doctors want to recoup for the long, lean years of their schooling), and he is no longer a likely candidate for a program like the NHSC, whose appeal necessarily lies in further public service and self-sacrifice. The success of such a Corps would therefore hinge on its ability to attract young doctors before they enter the military and to provide them an alternative to it. But because the Pentagon and its allies, particularly the Armed Services Committees of the House and Senate, would block any legislation attempting to substitute such service for a doctor's military obligation, no one who advocated an NHSC could seriously envision a change in the Selective Service law that would permit the Corps' creation. Consequently the NHSC concept had taken on the aura of other "antipoverty" proposals like the guaranteed minimum income: a nice idea, but legislatively an impossible one.

This was where the matter had stood, Bergman went on, until he and several other doctors who had served in the U.S. Public Health Service (PHS) realized that the PHS could run a doctor-corps program without a change in the draft law. He gave me a copy of a proposal developing this idea, and told me it had been written by Dr. Laurence Platt, a young commissioned officer of the PHS. Platt's scheme built on this unique concept of using PHS doctors—who serve in the PHS instead of in the military—to staff the NHSC. Technically, PHS commissioned officers do not have a draft *deferment*; under the terms of the Selective Service Act, their tours of duty in the PHS actually satisfy their military obligations. Of the 8,000 or 9,000 men and women who graduate from medical school each year, however, only about 600 (or roughly 7 percent) receive PHS commissions —not enough to inconvenience the military, which has 16,000 doctors.

The details of Platt's scheme presented many practical difficulties, Bergman said, and the medical philosophy underlying it clashed with Bergman's professional views ("Platt is a propagandizer for group practice," he declared scornfully). But the Platt proposal had developed that one kernel of brilliance: use of PHS doctors in the National Health Service Corps. No new draft deferment would be needed to create the Corps, saving a futile legislative struggle against the Pentagon, and a program that would fulfill a doctor's military obligation would be even better than one that merely provided a deferment: Peace Corps doctors had deferments, after all, but that didn't prevent them from being drafted after they returned to the United States.

Once Bergman had explained the key feature of the Platt proposal, I thought I understood the task that faced us. "Magnuson can introduce a bill," I ventured, "setting up a National Health Service Corps staffed by PHS doctors." It all seemed very simple, but Bergman smiled sadly at my premature confidence.

"No," he responded patiently, "I'm afraid it's a bit more complicated than that." Confused, I sat back unhappily in my chair.

"The problem with the Platt proposal," he resumed, "is that commissioned officers of the Public Health Service can satisfy their military obligations *only* if they perform traditional PHS duties. Caring for patients, unless they happen to be Indians or sailors or Federal prisoners, isn't a traditional PHS duty."

Obviously I didn't know very much about the Public Health Service. If PHS doctors didn't practice medicine, what *did* they do? Bergman explained that the PHS had grown out of the nineteenth-century Marine Hospital Service, but that throughout its long history it had engaged primarily in the types of activities its name implies: public health. Public health includes sanitation, pestilence control, and activities such as imposing quarantines during epidemics. But public health does not include health care in the sense of doctors treating individual patients. The only people whom PHS doctors treat directly, in fact, are "wards" of the Federal government—a category that includes merchant seamen, as well as Indians and prisoners, as an anomalous legacy of late-eighteenth-century maritime conditions. Everyone else in America is able (at least in theory) to visit a private practitioner; health care for the general population is thus completely outside the scope of public health—and, by law, outside the responsibilities and authority of HEW and the U.S. Public Health Service. Even though poverty areas and isolated towns have few or no doctors, in other words, the Public Health Service is powerless. Consequently, it would not be enough, Bergman explained, to create an NHSC and staff it with PHS doctors: somehow, the authority of the PHS itself would have to be broadened to include the care of individual patients in selected communities.

The problem was thus much more complex than I had

innocently thought. The NHSC would have to be part of the PHS—that much was clear. But somehow, Bergman added, Senator Magnuson would have to bring about a change in the mission of the PHS—and not so big a change that we ran afoul of the Selective Service Act, which set strict limits on what PHS doctors could do without getting drafted. The only alternative would be to change the draft law itself, and even Bergman, who admitted that his enthusiasm outstripped his legislative acumen, could not foresee the Pentagon submitting to a program that presented such an open threat to its supply of doctors.

Having outlined this puzzle, Bergman then recounted the steps he had taken before bringing his idea to me. First, he had rewritten the Platt proposal, leaving out the "group practice propaganda," and sent it in January to Magnuson's unofficial health-policy advisers. They had responded with universal enthusiasm for the NHSC concept and with uniform pessimism about its legislative prospects. Bergman had then taken a sheaf of their replies to Stan Barer (knowing that the legislative prognoses of amateurs would not trouble him), and tried to interest him in the project on its substantive merits alone. Barer, however, had asked that Bergman devote his energies instead to writing a national health-insurance bill, which Magnuson was impatient to introduce. The Senator had advocated national health insurance publicly for many years, Barer explained, and now the legislative climate was warming to the concept. Awed by such a massive project, however, Bergman had demurred, then taken his NHSC proposal to one of Magnuson's other aides (and Barer's subordinate), Norm Dicks. Dicks agreed to draft a bill with Bergman, but in the end neither of them was satisfied with it; the program the bill outlined resembled a domestic Peace Corps, and would have required that impossible change in the Selective Service law. Before Dicks could redraft the bill, however, he had become mired in another major task: to prepare Senator Magnuson's defense of the supersonic transport, the SST, over which a Senate battle seemed imminent. So, doggedly, Bergman had returned to Magnuson and Barer, this time asking (without my knowledge) that I replace Dicks, my preoccupied superior, on the project. Sensing Bergman's determination, perhaps, the Senator and his top aide finally agreed, giving Bergman—in the terminology of Professor Richard Neustadt—a "hunting license" to pursue the establishment of the National Health Service Corps. And Bergman intended to hunt.

So the National Health Service Corps had become "my baby." The choice of a staff man could not have been less auspicious. I was busy. I was young and relatively inexperienced. Worst of all, I was ignorant—ignorant of the field of medicine, ignorant of the workings of HEW and its Public Health Service component, and consequently ignorant of the environment in which we would be working: the politics of health legislation.

The one thing I did know (or at least the one thing I thought I knew) was that for Magnuson to propose a National Health Service Corps might be risky from a political standpoint; one particularly implacable interest group—organized medicine—seemed certain to oppose the scheme. Tentatively, I expressed my apprehensions to Bergman.

"You've shown me the need for this Corps, Abe," I said, "but it seems to me we have one big problem: it's 'socialized medicine!' "

Bergman looked at me with withering disdain, as if this were too trivial an objection to dignify with a response. "Sure it's 'socialized medicine,' " he replied impatiently, "but if doctors who serve in the Corps go on to set up their own practices in poverty areas, then obviously the effect of the Corps will be to strengthen the private-practice system. The Corps isn't going to take over the care of poor people; it's going to help redistribute doctors. Anyway, the important thing is what you just said: there's a need for it."

So that was where Senator Magnuson's National Health Service Corps plan stood on March 11. Bergman had done the "hard" work already: he had come up with a vaguely defined proposal and persuaded the Magnuson office—from the Senator down to the most junior legislative assistant—to undertake it. All Senator Magnuson and his staff had to do was set it up: a socialized-medicine scheme that would strengthen the system of private practice in America.

Somehow I couldn't help thinking that Bergman's had been the easier task.

II

BEGINNER'S LESSONS

1.

Confronted with a National Health Service Corps scheme
that purported to strengthen the system of private practice,
a sufficiently paranoid member of the American Medical
Association might have recognized it immediately as the
Trojan Horse of socialized medicine. In Senator Magnuson's office, however, the Corps proposal seemed singu-
larly undramatic at first, and we hardly pursued it with the
zeal one would expect of conspirators. In fact, we agreed
from the first that the NHSC should not be as grand in
scale as it might be in philosophy; even Bergman did not
want it to begin as a massive new program, for he doubted
any single approach could solve the complex "doctor distribution" problem. So we settled for what we hoped would
be a small but imaginative experiment: an NHSC in which
several dozen Public Health Service doctors would run a
handful of health-care projects in a few selected communities scattered throughout the United States. If this limited

program proved successful, we reasoned, Senator Magnuson could eventually persuade Congress to expand it.

One reason our plans were so modest was that our initial strategy called for Magnuson to create the NHSC without any new legislation. Legislation would have been "best," of course, in the sense that legislation alone could give visibility, coherence, and an unambiguous mission to the new Corps. But an NHSC bill, unlike earlier Bergman-inspired legislation, would not fall within the jurisdiction of the Senate Commerce Committee, where Magnuson, as Chairman, could pass virtually any bill he liked. Instead, such a bill would automatically go to the Committee on Labor and Public Welfare, which considers all health legislation in the Senate—and Magnuson was not a member of that Committee. Nor did Magnuson sit on the Senate Armed Services Committee, which might ask to review the bill no matter how carefully we tried to skirt the draft law. So the one thing we knew for certain was that we didn't want to establish the NHSC through new legislation; this reinforced the seeming wisdom of aiming for a small NHSC.

Fortunately, Magnuson could create the Corps without writing a bill—or so we thought. Through the HEW Appropriations Subcommittee, the Senator controlled HEW's funds and the funds of its relevant subdivision, the Public Health Service. Our initial strategy, therefore, was simple: Magnuson would merely add a few million dollars to the HEW Appropriation bill and "earmark" the money (i.e., specify its use, in the bill or in the accompanying Report) for an NHSC-type experiment under Public Health Service auspices. Since the total HEW Appropriation involved approximately $20 billion, and since Congress habitually adds a few hundred million dollars to the President's annual budget request for HEW, a small increase for the NHSC might go unnoticed, or at least cause little controversy.

We knew Magnuson would have no difficulty earmarking

the funds; the question was whether HEW would cooperate thereafter. The whole strategy hinged on HEW's willingness to play along: if the Department was inclined to balk, it could refuse to spend the money, on the ground that the Public Health Service law did not explicitly authorize any program like the NHSC. But if, on the other hand, HEW did want to establish the Corps, it could quietly agree with Senator Magnuson that, yes, the law *could* be interpreted broadly as allowing this new experiment.

Obviously, we needed to reach an understanding with the Department of Health, Education and Welfare. This would have been true even with a less covert strategy, however, because in practice hostile Departments can effectively scuttle even the firmest of Congressional directives. Moreover, I had been taught in college (and consequently insisted to Bergman) that a prerequisite of "good" public administration is that the Executive Branch, with all its expertise, participate in designing the programs it will eventually have to administer. Whenever I passed the vast HEW Building at the foot of Capitol Hill, I couldn't help thinking that somewhere within that labyrinth there must be people who understood the "doctor distribution" problem better than Bergman and I did (particularly since all *I* knew was what Bergman had told me).

We anticipated that HEW would want to cooperate. First of all, the Department would be stupid not to "play ball" with Magnuson, the Chairman of the HEW Appropriations Subcommittee. But more important, we thought HEW would like the Corps proposal itself. Top HEW officials were already feuding publicly with the White House, asserting the need for new health programs but checked by fiscal and policy constraints from the President and the Office of Management and Budget (OMB). Dr. Roger O. Egeberg, the Assistant Secretary of HEW for Health and Scientific Affairs (and hence the "nation's number one doctor"), charged openly that the men on Pennsylvania

Avenue were "callous," "indifferent," or "insensitive" to America's health-care problems. Egeberg's criticism received widespread coverage in the news, not only as one of the first indications of dissension within the Nixon Administration, but also as evidence that Egeberg himself was not the docile yes-man observers had once thought. Nixon's first choice for the post Egeberg occupied had, after all, been the reform-minded Dr. John M. Knowles, but that nomination had provoked such an outcry from the American Medical Association (AMA) that Nixon had withdrawn it and substituted Egeberg, a seemingly innocuous academic administrator whom the AMA could accept. Nixon's capitulation to the AMA had seemed to indicate that no one in the Administration (least of all Egeberg himself) would challenge the status quo of American medicine—but now Egeberg was proving that judgment premature.

In addition to Egeberg's growing independence, the historical "alliance" between HEW and Congress encouraged us to seek the Department's cooperation in making plans for the NHSC. Throughout the 1950's and early 1960's,* Congress had consistently provided more funds for HEW than the President had requested, and the increases had been engineered through more or less open collusion between HEW officials and the Chairmen of the HEW Appropriations Subcommittees in the House and Senate. Magnuson continued this pattern when he became Chairman in 1969, adding a standard $300 million to the Fiscal 1970 HEW Appropriation, but President Nixon promptly vetoed the entire bill. The veto (Nixon's first, and televised live to the nation) meant more work for Magnuson—he and his Subcommittee had to rewrite the whole appropria-

---

* President Eisenhower established HEW in 1953 (see Chapter III). In the mid-1960's, for a number of reasons (including the Vietnam war), HEW funding remained relatively stable.

tion during the Christmas holidays—but it stung HEW more severely. Speculation grew that HEW would seek to reforge its traditional alliance with Congress in order to resist Presidential "downgrading" of its programs—a classic textbook response for any out-of-favor Department, and one that HEW particularly had followed in the past.

Under the circumstances, we didn't hesitate to ask HEW's help in creating the National Health Service Corps, nor did the Department's initial reaction disappoint us. When we requested technical assistance, for example, in drafting the earmarking provision and in determining how much money to allot the proposed Corps, HEW promptly agreed to send us some of its top talent—a young doctor and a young lawyer from the Department's operating division, the Health Services and Mental Health Administration (HSMHA).

In order to elicit maximum cooperation from the HSMHA doctor and lawyer, Bergman and I carefully staged our first meeting to impress upon them the control Magnuson exercised over their Department's money. We picked as a conference site the cavernous hearing room of the HEW Appropriations Subcommittee in the New Senate Office Building, and in case the significance of the chamber should escape our visitors, we deliberately invited a fifth participant: Harley Dirks, the chief clerk of the Subcommittee and hence Magnuson's top aide in deciding the size and distribution of HEW's funds. Not a subtle show of power, perhaps, but one not easily dismissed.

We needn't have worried. Our doctor and lawyer readily endorsed the NHSC concept; in fact, they insisted, people in HSMHA had long been eager for just such a program. HEW welcomed innovative proposals for better health care, they said, but the White House and the OMB blocked the Department's own initiatives. Conspiring with Congress, however, could bring fast results; perhaps after we had set up the NHSC (an easy matter, they suggested), we could undertake some more substantial tasks together. The only caveat entered in this optimistic discussion was the lawyer's cautious remark, just before leaving, that the legality of our earmarking strategy was unclear; if the PHS lacked authority for patient care, Magnuson could not create that authority simply by giving the agency more money. Perhaps, the lawyer added, specific authorizing legislation might be needed, in which case the earmarking strategy wouldn't work. But this was only a possibility, and the lawyer promised to consult his books and produce a definitive answer.

With the technical details "farmed out" to the HSMHA doctor and lawyer, we began to consider the more rarefied politics of our earmarking strategy. We decided the next step was to visit Dr. Egeberg himself, the unexpected new advocate of innovative health-care programs. And we knew the most important person to include as a member of our delegation was again Harley Dirks.

Dirks is in many ways a legendary man on Capitol Hill. Rumor has it that he was once a shoe salesman in Othello, Washington, a drowsy little farm town in the dry Columbia Basin. A more likely version is that Dirks *owned* a shoe store in Othello, and if he occasionally fitted the customers himself, it was not because he lacked grander dreams. Othello is miles from anywhere, an oasis of sorts in prairie-like Eastern Washington, and its isolation—even from Seattle—cannot be adequately expressed in a mileage number on a road map. Othello was so slow, and Dirks so fast, that soon he found himself owning a host of its businesses and one of its banks—or so the story goes—despite the fact that he spent much of his time catching trout, shooting pheasant, and siring offspring. For whatever reason, Dirks eventually felt the urge to move on, and to a man of his imagination that did not mean bundling up the family and heading for Walla Walla. Instead, he worked for Senator Magnuson in the 1962 campaign and then followed him back to Washington, D.C.

Dirks became a "clerk" on the Appropriations Committee at a time when Magnuson handled the funds of HUD, NASA, and the many independent agencies and regulatory commissions. When Magnuson switched to the HEW Appropriations post, Dirks went with him, simply moving his pipe rack to a new office and confronting a new set of figures. At first, his nominal superior was the "Chief Clerk" of the Subcommittee, an irascible Southerner who had served under chairmen now almost forgotten on Capitol Hill. Before long, however, Dirks moved in behind the Chief Clerk's desk (his own had become an unworkable mountain of papers), and within a few months the Chief Clerk stopped coming to work altogether. Dirks redecorated the staid office with oils he had painted, and as a quiet joke he arrayed on his new desk such "authoritative" academic works as *The Power of the Purse* and *The Politics of the Budgetary Process*. He had neither the time nor the need to read books about appropriations; he ran a Subcommittee that appropriated nearly $40 billion each year (an amount second only to the Defense Department's).*

Like other Appropriations Committee clerks, Dirks is unknown to the public and to much of the Washington press corps. Tourists do not call at his office (although Senators and Secretaries do), and at appropriations hearings members of the audience sometimes whisper, "Who is that man sitting next to the Chairman?" That Dirks carries his power so judiciously says much about his fierce loyalty to Senator Magnuson, his sole constituent. Magnuson relies on Dirks heavily, not simply because he is loyal, or because a chairman has little choice, but also because Dirks is thorough, alert, and discreet. The only outsider, in fact, who has ever sensed Dirks's true influence was an academic researcher who interviewed him in connection with a study attempting to correlate appropriations figures with Sena-

---

* When trust fund expenditures are included, the HEW appropriation totals some $80 billion, an amount in excess of the regular Defense Department appropriation.

tors' backgrounds; amused, Dirks simply jotted down for his visitor his own prediction of dollar amounts, by program, in an appropriations bill the Senators themselves had not yet even discussed. When the bill finally passed, Dirks's projections corresponded uncannily with the approved figures.

Dirks's anonymity does not extend to the Department of Health, Education and Welfare. Bergman and I witnessed a revealing, if somewhat comic, demonstration of this as we walked with Harley down HEW's long corridors on our way to discuss the earmarking strategy with Dr. Egeberg. From one doorway after another, men and women emerged to intone respectfully, "Good morning, Mr. Dirks," or "Hello, Harley!" and so on down the list of ingratiating pleasantries. Bergman and I felt obscure and incidental, as if we were Secret Service escorts; Dirks, for his part, smiled and waved like a Presidential candidate. It was hard to imagine him ever going back to Othello.

Even Dr. Egeberg, when we arrived, seemed sensitive to Dirks's presence. He welcomed us warmly and ushered us immediately into his inner office, hastily summoning aides and ordering coffee. A huge, bald man in his late sixties, Egeberg sported a jaunty yellow BULLSHIT button on his lapel. Hardly giving us time to sit down (much less to broach the subject of our visit), he launched into an animated monologue, designed (I supposed) to establish his credentials as a critic of the President and Presidential health policies.

"I had an appointment to see the President a month or so ago," he began, "because I wanted him to add a hundred and fifty million dollars to our budget for training more doctors. I was sitting outside the door to the Oval Office, waiting, when John Ehrlichman [the President's top aide for domestic affairs] came up and asked, 'This visit doesn't have anything to do with money, does it?' I said, 'Of course it has to do with money—we need a hundred and fifty million dollars to train more doctors.' 'Oh, well,' Ehrlichman said, 'if it has to do with money, we'll have to reprogram this appointment. No one can discuss money matters with the President unless George Shultz [Nixon's fiscal adviser] is here.'

"Now, I've called every single week since," Egeberg concluded, "and I still haven't been able to get the appointment 'reprogrammed.' And the hell of it is, I *know* the President of the AMA can walk in and see Nixon anytime he wants!"

The anecdote suggested Egeberg might cooperate with us; so did his eagerness in turning to Harley to ask why we had come (evidently he hadn't been briefed). Harley, adopting the role of silent sage, nodded to indicate that I should explain our plan. Somewhat nervously (this was the "nation's number one doctor"), I told Egeberg what we hoped to establish: a National Health Service Corps, within the Public Health Service, created solely through an earmarking of funds in the HEW Appropriation. Would Egeberg and the Department help?

Egeberg responded without hesitation. "I've always wanted a program like that," he said, "but I can't come right out and ask for it myself. I've got certain problems down *there*, you know [he motioned toward the White House]. But if *Maggie* proposed it," he went on, in mock conspiratorial tones, "and if he provided the *money* for it, well then I'd *have* to set it up, wouldn't I?

"We need a new mission for the Public Health Service," he continued, after exchanging broad smiles with Dirks, "and in fact, I've got a committee looking at the problem right now. I think the answer has got to be some kind of doctor corps. So let's hear your plan."

The plan we agreed upon, after a brief discussion, was simple. Egeberg's staff would write some questions, based on the HSMHA doctor-lawyer team's research, and give them to Magnuson so that he could "spontaneously" ask

Egeberg about an NHSC when the doctor came to testify during the HEW Appropriation hearings in June. Magnuson would describe his idea briefly, then ask Egeberg (for example), "if Congress provided you with three million dollars for this type of program, staffed with Public Health Service doctors, how would you spend it?" Egeberg would then reply, "Well, Mr. Chairman, of course the Department has not *asked* for any such program, but if you and the Committee feel so strongly about it that you provide three million dollars, I guess this is what we would have to do. . . ." Then Egeberg would outline the details of the hypothetical Corps, prompted occasionally by carefully prearranged questions from Magnuson. The exchange, printed in the hearing record and in the Report accompanying the appropriation, would serve both to define the "Congressional intent" behind the NHSC (since no legislation would be available for this purpose) and to create the impression that Magnuson had "forced" the new program upon a reluctant but ultimately pliable HEW officialdom. The scheme was so clever that we wondered if Magnuson and Egeberg would be able to keep straight faces while reciting their lines.

After chuckling over the impending "drama" in the hearing room, Egeberg rose and walked us to the door. As we left, I mentioned to him the HSMHA lawyer's warning that the strategy might prove impossible for legal reasons. Egeberg replied that he hoped the lawyer was wrong, and that if not, we could still count on the services of HEW's General Counsel in drafting any legislation we might need. "Let's keep in touch," he added, and bade us goodbye.

I had to admit, as we walked away, that I felt better about our enlisting Egeberg as an ally than I had before the visit. My misgivings had stemmed from my only previous exposure to him, at a press conference in 1969 when HEW announced a partial ban on cyclamate sweeteners, which had just been found to cause cancer in rats. In later weeks, the cyclamate "ban" became the object of Washington humor, but the press conference had been tense (and held on a Saturday for a deliberate reason: the stock market would be closed). "This is going to be ten times worse than when Thalidomide hit," confided a White House aide I knew, and HEW Secretary Robert Finch, who had spoken first, gripped the podium tightly; sweat showed all over his face. Yet Dr. Egeberg, speaking next, treated the issue nonchalantly from the first, pointing out that everything—cyclamates, the Pill, cigarettes—had its advantages and disadvantages from a health standpoint. This attitude had surprised the press corps, and reinforced my distasteful image of Egeberg, an image I had picked up during the earlier "Knowles Affair."

Now, however, I found I liked Egeberg. I could even interpret sympathetically his position on cyclamates, something I had judged too quickly in any event. I could see why Magnuson liked Egeberg too, almost alone of the HEW officials he confronted each year (the indecisive Finch had become "Secretary Flinch" in Magnuson's vocabulary). What struck me most about Egeberg was his good nature and his obviously good intentions. Climbing into a cab for the brief ride back to Capitol Hill, I confided all this to Bergman and Harley Dirks.

Harley looked at me and grinned. "Wait and see," he admonished. "You like him because he's barking at the White House, but he's barking because the White House keeps him on a very short leash."

2.

From the beginning, a chief attraction of the earmarking strategy had been that it required so little effort on our part. With HEW doing all the technical work for us, and with only a simple legislative maneuver ahead, the National Health Service Corps seemed ideal: a worthwhile project, yet an undemanding one. I could concentrate on my other assignments, Harley could get back to the HEW Appropriation, and Bergman would be satisfied if HEW devised a proposal that fulfilled his general conception of what the new Corps should be. Best of all, Magnuson could gain a significant (and newsworthy) victory for poor people, and all at the cost of a half-hour dialogue with Dr. Egeberg during the appropriation hearings.

The catch, of course, was that HEW actually had to do what it had promised in the way of preparations. And, as if to confirm Harley's original skepticism, this is precisely where the Department failed. Maddeningly, the HSMHA doctor kept delaying his outline of the NHSC program, and the HSMHA lawyer, for his part, seemed unable to find a definitive answer to the critical legal question. One day, when I called the lawyer yet another time, I found that he and his brother (another HSMHA doctor) had been sent to New Mexico to make a lengthy study of an Indian health clinic. When I called the HSMHA doctor to ask who could replace the lawyer, I learned that the doctor had embarked on an even stranger journey—a month-long trip to study health services in Yugoslavia.

Annoyed at having lost so much time, I turned for the legal opinion to an expert we should have consulted at the outset: Hugh E. Evans, a lawyer in the Senate Legislative Counsel's office (which provides technical assistance to Senators in drafting bills). Unlike the HSMHA lawyer, Evans could give me an answer at once: the earmarking strategy wouldn't work. He emphasized that the Public Health Service had no legal authority to treat patients except "traditional beneficiaries" (i.e., Indians, prisoners, and merchant seamen). If Magnuson earmarked funds for treating other types of patients, a hostile or legalistic Senator could make a "point of order" when the HEW Appropriation came up for a vote; insisting that the PHS had no authority to spend the funds, such a Senator could force the President of the Senate to rule that the money must be deleted. But what if no one *noticed* the money, I asked; wasn't it at least conceivable that we could sneak such a small amount through? Evans thought not; "a lot of Senators can be pretty fussy about legislating on an appropriations bill," he advised.

Evans's opinion—disappointing but obviously correct—should have made us abandon the earmarking strategy outright. But by this time our preparations seemed too extensive, and the alternative of writing a bill too hopeless. So instead we searched for some tactic that would reconcile the strategy with the legal constraint, and for a brief but exciting moment, we thought we had found one.

Evans had said only that Magnuson could not earmark funds for the NHSC in the absence of a law authorizing the PHS to carry out an NHSC-type function. But what if there already existed, somewhere in the mass of PHS statutes, an obscure section of some law that a smart lawyer could demonstrate *did* authorize such a function? All we needed was something that could be very liberally construed as "authorization," something that Magnuson could contend made the earmarked funds legitimate. Surprisingly, we managed to find just the law we were looking for: section 314 (f) of Public Law 89–749, the "Comprehensive Health Planning and Public Health Service Amendments of 1966."

Section 314 (f), entitled "Interchange of Personnel with the States," authorized HEW to assign employees—including PHS doctors—to state health-care programs; the only restriction, which seemed a mild one, was that the state programs had to "aid the Department of Health, Education and Welfare in more effective discharge of its responsibilities in the field of health as authorized by law." Since Congress had never funded section 314 (f), it had never been used, so there were no precedents to restrict us. We reasoned that Magnuson could fund it, and that states could take advantage of it by establishing token health-care programs—the Federal government would supply all the funds, and all the medical personnel in the form of PHS doctors. The National Health Service Corps, in other words, could be established in everything but name. All we needed was Hugh Evans's opinion that this new earmarking strategy would be legal.

Hugh Evans is a soft-spoken and kind lawyer. He had been uncomfortable, I knew, in his forced role as "naysayer" to our original strategy. This time he was even more uncomfortable, but he had to tell us that section 314 (f) wouldn't work either. First of all, he reminded me, the draft law stated that PHS doctors could fulfill their military obligations only if they served in an "office or bureau" of the PHS itself; a state program, even one over which the PHS exercised de facto control, could not afford them protection from the draft. Moreover, he pointed out patiently, section 314 (f) itself said the state health-care programs had to "aid the Department of Health, Education and Welfare in the more effective discharge of its responsibilities in the field of health as authorized by law." But our whole problem was that the Department did not have the responsibility, or the legal authorization, to provide health care to anyone except "traditional PHS beneficiaries." Earmarking strategy number two, in other words, foundered on the same lack of legal authority that had wrecked earmarking strategy number one.

Then Evans gently made the inevitable suggestion, the suggestion we had resisted from the first because we knew it to be futile.

"Eric," he said, "I think you're going to have to write a bill."

III

GETTING SERIOUS

1.

The earmarking strategy had taken five weeks to die; now, at the end of April, the 91st Congress itself had only four or five months to live—too short a time in which to write and pass a new bill even in ideal circumstances, and circumstances were hardly ideal. Magnuson did not belong to the Labor and Public Welfare Committee (which would have to bless his bill before the Senate acted); the House of Representatives would somehow have to pass the bill too; and worst of all, Congress was anxious to adjourn. With elections in November, and with Democratic control of the House and Senate at stake, only the most pressing legislation would become law; the rest, including a National Health Service Corps bill, would have to wait until the 92nd Congress convened in 1971.

In Senator Magnuson's office, as in every suite on Capitol Hill, the prospect of adjournment meant some projects had to be abandoned in order to save more promising ones. Of my particular assignments, the National Transportation Act and the World Environmental Institute Resolution had come the farthest; we had held five days of hearings on the former in March, and Magnuson's introduction of the latter on April 27 had quickly brought a deluge of inquiries, invitations, and visitors. In addition, Stan Barer had reluctantly returned me to another job: helping answer the mail. One of Magnuson's other aides was joining the Army, and someone had to assume his daily allotment of letters and telegrams. Since Senators and Congressmen have become the ombudsmen of American government, answering the mail is an important political function—more important to constituents, perhaps, than legislation itself. Yet answering the mail threatens to become the *only* function if, as in Magnuson's office, all correspondence receives thorough and conscientious treatment: an aide who spends only half his day researching and drafting replies for the Senator's approval soon finds the stack of unanswered mail overflowing his desk onto the typewriter, the telephone, the chair, and ultimately the floor.

For all these reasons, I had little personal interest in prolonging the National Health Service Corps project once Hugh Evans had pronounced the earmarking strategy unworkable, and my superiors seemed to agree. If Magnuson could create the Corps only through legislation, it would have to wait until the next Congress. But this decision failed to take account of Bergman. Far from being dissuaded, Bergman seemed determined to redouble his efforts, and since he had no formal staff position, his "efforts" consisted largely of badgering and cajoling me. The World Environmental Institute, for example, attracted him no more now than it had before it received international attention, and he seemed to think that answering the mail was completely unimportant. Whenever I tried to reason with him, Bergman had a petulant and inflexible reply:

"There *has* to be a way." Silently, I cursed doctors in politics, particularly monomaniacal ones.

In fact, however, Bergman was right: there *was* a way, and an easy one, too. The Health Subcommittees of the House and Senate, we discovered, were considering a bill known as the "Public Health Service Amendments of 1970." This legislation, a fairly minor concern of the Subcommittees, simply revised and updated PHS procedures, but there was no reason why the Subcommittees could not amend it to include a National Health Service Corps. Instead of Magnuson having to introduce his own bill and push it to passage, the Subcommittees—if they felt so disposed—could simply incorporate the NHSC proposal into this legislation, which was certain to pass. Members and staff of the Senate Subcommittee, when we discussed this plan with them, encouraged us to proceed, and we easily arranged for Congressman Paul Rogers of Florida (the de facto leader of the House Health Subcommittee) to carry out a parallel maneuver on the other side of the Capitol.

So the "amendment in committee" strategy replaced the failed earmarking strategy, and we wished we'd thought of it in the first place. All Magnuson had to do was introduce a rough bill giving the general outline of the NHSC—the Subcommittee staffs and HEW would work out the details, then graft the proposal onto the Public Health Service Amendments of 1970. The strategy was simple and sound, and might even have worked, but something unexpected happened in early May: President Nixon decided to invade Cambodia.

Militarily, the invasion of Cambodia encountered surprisingly little resistance—the enemy "headquarters," if they ever existed, had vanished by the time American troops swept into the Parrot's Beak. The real opposition, instantaneous and outraged, came on the home front, from substantial portions of the public and hence the Senate (the House, although shaken, kept silent beneath the muzzle of its hawkish "leadership"). Nixon had fought the Senate before, sniping with periodic vetoes and forcing major confrontations over the anti–ballistic missile (ABM) and the Supreme Court nominations of Haynsworth and Carswell. This time, however, his seeming recklessness offended as much as his policy itself, and the battle between the Senate and the White House escalated dramatically. The angry Senate sessions, hot debates over the Constitutional division of the (so-called) "war power," lasted far beyond midnight; cots and bedding appeared in the cloakrooms and lobbies. The Church-Cooper Amendment, to block any similar invasions in the future, immediately became the only order of Senate business.

But the invasion destroyed the legislative agenda in another, less direct way. With a wider war in Asia, and with students shot dead at Kent State, thousands of angry youths, lawyers, doctors, mothers, civil servants, and others streamed into the narrow halls of Congress, demanding that "business as usual" cease. The demand was self-fulfilling in any event; groups of petitioners blocked the corridors and doorways in impenetrable knots, while piles of mailbags choked passageways and office space. People who came for only one day undoubtedly left remembering one day's congestion and chaos; solons and staff members, on the other hand, lived and worked in a state of siege that lasted three weeks at its worst, then continued weeks longer at lesser but still unmanageable levels.

Staff duties, in those tumultuous days of May, included everything except normal tasks. So many people poured into the office that we became substitute Senators, meeting with twenty enraged mothers in the hall, for example, while the Senator himself dealt with sixty students around his desk. Even when we found time to work, we worked only on the war: searching statutes, poring through legal briefs, drafting position papers, all to find out what the Senate—and the Senator—could and should do about Cambodia. We ran between offices with the latest draft of the ever-changing Church-Cooper Amendment, and we ran (too slowly; our CONGRESSIONAL OBSERVER armbands could not protect us) from the tear gas at Lafayette Park during the March on Washington. Answering the mail was not even a possibility; we had difficulty finding enough volunteers just to open and classify it—"pro-Nixon," "anti-Nixon," "constituent," "out-of-state," "war in general," and "routine business" (the smallest category).

In June, at last, a measure of peace returned to Capitol Hill, if not to Southeast Asia; we had time enough to sit down and count the legislative casualties of May. One of the first victims, we discovered, had been the amendment-in-committee strategy for the National Health Service Corps.

The strategy's demise had been simple enough. While the events of May had occupied the *personal* staffs of the Senators, the *committee* staffs had been insulated from the barrage of visitors and letters (no one had come to see Harley Dirks about Cambodia, for example). As a result, despite the war critics' demands, the committee staffs *had* continued "business as usual." The staff of the Senate Health Subcommittee had finished drafting the Public Health Service Amendments of 1970, and the Subcommittee members, followed by the members of the full Labor and Public Welfare Committee, had hurriedly approved the legislation at the first opportunity, thus sending it to the Senate for final action once the Cambodia storm cleared.

In other words, the bill we had planned to amend in committee was no longer there.

2.

So the amendment-in-committee strategy, like its predecessor, failed even before we had a chance to test it. At this point, Bergman himself might simply have cursed Cambodia and abandoned the NHSC until the 92nd Congress, but unfortunately we had denied ourselves that option when Congressman Paul Rogers had become part of our plan. Whether or not Magnuson acted, Rogers could now introduce his own NHSC bill in the House, and even amend the House version of the Public Health Service Amendments of 1970 to include it, since the House Health Subcommittee (unlike its Senate counterpart) had not yet passed that legislation. Without parallel action in the Senate, of course, Rogers couldn't get the NHSC enacted, but he *could* get publicity and credit for an idea that Magnuson's office had developed. We simply couldn't allow that to happen; Capitol Hill possessiveness precluded Rogers' becoming anything more than Magnuson's needed ally, his coequal in the venture. To preserve Magnuson's identification with the NHSC proposal, we needed a new strategy, and if we had to devise a new strategy, we might as well find one that included both Congressman Rogers and the possibility of the NHSC becoming law during the 91st Congress after all.

And so, of necessity, the "Floor amendment" strategy was born. Instead of amending the Public Health Service Amendments of 1970 in committee, which was no longer possible, Magnuson would try to amend the legislation when it came to a vote on the Senate Floor. If he succeeded, and if Rogers could still amend the bill in committee or on the House Floor, the NHSC would become law. But could Magnuson succeed?

The major obstacle to a Floor amendment is that it represents an attempt to "short-circuit" the legislative process. After they are introduced, new bills are supposed to go to committee (and subcommittee) for consideration before coming back to the Senate for a final vote. Floor amendments usually succeed only when they represent technical changes or a necessary compromise, or when a committee has clearly thwarted the majority will of the Senate. The

Senate rarely adopts Floor amendments of the type we envisioned, because to create a new program so summarily
involves too much uncertainty ("What is this thing, anyway?") and too great an infringement on committee
prerogatives. Without the acquiescence of the relevant
committee chairman, in fact, our Floor amendment would
be doomed, and in any case the strategy might fail if a
hostile Senator pleaded for traditional procedure. I could
easily imagine, for example, the following speech (having
heard it, in substance, many times before):

> Mr. President, the amendment in question may have much
> to recommend it. I do not want to be misunderstood. I do
> not say it is a bad amendment; I merely say that it is impos-
> sible for me to know much about it, one way or the other,
> without hearing from the Committee on Labor and Public
> Welfare first. I would say to the distinguished Senator from
> Washington, my able colleague, that if I were not forced to
> choose today, if I could first see some hearings or a report
> from the Committee, I might very well wish to associate my-
> self with this program he proposes, as I have on so many
> occasions in the past.
>
> But Mr. President, why must the Senate rush to create this
> program without having a chance to learn more about it? If
> it is a worthwhile program, as it may well be, then the Com-
> mittee will certainly act upon it, and in the process the
> Senator's bill will undoubtedly benefit from the wisdom of
> the Committee and from the testimony of expert witnesses.
> Then we might enact this program, knowing that it is needed
> and worthwhile; but to enact it now, knowing nothing about
> it, would simply not be responsible. If it goes to Committee,
> and the Committee approves it, then we can support the
> Senator in conscience, but if we must decide now, on the
> basis of a mere amendment we have hardly seen, then—and I
> say this with all respect for my friend, the distinguished
> Senator—I am afraid I must oppose it. . . .

If we could not forestall such a speech, we at least had to
be capable of rebutting it. If the Committee Chairman,

Senator Ralph Yarborough, endorsed Magnuson's proposal, and if some other Committee members also spoke in its behalf, the amendment might succeed, even if it required a roll-call vote. But although Magnuson, as the fifth-ranking Senator and a committee chairman himself, had plenty of power to help persuade Yarborough and the Committee, he would need something else, too: an amendment so well drafted that no one would object to it on technical grounds, and a mastery of the subject matter so complete that he could counter easily any substantive criticisms of his proposal. Unfortunately, our preparations to date were inadequate in both respects.

Before we could even approach Yarborough and the Committee, therefore, we had to have a very good proposal in hand, and this meant the Floor-amendment strategy required a great deal more effort from our office than had the earlier strategies. The earmarking strategy, and even the amendment-in-committee strategy, had left most of the work to HEW, especially the detailed preparation of the NHSC plan itself. Now, however, Magnuson himself would have to outline his proposal in detail, and be able to answer even the most difficult questions from his colleagues. True, he could have an aide with him on the Floor if he wished, but one aide was hardly equivalent to a battery of HEW experts, and in any event the amendment's chances would diminish the moment Magnuson had to consult an aide when asked, "Won't this program take doctors away from our boys in uniform and put them to work for people who ought to receive care from private practitioners anyway?" Friends of the AMA would pose worried questions about "socialized medicine" and the possibility of doctors already in practice being drafted to make up for a shortage the NHSC might cause, while Senators who styled themselves experts in public policy might inquire whether or not tax incentives, "loan forgiveness," or subsidies would be better methods of attracting doctors to needy areas. And if Magnuson faltered in reply, or if he merely failed to satisfy the doubters among his colleagues, the sticklers for legislative propriety would inevitably rise to intone, "Since a number of uncertainties seem to surround this proposal, perhaps it would be wise for us to send it to the Committee on Labor and Public Welfare for study instead of trying to make a final judgment here this afternoon."

Bergman and I knew we could provide Magnuson only general answers to such questions, and we certainly couldn't draft the needed legislation ourselves. But since Dr. Egeberg had promised to help, and since we had no reason to suspect that our earlier disappointment with the HSMHA doctor and lawyer had been anything other than accidental, we unhesitatingly turned to HEW again for assistance. Unfortunately, we never paused to consider the implications of our growing dependence on the Department.

3.

So far we had thought of the NHSC's political problems solely in terms of Congress; we knew the White House and the budget officials might become a problem, but for the time being, HEW's cooperation met our immediate needs from the Executive Branch. Our naïveté consequently astounded a senior officer of the Public Health Service, the first HEW official to visit us after Cambodia. As soon as he arrived on Capitol Hill and heard our plans, he warned us to expect not only the President's opposition, but that of many people in HEW as well.

HEW, the officer advised us, was not one big happy hierarchy. Instead, the Department had dissolved into warring factions, fratricidally destroying any possibility of effective policy-making. Not only would the opposing sides fail to

unite on the NHSC scheme, he said, but the proposal
would invoke, uncannily, the very issues in greatest dispute.
First of all, he explained, "socialized medicine" raised
ideological hackles at HEW as well as in the White House.
Of course, no one used the phrase "socialized medicine"
itself—no one wanted to relive the agonies of the Medicare
battle—but the debate was nearly as bitter, couched in
terms of whether or not the Federal government ought to
be "in the business of providing health-care services directly." Conservative diehards might now admit the legiti-
macy of government programs (such as Medicare and
Medicaid) to help old or poor people pay their medical
bills, but even this had taken a prolonged struggle, and for
the government actually to employ doctors was out of the
question. In theory, the distinction between the government paying patients' fees and the government paying doctors' salaries might seem unimportant or even ridiculous,
but in practice it had crucial significance for physicians'
incomes (and, the AMA might contend defensively, for the
quality of care patients receive). And even though the
NHSC would hardly make *all* physicians government employees, it would pose an immediate ideological threat to
them. If, during the Johnson years, the government had
nonetheless come close to trying a doctor-corps experiment,
the Nixon Administration would fight any such proposal,
our visitor advised. If Dr. Egeberg had given us the opposite impression, he added, that was because Egeberg led the
"progressive" HEW faction. But the "progressives" were a
minority in the Department, and the PHS officer cautioned
us against assuming that Egeberg's post gave him effective
control over Administration health policy: the White
House and the OMB ran things, he said ruefully, and they
had plenty of help from certain HEW underlings, including some of Egeberg's own lieutenants.

Even if prevailing Administration policy on "socialized
medicine" inexplicably reversed itself, the officer contin-

ued, the NHSC also raised the second-most-divisive issue at
HEW: what to do with the Public Health Service. The
Administration wanted to abolish the PHS altogether, he
said, so how could we expect Nixon officials to help us es-
tablish a new program specifically designed to be *part* of the
PHS?

"But wait a minute," I interjected; "we want HEW to
help us, and HEW can't agree with the White House that
the PHS should be abolished. After all, the PHS is one of
HEW's biggest agencies."

The PHS officer smiled sadly, then replied, "Our biggest
problem at the moment, in fact, is that too *many* people at
HEW can't wait to see us abolished."

Obviously Bergman hadn't taught me everything about
the PHS in my first lesson on March 11. Now the PHS
officer explained that the current controversy stemmed
from a historical fact: the PHS was a *uniformed* personnel
system, not a modern Civil Service system. The head of the
PHS, the Surgeon General of the United States, had traditionally been a Presidential appointee with military command over an elite Commissioned Officer Corps of doctors,
laboratory scientists, and other health professionals. The
Commissioned Corps had performed its disease-control and
sanitation functions with little change until the 1930's,
when it began to undertake research into the causes of disease. Soon, with the growth of the National Institutes of
Health (NIH) throughout the 1940's and early 1950's,
medical research became the PHS's major activity, and
NIH employees began to include civil servants as well as
uniformed officers. When President Eisenhower created
the Department of Health, Education and Welfare in 1953,
the PHS and all its components were subsumed into it, and
the Surgeon General began to lose effective control over
his former domain, of which NIH was only the most conspicuous portion.

By 1968, our visitor continued, the Surgeon General and

the PHS held formal positions on the HEW organizational chart totally out of keeping with their diminished importance. Civil servants greatly outnumbered commissioned officers, many of whom no longer wore uniforms and none of whom still reported to the Surgeon General. President Johnson, in fact, nearly eliminated the Surgeon General, the PHS, and HEW's "dual personnel system" (as the conjunction of civil servants and commissioned officers had come to be called), but after a protracted battle, his 1968 Executive Reorganization Plan retained all three. The Plan did recognize the de facto redistribution of power, however; the Surgeon General, for example, became a subordinate of the Assistant Secretary for Health and Scientific Affairs (the post Egeberg now occupied), and he lost the last vestiges of "line authority" over the operations of the PHS and its Commissioned Corps. To signal that the PHS would soon disappear altogether, the functional intermingling of PHS officers with civil servants increased, while the Budget Bureau succeeded in forcing the closure of many "uneconomical" PHS hospitals and outpatient clinics throughout the country.

Under the Nixon Administration, the PHS officer added, these trends had sharpened. The Surgeon General had no true function, and the once-proud, once-elite corps of commissioned officers had become somewhat idle, a haven for young doctors eager to avoid the draft (90 percent quit the PHS after their two-year draft-obligated tour). The idleness was not the doctors' fault: there was nothing for them to do, at least if they wanted to practice medicine. A few were lucky enough to get into the Indian Health program, a few more into the Federal prisons or marine hospitals, but most simply served out their time behind a desk in HSMHA or a microscope in an NIH laboratory. Unlike their predecessors in the 1950's, who had been "farmed out" to work in non-PHS health-care programs, PHS doctors were now restricted by a 1967 amendment to the draft

law forbidding such assignments—the same provision that
had foiled our earmarking strategy number two. The AMA
had inspired the change in the draft law; AMA members
had been drafted to meet the military's needs in Vietnam,
and the AMA had only to look around to see dozens of
young PHS doctors avoiding military service (and treating
patients, too). So the draft-law change had made the AMA
more secure, in terms of both national service and clientele,
and now no one—the PHS officer told us wearily—could
hope to succeed in getting that provision of the draft law
repealed.

Since the PHS no longer served a function important
enough to justify its existence to the cost-conscious and
efficiency-minded men at the OMB (the former Budget
Bureau), the question had become what to do with it: abolish it outright (as the Administration preferred), or find a
new mission for it to perform? Friends of the Service advocated the latter course; the Platt proposal for an NHSC, in
fact, had stemmed from the same vision of the PHS's proper
future. The commission now studying the PHS (which
Egeberg had mentioned to us) also wanted to establish a
doctor corps, the officer told us.

"But," he concluded wistfully, "I don't think the people
who want to save the PHS have the power to match Nixon
and the OMB—even if Senator Magnuson wants to help so
that he can get his National Health Service Corps."

Having imparted his gloom to us, the PHS officer left
Capitol Hill. Bergman and I pondered what he had said,
and began to understand the irony of Magnuson's position.
On the one hand, we didn't really care what happened to
the PHS; we were concerned with creating a National
Health Service Corps. On the other hand, the draft law and
legislative reality meant the NHSC would have to be part
of the PHS, so if we wanted the NHSC, we would have to
help resuscitate the Public Health Service: a classic case of
the tail wagging the dog. It didn't occur to us at the time

that the old dog might still have the strength to wag the tail a bit too.

4.

Soon after our instructive tutorial with the PHS officer, Bergman flew home to Seattle and his hospital duties, while on May 26 I met with three HSMHA bureaucrats whom HEW had assigned to assist Magnuson in preparing the NHSC legislation. Bergman objected to the word "bureaucrat" in the memo I sent him after the meeting; he felt our potential opponents at HEW might deserve such a derogatory label, but not these men, who showed themselves to be our friends. They efficiently divided up the necessary tasks, for example: one would draft the Floor amendment itself, another would furnish current data on the numbers and categories of PHS and military doctors, and the third would summarize for us all statutes relevant to the PHS and to our proposal in particular. They also gave me a great deal of useful information and advice during our meeting, including suggestions for the program's administration and optimal initial size. They cautioned against seeking anything more ambitious than two pilot projects, one urban and one rural, at least in the early stages of the NHSC. A paragraph from my memo reveals how timidly we planned:

> Rather than fight the military to get manpower—perhaps 20 doctors plus the requisite number of supporting health professionals—we might provide that for the pilot projects the Secretary of HEW could hire individuals who had already satisfied their military requirement. The aim of this would simply be to get an evaluation and a report on the pilot projects that could lead to new legislation expanding the NHSC in future years and providing a draft deferment of some sort (perhaps after some favorable finding as to the "national interest" by the Secretary).

The men from HSMHA felt certain our discussion had been "realistic," and they appeared eager to perform their respective tasks, so perhaps, as Bergman scoldingly suggested, I had treated them unfairly in calling them "bureaucrats" initially. In subsequent weeks, however, Bergman and I both found worse terms of abuse, and for a simple reason: not one of the three bureaucrats kept his promises.

5.

A few days after meeting the HSMHA trio, and before I suspected I might not hear from them again, I received an unexpected phone call from a Dr. John Zapp. Zapp said that he was Egeberg's chief aide, and that *he* had been delegated to help us prepare the NHSC legislation. Although this news confused me somewhat, I soon discovered how amiable and charming Zapp could be. A dentist, in his midthirties perhaps, he seemed frank, decisive, and highly competent, although I might have appraised his abilities more critically had I known (as I was told only much later) that he owed his HEW appointment to the 1968 campaign, during which he had organized a "Dentists for Nixon" committee. At the time, however, the fact that Egeberg apparently remembered us seemed heartening in itself, and the affable Zapp made our hopes seem more realistic. Bergman too expressed pleasant surprise when I told him of our new partner and his status. Bergman had expected the Surgeon General, Dr. Jesse Steinfeld, to call me, since he had met Steinfeld by chance on a plane flight and told him of our plans. Perhaps Steinfeld and Egeberg had gotten together and chosen Zapp, we speculated; at any rate, he seemed the most capable of the individuals HEW had yet sent us.

Before I could meet with Zapp, however, another HEW

staff man named Harley Frankel visited our office, Frankel, it turned out, directed the commission that Egeberg had told us was studying the future of the PHS and its Commissioned Officer Corps. He had heard of our plans, and wanted more details. Frankel told me that as staff director of the commission, he would write virtually all of the forthcoming report, and he intended to recommend strongly that the entire PHS be converted into a massive National Health Service Corps. Every PHS doctor, he insisted, should be out serving the poor and the needy; let NIH hire laboratory technicians for its medical research, let HSMHA employ public administrators for its desk jobs, but let the doctors get out there in the field with their stethoscopes and tongue depressors. With such a grand design in mind, Frankel could hardly contain his disbelief when I told him, somewhat sheepishly, how modest our legislative plans were. He was thinking in terms of an NHSC three or four hundred times as large as the minuscule pilot-project program we had conceived, and he scornfully opined that the projected Magnuson plan would be worse than no legislation at all. I could defend our proposal only on the ground of legislative reality as we understood it, but Frankel simply scoffed and left the office in disgust.

Almost immediately afterward, Dr. Laurence Platt appeared. His plan had made use of the unique idea of employing PHS doctors to staff the NHSC, and consequently appealed to Bergman. He seemed startled, however, that Senator Magnuson had seized upon "his" idea; he would have preferred one of the younger Senate liberals whose names he knew from the newspapers. And although he regretted that we had deleted most of his plan and retained only its key feature, he generously offered to help if he could; like Bergman, he was a doctor who felt health legislation was too important to be left to the legislators. In fact, he did help a great deal, bringing with him on his next visit six of his young colleagues from the PHS. The group of us held an extended "rap session," sprawled around the windowsills, desktops, floor, and few chairs in my cramped working quarters. In calm, professional tones—a soothing contrast to the stridency of our recent Cambodia and Kent State visitors—Platt and his friends patiently explained many aspects of the NHSC that hadn't occurred to me. I asked Platt to draw up an example of a possible NHSC project, and within a few days he supplied me with a detailed description of how the NHSC might work on a particular Zuni Indian reservation. While not directly relevant, the Zuni Indian proposal was an illustrative example, and I carefully filed it for use in explaining the NHSC to others.

In early June, I finally met with Dr. John Zapp and one of his assistants. Using the same old techniques (and hoping for better results), I staged the meeting in Harley Dirks's office, the headquarters of the HEW Appropriations Subcommittee. Harley couldn't join us around the table, but we could see him at his desk nearby, clenching his pipe firmly between his teeth or answering the phone, "Yes, Senator . . ."

Zapp seemed eager to help, mindful perhaps of Dirks's presence, but he soon had me thoroughly flustered with a series of questions too technical for me to answer. How did we wish to define a "physician deficient area" in the Floor amendment? How should the scale of fees be determined, who should have to pay them, and should they go to the NHSC or simply to the Treasury? Had we thought about how NHSC doctors were to acquire hospital privileges? Apparently my simple, straightforward conception of the pilot projects would not do; Zapp decided to leave me with a long list of issues to resolve before proceeding further.

At the end of our disappointing meeting, convinced that I was incompetent, I walked with Zapp out into the bright sunshine along Constitution Avenue, where he searched for a cab to carry him back to HEW. In an effort to compensate him somewhat for the time he had evidently wasted, I asked him if I could do anything to help cement the alliance between our respective employers, Magnuson and Egeberg. I told him Dirks had asked me to draft Magnuson's opening statement for the HEW Appropriations hearings that would begin on June 16; was there anything Egeberg might particularly like to hear the Chairman say—anything that might aid him in dealing with the White House and the OMB?

Zapp thought for a moment, then brightened. "Yes," he said avidly, "we'd sure appreciate something in there about health manpower—that's Dr. Egeberg's big concern at the moment. It would really be helpful if Magnuson pointed out that we could double the size of our medical-school class by 1976 if we doubled our funding for health manpower."

I told Zapp, as he climbed into his cab, that I would try; Magnuson and Dirks would have to agree. And a week later, Zapp was able to read Magnuson's speech—containing the key suggestion—in every major newspaper in the country.

6.

But "team spirit" did not catch on at HEW. None of the HSMHA bureaucrats completed the assignments they had voluntarily assumed, and Dr. Zapp stopped returning my phone calls. Finally, several weeks later, Zapp did call for once, apologizing for the delay and excusing himself on the ground that all his time had been taken up preparing testimony for HEW bigwigs to deliver at Magnuson's appropriation hearings (the implication being that Magnuson would get more help on the NHSC if he eased up on his HEW hearing schedule). Zapp asked me to come to his office the next day for another meeting. Despite the minor deviation from protocol (he should have come to Capitol Hill again), I felt happy just to arrange a second meeting, and anyway he was busy and I had a position of little status in the Senate. The NHSC was well worth a short cab ride.

When I arrived for the scheduled appointment, however, Dr. Zapp had been "unavoidably detained" elsewhere; would I mind talking with his assistant? I certainly *would* mind. Angry for the first time, I left immediately and returned to Capitol Hill. A few hours later, my temper cooled, and in place of anger I felt distinct uneasiness about our relationship with HEW. Something was definitely wrong.

The next day, one of the HSMHA bureaucrats unexpectedly came to Magnuson's office. "Here's the National Health Service Corps proposal," he said nervously as he handed me a sheaf of papers. I noticed it was typed on plain white stationery instead of under the HSMHA letterhead; it bore no identification as to author or source.

"I'm leaving the country for a few weeks," he added hurriedly, "and when I get back, I'd appreciate it if you called me at home, not at the office, if you have any questions about this." Then he rushed away, stricken with that strange HSMHA disease that requires a cure remote from Washington, D.C.

Puzzled, I leafed through the papers. To my consternation, it was not an NHSC proposal at all, much less a draft of legislation: it was Dr. Platt's Zuni Indian Reservation scheme, retyped and with no reference whatsoever to Platt himself.

Furious now, I immediately stormed over to Harley Dirks's office, and when he saw my face, he quickly concluded the telephone conversation he was having. Sitting across his desk, I blurted out in a confused stream the frustrations, the double crosses, and the broken promises of HEW. What the hell should I do? I asked.

"Ric," Harley replied firmly, "I think you're being 'had.'

HEW's conning you. They've gotten a damned sight more information out of you than you have out of them, and I don't think they have the slightest intention of coming through for Magnuson now. Either they want to nip the Corps in the bud, or else they want to steal the idea so Nixon can propose it himself.

"My advice to you," he concluded, "is to write a bill without HEW. I'll talk to Magnuson with you, and we'll figure some way to get this damned thing passed. It sounds as if we've got to teach these boys a lesson or two."

Harley's analysis seemed obviously correct, except for the notion that Nixon might advocate an NHSC himself. Yet only a day or two later, Dr. Egeberg announced to *The New York Times* that the Administration might soon propose a "national doctor corps." Fortunately, Bergman arrived in Washington at the same time. On the night of July 8, having reached such a pitch of anger that we became clearheaded, we sat down in the deserted Senate Office Building and typed out the legislation we wanted.

We had spent four fruitless months trying to extract a draft from the "experts" at HEW. It took us precisely an hour to write it ourselves.

IV

A FRESH START

1.

Like many others in Washington State, my family often celebrates summer with an alpine hike in the Olympic Mountains. Our favorite trail runs along the top of a high ridge, far above timberline, on the outer rim of the jumbled and seemingly infinite Olympic range. Once, looking out across this vast and roughly leavened expanse of rock and ice, my father paused and said, "Just think: if you'd been here when all of this was created—if you'd seen the lava flowing and the mountains pushing up—you would have thought the end of the world had come. But really it was just the beginning."

I should have remembered that remark in the summer of 1970, even though the hot asphalt and suffocating humidity of Washington, D.C., had little in common with the Olympic Mountains. For it seemed to me that the end of the world *had* come, at least for the National Health Ser-

vice Corps. When the burst of anger in which we had
drafted the NHSC bill subsided, and when Bergman had
flown home again to Seattle, I lapsed into mild depression.
Although Hugh Evans would polish up our draft, number-
ing its sections properly and sprinkling it with legal jargon,
and although Magnuson would soon introduce the bill in
the Senate, we all realized that HEW's noncooperation had
virtually eliminated any chance that the proposal might
become law. Now it would be too "controversial" for a
Floor amendment, and without HEW we wouldn't have all
the technical information we'd need. What had seemed in
March a promising and relatively simple legislative effort
now seemed futile and not worth Magnuson's time. For
even if, by some legislative miracle, the Senator managed to
pass the NHSC, HEW now appeared unlikely to administer
the program with imagination or enthusiasm, and this discouraged us most of all. A news item in the weekly *Washington Report on Medicine and Health* reinforced our
gloom; indicating that Harley Frankel would soon submit
his report recommending that PHS doctors "provide direct
medical care to . . . the poor in areas where medical services
are inadequate," *Medicine and Health* added cautiously:

> Whether or not this recommendation is ever implemented
> may depend on the outcome of a major policy decision.
> That is, should the Government provide medical services at
> all, even to the poor, or should it help the private sector to
> do the job? In its actions so far, HEW appears to favor the
> latter course.

The "major policy decision" came soon enough. Frankel
handed in his report a few days later, and *Medicine and
Health*'s editor, Jerry Brazda, called to tell me HEW's reaction: far from accepting the document, or even releasing
it to the press, Deputy Under Secretary Frederick V. Malek
had "literally tossed Frankel's report in the wastebasket"
(other sources said Malek had "literally torn up the re-

port"). HEW appointed a wholly new committee and instructed it to come up with different recommendations—including, presumably, the outright abolition of the PHS and its Commissioned Corps. Harley Frankel, who had contemptuously dismissed Magnuson's NHSC plan as "too conservative," was relieved of his duties and transferred to the Office of Education.* Dr. Egeberg, who only a few days before had confided publicly that the Administration would propose a "doctor corps," now had no comment.

Under the circumstances, the NHSC seemed almost hopeless, but now principle and politics—if not legislative feasibility—forced us to continue. HEW had treated us badly; the Department should have responded fairly (if not, indeed, obsequiously) to a request from the Chairman of the HEW Appropriations Subcommittee, and instead it had handed us an insult that would have shocked even a freshman Congressman. As Harley Dirks had said, we needed to teach HEW a lesson, not only to ensure responsiveness to Magnuson and Congress in the future, but also to check the bureaucratic tendency toward arrogance. Magnuson could have cut the Department's funds as punishment, of course, but he wanted HEW to do more in the field of health, not less. So our only choice was to demonstrate that Magnuson would legislate with or without the Department's cooperation, and that it would require more than harassment to stop the NHSC.

We couldn't abandon the NHSC anyway unless we were willing to give up Magnuson's identification with the issue. The proposal was simply too logical, too attractive; some other Senator or Congressman would soon introduce a

---

* Malek, on the other hand, soon joined the White House staff and became the Administration's chief "hatchet man." When Interior Secretary Walter Hickel was fired later in the year, for example, it was Malek who then sat behind Hickel's desk and summoned top Interior Department aides, ordering them to "be out of the building by five o'clock."

"doctors corps" bill if Magnuson didn't. We couldn't accept the prospect of someone else garnering credit for a progressive and humanitarian measure that the Magnuson office had pioneered at such a great cost of time and frustration. More important, we honestly could not imagine the NHSC becoming law except if Magnuson sponsored it—almost no one else in Congress had enough power.

And so, despite its poor legislative prospects, we pressed ahead with the NHSC. Ironically, I relished the task more now than ever before. I felt keenly that I had failed Magnuson, and that it would be my fault if HEW officials concluded they could thwart him with impunity. In addition, however, I felt by this time personally committed to the NHSC—not merely as a legislative enterprise in which my employer had a stake, but also as an important program in its own right. Since my original conversation with Bergman, dozens of other doctors had emphasized the need for such a corps, and I had read a great deal of literature on the medical plight of the poor. Whatever the bill's legislative outlook, the plan itself was neither grandiose nor unrealistic: it was still a modest, practical program that willing administrators could easily carry out once legislation was passed. Although the NHSC would not, in itself, eliminate the disparities in health care between poor and middle-class communities, at the very least it would provide some medical care to people who needed it desperately. In melodramatic fashion I began to think. There are people alive today who will die because they can't find a doctor; creating the Corps means saving at least a few lives. Cast in terms of human life, HEW's little games seemed all the more irresponsible, and passage of Magnuson's legislation all the more important.

We realized, moreover, that if Magnuson's bill did pass, HEW might relent and decide to administer it faithfully. A new Secretary, Elliot Richardson, had taken office in late June, and he had a reputation as a "progressive." And if the bill couldn't pass in the 91st Congress, we could start making progress toward its passage in the 92nd. Then, if the Nixon Administration still refused to implement the law, at least it would be on the books; the next Administration might have a different attitude, and if so, there would be assurance of doctors for the poor the day Nixon's successor (and a new HEW officialdom) took office.

And so, with thoughts such as these, our cyclical pattern of determination and disappointment continued. When Hugh Evans promptly returned to us a proper draft of the NHSC bill, we forced ourselves to recognize that only the abortive pas de deux with HEW had ended. The "dance of legislation" had just begun.

2.

Like a college mixer, the "dance of legislation" first becomes earnest and fascinating with the search for partners. In Congress, however, unlike a college dance hall, one is permitted as many partners for each dance as one can muster, and since every partner helps, there are rarely any wallflowers except by choice. In fact, a Senator about to introduce a bill routinely asks all of his colleagues to join him as "cosponsors" of the bill. He sends to each of them, or at least to those whose consent he considers likely, a copy of the proposed legislation and a draft of his "introductory remarks" (i.e., the explanatory and exhortatory speech he will deliver in the Senate when he introduces the bill). Other Senators and their staffs read these materials carefully, and if a Senator (for whatever reason—and there may be many) wants his name on record as a backer of the proposal, one of his aides will call to say, "My Senator would like to have his name added as a cosponsor of your Senator's bill." Alternatively, if a Senator becomes interested in another's bill only after its introduction, he simply asks to be listed as a cosponsor in the bill's subsequent printings.

From a legal standpoint, the institution of cosponsorship is entirely superfluous. Senators needn't cosponsor a bill in order to vote for it, and in fact a Senator sometimes votes *against* a bill bearing his name at the top. Cosponsorship fulfills no formal legislative requirements, nor does it afford the opportunity for formal legislative shortcuts. Even if every Senator cosponsors a particular bill—as was true in 1937, for example, in the case of the National Cancer Institute Act—it still must go to the appropriate committee and receive that committee's approval and then the Senate's (and, of course, pass the House and be signed by the President) before becoming law. A large number of cosponsors does not even guarantee that consideration of the bill will proceed quickly: the proposed Women's Rights Amendment to the Constitution languished for years in the Senate Judiciary Committee, even though 77 of the Senate's 100 members had cosponsored it (one women's organization, however, misguidedly devoted its lobbying efforts to securing a 78th and then a 79th cosponsor).

Why, then, do Senators bother to solicit cosponsors at all? The answer, of course, is political. Cosponsorship is one of the lubricants of the legislative process. Among other things, a solicitation for cosponsorship carries with it this implicit offer: "In return for your support of this bill—which I need—I will give you the opportunity to associate your name with it and thereby get some of the credit and publicity, plus something to write in your letters to constituents—all of which *you* need." Besides distributing laurels widely in return for widespread support, cosponsorship may also help two or more Senators cooperate on a single bill when each would otherwise have introduced his own. Or it may dispose a key chairman to act favorably on a bill that comes before his committee (a possibility, like the preceding one, that we anticipated in the case of the

NHSC). In the most general sense, cosponsorship often becomes the medium of exchange in the political balance of payments: it may create, or it may discharge, debts between various Senators. (Just who becomes indebted to whom, however, depends upon the relative influence of the Senators involved: a high-ranking Senator *deigns* to cosponsor the legislation of a junior colleague, while a freshman is *privileged* to cosponsor a Chairman's bill.)

With so many ambiguities, a Senator rarely knows the precise motives of those colleagues who cosponsor his legislation. Some may genuinely find merit in his idea; some may simply feel they "owe him one"; and some may even be attempting to propitiate him in advance when they know they must disappoint him on some other impending issue of great importance. From his point of view, however, the cosponsors' motives matter less than their numbers, particularly if the list includes Senators in a position to help the bill's chances. A show of bipartisan support—and even better, what might be called "transideological" support—is always useful, since Congress tends to avoid legislation tinged with a party label or an "-ism." If Harold Hughes and Strom Thurmond both cosponsor a bill, for example, other Senators will consider it "safe," and probably vote for it whether or not they know anything about the bill's content.

For the NHSC, we wanted as many cosponsors as possible, of course, and we hoped particularly for Republicans (to make the bill appear less "radical") and members of the Labor and Public Welfare Committee (without whose support no health legislation can pass). Beyond these general aims, we felt we needed the cosponsorship of three specific men, all Democrats. The first, Senator Gaylord Nelson of Wisconsin, apparently intended to introduce his own NHSC bill; somehow we had to persuade him to cosponsor Magnuson's instead. The second, Senator Henry M. ("Scoop") Jackson, was Magnuson's junior colleague from

Washington State and a leader of the Armed Services Committee; we hoped he could calm the Pentagon if the military chiefs interpreted the NHSC as a threat to their own supply of doctors. Finally, we knew we needed help—or at least a blessing—from Senator Ralph Yarborough of Texas, the overlord (as Chairman of both the Labor and Public Welfare Committee and its Health Subcommittee) of all health legislation in the Senate.

We approached Nelson first, for although he lacked Jackson's or Yarborough's legislative influence, he could have wrecked our plans with an NHSC bill of his own. Not until mid-June, and then only by chance, had we learned of his interest in the health-corps concept: one of his aides unsuspectingly sent Bergman a letter asking for help in drafting an NHSC bill. The aide may have picked up Bergman's name from Dr. Laurence Platt of the PHS, but if so, Platt must have neglected to mention that the Seattle doctor worked solely for Senator Magnuson. Instead of answering the letter, Bergman quickly sent it to me, covering it with frantic red question marks, exclamation points, and orders to "DO SOMETHING!"

Bergman's alarm was justified: if Nelson acted first, Magnuson would not get credit for the NHSC idea, and more importantly, the idea itself would probably become impossible to pass. Unlike Magnuson—a "Senator's Senator," member of the "Inner Club," and formidable legislator— Nelson enjoyed little seniority (he had entered the Senate in 1963) and, as yet, even less influence. Among his colleagues, he had a reputation as a well-intentioned but "wild-eyed" liberal, successful as a popularizer and "idea man," but often moody and diffident in legislative matters. Were Nelson to introduce an NHSC bill, it might easily be ignored, or considered laughable, or denounced as "dangerous and unrealistic"—the antithesis, in any case, of the normal reaction to Magnuson's legislation. Once the NHSC bore Nelson's stamp, Magnuson would very likely consider the proposal lost, and his prognosis would probably be accurate.

To avert this breakdown, I called the Nelson aide who had written Bergman and invited him to Magnuson's office for a talk. He turned out to be a young medical student working in Nelson's office as a summer intern, not a bona fide legislative assistant, and I could see he felt just as inexperienced and uncertain of himself as I had a year earlier. With this in common, as well as a mutual belief in the NHSC, we had a friendly and candid conversation in which he admitted he had undertaken the project on his own, without instructions from Nelson. He knew he couldn't write a comprehensive NHSC bill by himself, but he hoped to persuade Nelson to introduce a rough bill and so call attention to the concept. Apparently he had already inserted an allusion to the NHSC in one of Nelson's speeches, and I didn't doubt that he could draft a bill of some sort for his employer to introduce. This type of legislation (known uncharitably as "garbage" in Senate jargon) sometimes succeeds in stimulating public discussion, but more often it is simply a legislative form of prospecting: like a small mining claim staked in a potentially rich area, it costs almost nothing and pays handsome returns (in the form of credit for the idea) should someone with better resources come along later and develop it.

Because the Nelson aide did not believe the NHSC could possibly pass in the few remaining months of the 91st Congress, his strategy had logic and consistency: calling attention to the proposal would be a good beginning, a sufficient goal for 1970. Looking back on my own experience, I realized he probably thought of the legislative process as a mysterious black box, into which proposals could be thrown indiscriminately and out of which—for no explicable reason—laws would one day emerge. He understood, I think, how little Senator Nelson could influence this input-output process, and in any event, he knew his own summer on Capitol Hill would be too short for a complete "dance of legislation." So he felt, quite naturally, that he would have done his job well merely to get an NHSC bill introduced.

Our office, on the other hand, assumed the NHSC *could* become law during the 91st Congress, but only with luck and with an influential author like Magnuson, whose legislation the Senate always takes seriously. The difference in outlook was as comprehensible as it was extreme ("You don't appreciate what it's like to work for a powerless Senator," a friend of mine, aide to a very junior Senator, once said. "You guys can pass laws; all *we* can do is sit around writing press releases"). Although I liked Nelson's aide, I realized we would have to trick him into believing that Magnuson would introduce an NHSC bill before Nelson's office could even write one.

The deception was relatively simple. Through some fast talking, some intimations of superior knowledge, and an apparently magnanimous offer to allow Nelson the consolation of being a "prime sponsor" (whatever that is) of the Magnuson bill, I soon persuaded the Nelson aide to give up trying to write a bill of his own. Actually, if he'd been more skeptical he could still have written a bill, for our conversation took place some weeks before Bergman and I had drafted Magnuson's. But he believed me happily enough, and seemed delighted that Nelson could still salvage some identification with the issue. The knowledge that the aide cared most about the NHSC eased my conscience a bit; if our bill made progress in the coming months, I knew my momentary disquiet over the tactic would probably disappear.

With Senator Nelson safely "on board" Magnuson's bill, we turned our attention to Jackson and Yarborough, the two men who could help us most; this time our approach was completely honest. Bergman had recognized Jackson's potential importance from the beginning, for we feared the

Pentagon's opposition and needed someone to reassure the military chiefs of the NHSC's modest and experimental nature. Moreover, the Senate Armed Services Committee might demand a look at the bill, even though it did not affect the draft law directly, and with so little time remaining in the 91st Congress, sending the legislation to that Committee would effectively kill it. As a ranking member of the Armed Services Committee and the Senate's leading "hawk" (a label he disclaimed), Jackson could prevent these difficulties; if worse came to worst, he could draw on his unique relationship with Defense Secretary Melvin Laird (himself a former health-oriented Congressman) to help the bill.

Although we needed Jackson's assistance for these reasons, we had other, less selfish motives in asking him to cosponsor Magnuson's bill. Bergman, in fact, was almost wholly altruistic: he supported Jackson politically, and wanted to help him bolster his liberal image and answer his antimilitary critics with a health-care bill that served the poor and provided young doctors an alternative to military service. Jackson might have considered Bergman's suggestion gratuitous—he was electorally secure, and his few detractors never seemed to bother him—but he probably would have agreed on the desirability of our other ulterior aim: strengthening the spirit of cooperation between his office and Magnuson's. In the summer of 1970, somewhat uncharacteristically, that spirit often seemed surprisingly weak.

Junior and senior Senators from the same state rarely enjoy a warm relationship; they must compete for publicity, campaign resources, and esteem, and often end up bitter rivals. Magnuson and Jackson generally appear to be an exception. They ranked, in 1970, fifth and fourteenth in seniority and chaired two of the Senate's sixteen standing committees, and they make a devastatingly effective legislative team. They vote together—on nonmilitary issues, at least—nearly 90 percent of the time. They also relax and joke with each other frequently, in private as well as in public. All of this makes them unusual among men representing the same state.

Yet the Magnuson and Jackson staffs sometimes fail to reflect this amity, and even the Senators themselves occasionally lose patience with each other. Magnuson's staff tends to resent Jackson's phenomenal popularity in Washington State; whereas Magnuson received a remarkable 65 percent of the vote in 1968, Jackson got fully 72 percent in 1964 (and later, 84 percent in 1970). Moreover, virtually all of Magnuson's aides disagree with Jackson on military matters, his legislative specialty, and consequently Jackson's staff members often seem to consider their counterparts down the hall disloyal. Jackson's aides also envy Magnuson's greater seniority and his choice seat on the Appropriations Committee—a post only one Senator from each state can hold if both belong to the same party. Magnuson, too, had better luck than Jackson: he became Washington's senior Senator after only two years (in 1946), while Jackson has been the junior Senator since his election in 1952. Given these circumstances, it is perhaps understandable that occasional strains develop within "the best-working team in the U.S. Senate" (as Magnuson and Jackson often advertise themselves in their campaign literature).

What aggravated these chronic but generally mild tensions in mid-1970 was that military issues—the one subject on which Magnuson and Jackson cannot reconcile their views—suddenly dominated Congressional activity and debate. When Cambodia and Kent State thrust Senate resolutions and amendments into prominence on editorial pages and the evening news, Magnuson's developing dovishness contrasted sharply with Jackson's leadership of the "hardliners," and both offices grew increasingly uneasy. Jackson, who faced a "peace" candidate in his reelection campaign, apparently feared that Magnuson's independent position

and antiwar speeches might be used against him, yet neither Senator could, in conscience, change his views to
accommodate the other. Magnuson supported the Church-
Cooper Amendment on Cambodia, the McGovern-Hatfield
"Amendment to End the War," another amendment to
halt deployment of the anti–ballistic missile (ABM) that
Jackson championed, and finally, he led a successful Senate
fight to cut off funds for a proposed shipment of nerve gas
through the Pacific Northwest.* The nerve-gas issue worried Washington State voters even more than the war, for it
threatened them more directly, yet Jackson actually voted
against Magnuson's legislation to block the shipment. Jackson was told first, however, when the Pentagon finally relented, and in announcing the news he omitted any reference to the long struggle Magnuson had led; ironically, the
press gave Jackson most of the credit for stopping the gas.
While this incident irritated Magnuson's office, Jackson's
staff felt outraged in turn when Magnuson suggested publicly that Washington State colleges should provide a pre-
election recess to enable students to work in political
campaigns; evidently they assumed the students would not
work for Jackson. (Magnuson had recommended the recess
for the November general election, however, not for the
September primary in which the "peace" candidate opposed Jackson.)

We had drafted the NHSC at the height of these inter-
office hostilities, and the bill seemed like an appropriate
olive branch to offer. Both offices would benefit through
reconciliation and cooperation, and I particularly wanted
to be part of a joint legislative venture because some of
Jackson's staff believed (mistakenly) that I had been re-

---

* Jackson and many other "hawks" did support the Church-Cooper
Amendment on the final roll-call vote, but only after they had succeeded in amending it to their own satisfaction. For Magnuson's
tactics on the nerve-gas issue and his earlier opposition to the ABM,
see Chapter X.

sponsible for the college-recess plan. Magnuson, who regarded the growing staff feud as childish in the extreme,
agreed that the NHSC bill should be shared with Jackson;
in fact, he wanted Jackson as a "coauthor" of the bill, not
merely as a cosponsor. He instructed me, as did Stan Barer,
to coordinate plans for the bill's introduction with Jackson's staff, and he promised to speak with Jackson personally when the latter returned from a week of campaigning
in Washington State.

With an electoral battle at home and legislative battles in
Congress, Jackson had divided his staff, as well as his time,
between Seattle and the Capital. The chain of command in
his office was temporarily unsettled, and I discussed the
NHSC not with one of his personal aides, but with Bill Van
Ness of Jackson's Interior Committee staff. Van Ness understood immediately all the reasons we wanted Jackson as
"coauthor" of the bill; he said he would read the legislation
first, then decide whether or not to approach Jackson about
it. In return, I agreed to draft an introductory speech for
Jackson and send it to Van Ness enough ahead of time for
him to alter it if he wished.

Within a week, Van Ness had the speech and Magnuson
had Jackson as a "coauthor" of the NHSC. Now only one of
our three original targets remained: Senator Yarborough,
the most important but also the most enigmatic. Yarborough had just been defeated in the Texas Democratic
primary, and consequently he had only a few months left to
serve in his unhappily truncated Senate career. Other Senators in the same position have frequently abandoned the
Senate and sulked, but Yarborough surprised observers by
working harder than ever before. As Chairman of the
Labor and Public Welfare Committee, he seemed determined to pass as much legislation as possible in the waning
weeks of the 91st Congress; his bemused aides speculated
(presciently, as it turned out) that despite his sixty-five
years, Yarborough probably had it in mind to run again.

Whatever his motives, we hoped to persuade Yarborough to include the NHSC bill on his ambitious agenda, but we knew we faced potential difficulties. Yarborough, his staff told us, suspected that Magnuson had once kept him off the HEW Appropriations Subcommittee (in fact, however, the Chairman of the Appropriations Committee, Georgia's Richard Russell, had blackballed Yarborough because he thought the HEW Subcommittee was becoming "too liberal"). In addition, Yarborough's aides claimed that Magnuson had failed to act on many of the Texan's bills in earlier years when Yarborough had been a member of Magnuson's Commerce Committee; might he not now seek revenge by ignoring a bill himself?

In order to mollify Yarborough and win his support, we decided to make him too a coauthor of the bill: "The Magnuson-Jackson-Yarborough Act" seemed an unwieldy nickname for a law, but without Yarborough it couldn't become a law at all, at least in 1970. This offer, however, hardly overwhelmed Jack Forsythe, the Chief Counsel of Yarborough's Committee. Nonetheless, he found the NHSC bill acceptable and, after all, he and Harley Dirks had become good friends through their past cooperation on the legislative and funding aspects of HEW affairs. So Forsythe agreed to raise the matter with Yarborough, although he emphasized that he couldn't commit Yarborough to support the legislation until the Chairman himself agreed. Moreover, he flatly refused to help if Magnuson tried to pass the NHSC as a Floor amendment. "The bill *must* come to this Committee," he asserted, "and if the Chairman and the Committee members like it, there's time enough left to pass it on its own."

So now we had to abandon the Floor-amendment strategy too, but Forsythe reassured us that the Committee could still pass the bill if it was suitable, and he predicted that Yarborough would agree to coauthor it. He told Harley he would try to get an answer from Yarborough quickly, and suggested that in the meantime I contact other members of the Committee and invite them to join as cosponsors. This latter suggestion encouraged us, for we doubted Forsythe would want other Committee members to cosponsor the bill if he thought Yarborough might oppose it. As it happened, the other Democrats on the Health Subcommittee cosponsored it almost immediately.

The Republicans, however, remained aloof at first. Even though they were in a minority on the Committee and in the Senate as a whole, and thus in theory could not block the bill if the Democrats agreed upon it, we knew that not all Democrats would support the legislation and that it would look suspiciously partisan without a few Republican names on top. I began to worry that HEW might have given the Republicans instructions, but Harley Dirks dismissed this with a laugh. "One thing you ought to know by now," he said, "is that HEW simply isn't that well organized." He guessed instead that some Republicans would soon begin to straggle individually to the bill's support.

At this point, according to Senate protocol, we should have waited as patiently as possible for Yarborough to make his decision. Protocol and prudence reinforced each other, for we might offend Yarborough if we moved prematurely, and to offend the chairman of a committee that must approve one's legislation is generally an act of legislative suicide. And yet, as we soon discovered, Senate protocol would be much easier to observe if only the Senate could enact laws without the House of Representatives.

3.

Senator Magnuson's chief partner in this particular legislative enterprise was not his junior colleague from Washington State, nor the Chairman of the Committee on Labor and Public Welfare, but rather a Florida Congressman, Representative Paul Rogers. Broadly speaking, Rogers controlled health legislation in the House the way Yarborough did in the Senate, although Rogers officially held no chairmanship. Representative John Jarman of Oklahoma chaired the House Health Subcommittee, in fact, but Jarman had gained the post through longevity rather than design. Having little interest in health affairs, Jarman had simply relinquished to Rogers all the Chairman's prerogatives except his title, and now Rogers unabashedly ran the Subcommittee from his personal office.

On most issues, Rogers was a thoroughly conservative legislator (his ADA rating sometimes fell below double figures), but he had progressive and ambitious goals in the field of health. Coincidentally, the House and the Senate both needed new health leaders: for twenty years, Representative John Fogarty of Rhode Island and Senator Lister Hill of Alabama had determined Congressional health policy as a two-man cartel, but in 1968 Fogarty had died and Hill declined to seek reelection. Yarborough's defeat left the Senate role vacant again, but in the House, Rogers still strove to assume Fogarty's fallen mantle. He needed ideas for new legislation, and welcomed any visitor with an imaginative proposal. Not surprisingly, Bergman had visited Rogers early in 1970 and mentioned the NHSC; Rogers had already heard of the concept, and agreed at once to introduce legislation jointly with Magnuson. Since then, I had been in almost daily contact with Rogers' top aide, a young lawyer named Bob Maher.

Although soft-spoken and unassuming, Maher had unusually quick political reflexes and an almost instinctive grasp of the dilemma of Rogers' career: how to be a progressive legislator, even in one policy field, with an archconservative Florida Gold Coast constituency. The NHSC appealed to Maher and his employer, and they believed the legislation wouldn't worry conservatives if it was properly described (Maher liked the bit about "strengthening the system of private practice"). We agreed that our office would prepare the bill itself, and that Rogers could suggest wording changes before he and Magnuson introduced it. This spared Maher most of the preliminary work—and, as it turned out, most of the frustrations of dealing with HEW—but it relieved our office of the fear that Rogers might act without waiting for Magnuson if difficulties developed in the Senate (every Congressional office fantasizes that someone else will "steal" its legislative ideas; for example, we refused to show anyone a draft of the NHSC bill until we were ready to solicit cosponsors).

By mid-July, however, Maher was becoming impatient. Had the roles we agreed upon been reversed, he probably would have understood HEW earlier than I had, and drafted his own bill sooner. Now that I had sent him a copy of our bill, considerations of time and his employer's temper dictated that we set a date for the bill's joint introduction. But until Yarborough decided to support the bill, I couldn't give Maher a date: we could hardly hand Yarborough an ultimatum, informing him that Magnuson would introduce the bill without him if he hadn't made up his mind by such-and-such a date. And yet, unfortunately, this was precisely what we ended up doing, for now that Maher had a copy of the bill, *he* presented an ultimatum to *us*.

If Magnuson would not agree to introduce the bill on a specific date, Maher threatened that Rogers would introduce it himself and revert to the amendment-in-committee strategy, for the House Health Subcommittee had still not passed the Public Health Services Amendments of 1970. Yet this strategy could no longer work: even if Rogers steered the amended legislation through the House, the NHSC provisions would not be part of the State version. When the conference committee of House and Senate Health Subcommittee members met to reconcile differences between the two versions of the Public Health Service Amendments, the Senate conferees would insist that the NHSC sections be deleted. Forsythe had stated categorically that the Senate Committee would not support the NHSC if Magnuson offered it as a Floor amendment, and the same Senators would hardly accept the program if the Senate had not passed it at all. Only if the Senate Committee and the Senate as a whole passed the NHSC as a separate bill could it now become law.

From Maher's point of view, however, it was better to introduce the bill and make progress toward a law in the next Congress (or even to introduce it and hope the Senate Committee would relent) than to procrastinate and perhaps lose the opportunity for at least one House of Congress to pass the NHSC in 1970.* When I related this unhappy new development to Forsythe, I found not only that Yarborough had reached no decision, but that Forsythe had little sympathy with our predicament. So what if the legislative situation became unmanageable? It was our bill, not his.

At this point, Magnuson himself had to decide what to do. We talked about the problem, and he and Barer both agreed that Rogers acting on his own presented the graver risk. Yarborough happened to be out of town, and we couldn't predict whether or not he'd make a decision even when he returned. And as Magnuson pointed out, Rogers was an important ally to keep: he could help the NHSC next year, if it took more than one year to pass, but Yarborough would be gone.

Still uncomfortable, I called Maher on July 15 and set July 21, the following Tuesday, for the bill's introduction. Could Forsythe get an answer from Yarborough that

---

* Any bill that fails to pass both the House and Senate by the time Congress adjourns must begin again during the next Congress; but in practical terms, passage by one House often helps bring action more quickly the next time.

quickly? I called him to ask, and although the question irritated him unmistakably, he replied simply, "Yes, that ought to be enough time."

By Monday, July 20, however, we still had not learned of Yarborough's decision. Anxious, I called Forsythe again; he informed me curtly that he had asked Yarborough three times already without receiving a definite response. He said he would try once more, but promised nothing, and warned that in case Yarborough made a last-minute decision, I should instruct the Recording Clerk of the Senate to "keep the *Record* open": that is, the Clerk should be prepared to add Yarborough's name to the bill even after Magnuson introduced it, provided the day's *Congressional Record* had not already gone to print.

Maher called as soon as Forsythe hung up; Congressman Rogers wanted to discuss the bill, he said. Rogers picked up the phone and reassured me immediately that he liked our draft of the bill and had studied it carefully. He did want to make some minor technical changes, however. For example, in our draft the authorized funding for the NHSC would be "$5,000,000 annually"—a figure we had set somewhat arbitrarily simply by doubling the cost estimate (and hence the number of doctors) in Dr. Platt's Zuni Indian proposal. Rogers wanted this to read "$5,000,000 for fiscal years 1971, 1972 and 1973." This change, he said, would reassure any Congressman who might fear the program would mushroom into a wasteful and sprawling bureaucracy; also, the three-year authorization was customary, for it provided a definite date on which the legislation itself could be renewed (we had drafted the bill so that Congress could expand the NHSC simply by increasing the funding level).

Then Rogers told me he intended to ask for cosponsors at a meeting that afternoon of the Health Subcommittee. I said we would be grateful if he'd allow Representative Brock Adams of Seattle to join as a cosponsor too; although Adams didn't belong to the Health Subcommittee and

could do little to assist Rogers with the bill, he did belong
to our state's Congressional delegation, and we hoped to
help him with his constituents. Rogers graciously acceded
to this request, and also gave his enthusiastic approval for
me to proceed with the publicity we had carefully arranged
to herald the bill's introduction.

4.

Although we had planned the publicity elaborately, as is
customary on Capitol Hill, serendipity had influenced our
selection of the reporter who would "break" the NHSC
story. In mid-June, I had substituted for Senator Magnuson
and delivered a speech on the World Environmental Institute to the Environmental Health Association at its annual
convention in Las Vegas' Sahara Hotel. I had shared the
platform for a time with Craig Palmer, a journalist who
covered HEW affairs for United Press International
(UPI). Palmer wanted to find a story more than he wanted
to gamble or ogle the nude dancers elsewhere in the hotel,
but unfortunately, I could answer very few of his questions
about Magnuson's HEW Appropriations hearings, then
under way in Washington, D.C. When I mentioned Magnuson's NHSC plans, however, Palmer immediately began
to scribble notes on his loose-leaf pad; as a professional
commentator on American health policy, he well understood the bill's significance. We quickly agreed that when
the bill was ready, Palmer could have an exclusive "scoop."

Palmer's interest in our plans meant that Magnuson
could achieve nationwide publicity when he introduced the
bill. Without Palmer or someone like him, we could only
have issued a standard press release, and even if the Senate
press corps understood the proposal, they would probably
ignore the press release as self-serving and as the product of

a Senator on whom public attention rarely focused. Because Washington newsmen generally devote most of their stories to men whose ambitions are Presidential rather than legislative, bills like the NHSC often progress methodically toward passage—or expire anonymously in committee—without the general public ever learning of their existence. A reporter like Palmer, however, can draw on his specialized knowledge and his position with a major wire service to alert thousands of potential supporters (and, of course, potential opponents) in the lay and professional communities to a bill that interests them. And because it is more difficult to kill "public interest" legislation if the public knows about it, we anticipated that Palmer's story would help the NHSC.

After we had drafted the bill itself, I called Palmer at his Washington office to arrange another meeting. Ironically, convenience dictated that we lunch in one of Palmer's haunts, the basement cafeteria of HEW, where I gave him a copy of the bill, Magnuson's and Jackson's speeches, and a section-by-section analysis of the legislation. In parting, I asked that he not release his story until we told him we were ready, and I gave him this final go-ahead within minutes of talking with Congressman Rogers on Monday, July 20.

I had anticipated that Palmer's story would achieve prominence; what startled me was how quickly he got it "on the wire." Only four hours after I had spoken with him, I happened to glance at a Washington *Evening Star* during an afternoon break in the Senate coffee shop. BILL SEEKS CARE OF POOR BY GOVERNMENT DOCTORS blared a two-column headline on the front page. Stunned, I thought at first some *other* bill had appeared on the eve of the NHSC's planned debut (that paranoid fantasy of stolen legislative ideas is persistent). But Palmer's by-line, and the opening paragraphs of the story, assured me immediately that our bill was indeed the subject of the article. As I read, I found to my relief that Palmer had not portrayed the bill as exclusively Magnuson's: "the plan will be introduced tomorrow by Senators Warren G. Magnuson and Henry M. Jackson, both Washington Democrats, and by Representative Paul Rogers, D.-Fla." This would please Van Ness and Maher, I reckoned; the venture was truly cooperative.

Since we had planted the news story ourselves, my excitement had no more logic than that of a businessman reading an advertisement for his company's product. But I felt rewarded that the NHSC, after months of obscure and laborious preparations, had finally received its due acclaim. Without finishing my coffee, I rushed upstairs to Magnuson's office, clutching the *Evening Star* tightly in both hands. The story's status on the front page and its general accuracy pleased Stan Barer, although we admitted to each other that we'd never thought of the NHSC simply as a bill seeking "CARE OF POOR BY GOVERNMENT DOCTORS." We reasoned, however, that the headline writers could hardly have said BILL SEEKS TO STRENGTHEN SYSTEM OF PRIVATE PRACTICE IN AMERICA; there was nothing very dramatic about that. So we took the paper to Magnuson, sitting at his desk, and although the Senator feigned nonchalance when he read the article, he nonetheless put the entire newspaper under his paperweight rather than relinquish it. I had to go downstairs again to buy another copy.

The next morning Senator Magnuson made an honest man of Craig Palmer. He rode the subway to the Senate, waited to gain the Floor, and then handed the Presiding Officer a copy of the bill and his typewritten speech (to save time, introductory speeches are seldom read aloud, but they are printed in the *Congressional Record* as if they had been). Senator Jackson also handed in his speech—in which, to my satisfaction, Van Ness had found it necessary to make no changes. Senator Nelson and Senator Edward

M. Kennedy also submitted speeches (the latter surprised us); only Senator Yarborough had not yet been heard from.

Duayne Trecker, Magnuson's Press Secretary, issued an explanatory press release for reporters whom Palmer's article might have intrigued; the release, as well as Magnuson's speech, called attention to the fact that Rogers and Congressman Adams had introduced the bill simultaneously in the House, and emphasized that Senator Jackson had "coauthored"—not merely "cosponsored"—the Senate bill. Even though we'd written the bill exclusively in Magnuson's office, we wanted our allies to know we considered them equal partners.

After reminding the Recording Clerk that Yarborough might make a belated decision to get his name on the bill, Magnuson turned to his Press Secretary and made what was, for him, an almost unprecedented concession: he agreed to tape an announcement of the bill for television. Trecker was stunned; Magnuson *never* agreed to make tapes for television news programs, and Trecker had almost resigned himself to the fact that he was a publicity agent for a politician who shunned publicity. Magnuson, after all, was something of a charter member in the Senate's reclusive "Inner Club," one of whose norms (as popular journals and scholarly tracts agree) is to disdain publicity; "Club" members should make laws, not headlines. Moreover, Magnuson occasionally seemed self-conscious about his no longer youthful appearance; he knew he didn't look like Bobby Kennedy or Mayor Lindsay in front of a television camera.

This time, however, Magnuson good-naturedly consented to cut a tape that Trecker could have flown out to Seattle in time for local screening that evening. Whether this decision grew out of enthusiasm for the NHSC bill or whether he simply felt the time had come to indulge his Press Secretary, Magnuson gamely endured the makeup men, the lighting crews, the cameramen, and the team of technicians who supervise filming and taping in the Senate Recording Studio, deep in the basement of the Capitol Building. Sitting before a backdrop painted as a window revealing a view of the Capitol Dome, and with the obligatory American flag planted at his side, Magnuson earnestly described the National Health Service Corps bill for an audience 3,000 miles away, most of whom probably had not yet awakened to begin the day whose news was already being prepared for them.

Magnuson did an excellent job on the tape, but as we walked back to the office through the underground tunnels, he seemed pensive and began to frown slightly. Probing, I remarked that the events surrounding the bill's introduction had been auspicious.

"Well," Magnuson replied reprovingly, "don't get your hopes up on account of all this stuff [he waved his hand disdainfully toward the Recording Studio]. We have a lot of problems with this bill, and it's not going to be easy to get it passed."

Later that night, at home in my Capitol Hill apartment, I puzzled over the Senator's pessimistic remarks and his sudden dourness after the taping session. He was right, of course, that the bill had a long way to go before reaching the President's desk (and who knew what problems might develop if it did?), but we had also made a creditable beginning, and perhaps surprised some of our acquaintances at the Department of Health, Education and Welfare. I wanted to savor the sensations of the past two days, not discourage myself with thoughts of the obstacles still facing us. Perhaps I had irritated Magnuson with my unrestrained and unseemly grins; he might have been embarrassed, walking along with such an amateurish aide. If so, I told myself, I'd have to strive for greater dignity and decorum the next morning, when I would go to the office early to review the day's events in the *Congressional Record*.

V

S. 4106: BORN OR STILLBORN?

1.

Twenty copies of the July 21 *Congressional Record* lay bound in twine just inside the door of Magnuson's office when I arrived the next morning. Using a letter opener from the receptionist's desk, I hastily sawed through the thick cord and removed the top copy, thumbing the pages rapidly until I caught the name "Mr. MAGNUSON." The speeches were there, printed in order, and at the top of the column stood the bill's official number: S. 4106. The list of cosponsors unfortunately did not include Senator Yarborough; while not unexpected, this omission prompted an audible curse. Continuing down the page, I skimmed Magnuson's and Jackson's speeches for typographical errors (we would reproduce these pages of the *Record* for interested constituents), then read what Senators Nelson and Kennedy had said about the bill. Everything seemed in order with respect to S. 4106; turning to the section entitled "Proceedings of the House," I scanned the pages to see how

Congressman Rogers had managed. Disconcertingly, I could find no mention of Rogers' name.

At first I thought I'd skipped a page or passed over Rogers' name without realizing it; I was notorious in Magnuson's office for my inability to locate things in the *Record*. So I turned back to the beginning of the House section, running my finger down each column to prevent another oversight. Yet I still couldn't find Rogers' name, or any mention of the "National Health Service Corps Act of 1970." Puzzled, I picked up the phone and called Rogers' office; oddly, the inane touch-dial melody suddenly annoyed me.

Maher came on the line, but volunteered no explanation. Had Rogers introduced the bill or not? I asked irritably. No, Maher replied brusquely, Rogers had not introduced the bill, and Rogers did not *intend* to introduce the bill. Stunned, I asked what had happened. Maher answered bitterly: " 'BILL SEEKS CARE OF POOR BY GOVERNMENT DOCTORS,' *that's* what happened!"

Resentfully, Maher described the past two days in the House. Rogers first took a draft of the NHSC bill to his Health Subcommittee meeting on Monday afternoon, just as he had planned. Instead of finding cosponsors, however, he found immediate opposition—and he saw, for the first time, a copy of Palmer's article in the *Evening Star*. Representative Tim Lee Carter of Kentucky, a Republican, had read the story on his way to the meeting; angrily, he accused Rogers of planning to "socialize" American medicine. The article and its headline shocked Rogers, and he stalked back to his office after finding Carter's sentiments widespread among the other Subcommittee members. Maher too had been upset; the purpose of the bill was to "bring doctors to needy communities," not—as the article suggested—to have the government take over the care of the poor. The next morning Rogers had refused to introduce the bill, ostensibly because the article had irrevocably prejudiced the Health Subcommittee against the legislation (later, we also learned that a group of Florida doctors had seen the story in their local newspapers, passed a resolution opposing the bill, and immediately sent Rogers a telegram expressing their views).

Would it help if Magnuson talked with Rogers? I asked Maher in desperation. "Well," he replied doubtfully, "you might try it, but frankly I think you can count Rogers out, at least for this year." Magnuson did call Rogers minutes later, but Maher's appraisal proved accurate. "He's really shaken," Magnuson reported in frustration after hanging up.

I felt shaken too. We had always known that Rogers and Yarborough were the only members of Congress without whose support the NHSC could not become law in the 91st Congress. To appease Rogers, we had risked Yarborough's displeasure and fixed a date for the joint introduction of the bill. Since Yarborough had not reached a decision by that date, we had probably alienated him, and now Rogers had failed even to introduce the bill in the House. Ironically, S. 4106 seemed further from passage now than it had before its introduction. And no one in our office had any immediate idea about how to resurrect it.

2.

Unable to devise a new strategy, we soon found we had no choice but to attempt a reconstruction, however difficult, of the Magnuson-Rogers-Yarborough alliance. But my first call to Forsythe after the debacle of July 21 unfortunately revealed even greater animosity than we had anticipated. The introduction of S. 4106 without Yarborough's blessing irritated Forsythe, as we'd expected, but he expressed greater displeasure over a misunderstanding we hadn't foreseen. Apparently aides to other members of Yarborough's Committee had called Forsythe to find out the Chairman's views before cosponsoring the bill themselves; one of these aides told Forsythe that I had claimed Yarborough already supported the bill. This "misrepresentation" on my part infuriated Forsythe, and had I really made such a statement to anyone, his anger would have been justified. I tried to explain that I had mentioned Yarborough only when asked, and that I had confined myself to repeating Forsythe's opinion that Yarborough would soon give us his approval, although he had not yet done so (Forsythe himself must have said something similar to his callers, for their Senators did cosponsor the bill without waiting for Yarborough). Yet whether or not Forsythe believed my explanation, it failed to placate him.

"I've tried to help you," he said hotly, "and I've been to see Yarborough about this bill four times. I'm not going to stick my neck out any more. If Maggie still wants Yarborough's name on the bill, he'll just have to ask him himself."

Forsythe's adamant declaration discouraged us. Senators are uniquely proud individuals, and Senators in Magnuson's position are unaccustomed to asking favors humbly of their colleagues. The mere suggestion that Magnuson ought to plead with Yarborough for his support might have struck the Senator as both useless and humiliating, particularly since it now appeared likely that Yarborough's successor, not the Texan himself, would ultimately have the responsibility for S. 4106's enactment. Yet progress of even a limited nature during the 91st Congress required Yarborough's help, and to give up trying for his cosponsorship (now that his opportunity to "coauthor" the bill had passed) meant giving up the NHSC itself until the following year. But how could we circumvent Forsythe's demand that Magnuson make the request of Yarborough personally?

The thought struck us that Magnuson could write Yarborough a letter instead of talking to him directly; the

Senator might sign a letter willingly, and we wouldn't even have to raise the embarrassing topic of his making a personal request. But would a piece of paper satisfy Yarborough? Forsythe had seemed to hint that the Chairman sought the satisfaction of Magnuson coming to him. What did he want? A deal of some sort? A chance to redress real or imagined wounds? We couldn't know. And so, uncertain of the results it would produce, we simply drafted a short note that Magnuson signed and mailed to the mysterious Chairman.

We did not expect Yarborough's reply immediately, and in the meantime we pondered how to overcome Congressman Rogers' misgivings. He had advocated the NHSC so fervently, before the appearance of that unfortunate headline, that neither Bergman nor I could believe his refusal to introduce the bill was irreversible. When Bergman flew back to Washington, D.C., at the end of July, Maher arranged to have us talk with the Congressman in his office. Tall and bespectacled, Rogers welcomed us cordially when we arrived, and he reiterated his support of the NHSC "in principle" even before seating us on the overstuffed couch in his inner office. From behind his memorabilia-strewn desk, he chided us lightly for the form Palmer's article had taken, but he spoke in tones more wistful than acrimonious. Through a mishap none of us had foreseen, we had lost the easy opportunity to create the NHSC, and now he could do nothing, he said, to pass legislation on the subject without first changing the climate in the Health Subcommittee.

"What they don't like," he explained of his colleagues, "is the idea of another do-good antipoverty *corps*. It sounds too much like one of these hopelessly idealistic projects everyone was dreaming up around here a few years back. I still think we can find a way to accomplish the same ends, but we've got to find a different means now."

Bergman and I didn't want to press Rogers; it was enough, for the time being, to learn that the legislative goal still tantalized him. Maher, who had remained silent throughout the brief meeting, seemed apologetic afterward as the three of us left Rogers' office and walked toward the elevator. "You can see the problem," he said with resignation, "but you can also understand his position."

Yet Rogers' unwillingness to proceed had created another problem for us in the House. Magnuson's speech, television tape, and press release had all named Congressman Brock Adams of Seattle as a cosponsor of the House bill—and now, embarrassingly, there *was* no House bill. Ironically, the Seattle papers hadn't covered the bill's introduction anyway—although almost every other major American newspaper had—but the smaller papers around Puget Sound had reprinted the press release more or less verbatim. Consequently, Adams had begun to receive letters and requests for copies of the bill, and he had nothing to mail his constituents in response. Rather than try to explain why no House bill existed, Adams' staff let the inquiries accumulate, simultaneously seeking from Magnuson's office permission for Adams to introduce the bill in Rogers' stead.

This request from Adams' staff put us in an extremely delicate position. We didn't want to add to the Congressman's difficulties (after all, we had told him about the bill originally only to help him), nor did we wish to offend him, but realistically we knew that his introducing the NHSC bill would kill its chances in the House—much as Nelson's introducing it might have killed it in the Senate. Neither Adams nor Nelson, despite good intentions, had yet become an effective legislative advocate. Adams' legislative disability stemmed from his junior status in a rigidly hierarchical institution and from his outspoken attempts to achieve House reform. Only recently, for example, he had participated in the dismally unsuccessful effort to unseat the aging Speaker of the House, John McCormack. As a result, the House Leadership would inevitably block any bill Adams introduced.

Under the circumstances, we obviously hoped Adams

would not introduce the NHSC bill, but the difficulty lay in preventing him from doing so if he chose to. Any Congressman can introduce any legislation he wants; there are no copyrights in the legislative process. In fact, some Congressman, unknown to us, could easily have taken the text of S. 4106 from the *Congressional Record* and introduced it in the House as his own.* But of the more than 20,000 bills introduced in the House during the 91st Congress, only a few hundred would ever become public law, and those that did would have come from Congressmen like Paul Rogers. All we could do was ask Adams' staff to wait, to realize that Rogers was crucial to the bill's passage and that to proceed without him would be to alienate his potential support (we avoided, of course, any discussion of Adams himself, and talked instead about Rogers' legislative "quirks"). To make this vigil more hopeful, we portrayed Rogers as poised to introduce the bill once minor technical changes could be agreed to in its text—a fiction that grew less and less credible as Rogers remained silent and as unanswered constituent letters continued to mount in Adams' office.

For a brief but unsettling moment, the circumstances of S. 4106's introduction also seemed likely to incur the displeasure of an even more important member of the Washington State Congressional delegation—Senator Jackson. Although we had taken extraordinarily detailed precautions to make Jackson appear as Magnuson's equal in the NHSC venture, the official copy of S. 4106 returned from the printers in a form suggesting that Jackson was nothing more than an ordinary cosponsor. Instead of showing that the bill had been introduced by "Mr. MAGNUSON and Mr. JACKSON (for themselves, Mr. CRANSTON, Mr. HUGHES, Mr. KENNEDY, . . . and Mr. WILLIAMS)," the notation read "Mr. MAGNUSON (for himself, Mr. JACKSON, Mr. CRANSTON, Mr. HUGHES, . . . and

---

* See Chapter XI.

Mr. WILLIAMS)." Certain that Jackson's staff would suspect us of treachery even over such a minor matter, I hurriedly took the bill to the Senate Parliamentarian, with
whom I became involved in a heated altercation. Drawing
on his arcane specialty, the Parliamentarian maddeningly
rebuffed me. There can be only one *official* author of any
bill, he said. Senator Magnuson had physically handed this
bill to the Presiding Officer of the Senate; *ergo*, Senator
Magnuson was the author. The Parliamentarian added
(somewhat disingenuously, I thought) that Jackson was
clearly preeminent among the other cosponsors: his name
followed Magnuson's immediately, whereas all the others
appeared in alphabetical order.

Since this answer failed to satisfy me, I doubted it would
satisfy Jackson's staff, but when I apprehensively took a
copy of S. 4106 to Bill Van Ness, he reassured me at once
and dismissed the entire matter as too trivial for consideration. Since the *Congressional Record* excerpts that both
offices had had reprinted made the coauthorship clear and
also contained the text of the bill, in the end we simply
mailed these reprints to constituents instead of sending the
bill itself. (When the Senate Document Room depleted its
initial stocks of S. 4106, the bill was reprinted, and in this
second edition Senator Jackson's name was inexplicably removed from its "privileged" position and simply alpha-
betized along with the rest. *This* time the Parliamentarian
admitted a mistake—by the printers, of course).

3.

Although we continually reassured Congressman Adams'
staff to the contrary, we soon realized that Rogers would
not introduce a companion bill to S. 4106. Rather than let
Adams substitute for Rogers, however, we decided to ask

for help from another Congressman, one with enough "clout" to champion the bill successfully in the House: Harley O. Staggers, Democrat, of West Virginia.

We considered Staggers an ideal replacement, for two reasons. First, as Chairman of the House Commerce Committee (officially the "Committee on Interstate and Foreign Commerce"), he already enjoyed a working relationship with Magnuson, his counterpart as Chairman of the Senate Commerce Committee. Staggers and Magnuson understood each other; they had sat together on dozens of conference committees and negotiated privately over countless bills awaiting action in one Commerce Committee or the other. More important, because of a jurisdictional difference between the House and Senate, Staggers had ultimate control over health legislation in the House, where the Health Subcommittee belonged to the Commerce Committee (in the Senate, the Health Subcommittee came under Yarborough's Labor and Public Welfare Committee instead). Thus Rogers was Staggers' subordinate; and since Magnuson's Committee had to approve most nonhealth legislation emanating from Staggers' Committee, the basis for a quid pro quo between the two chairmen clearly existed.

But could we possibly persuade Staggers to take an interest in the NHSC? The white-haired Chairman had traditionally allowed the Health Subcommittee almost complete autonomy; why should he suddenly unsettle expectations—and rebuke Paul Rogers—by reaching down to manipulate a relatively minor and perhaps doomed bill? Magnuson might conceivably have won Staggers' grudging cooperation by holding hostage in the Senate Commerce Committee some bill that Staggers' Committee had already passed, but unfortunately, Staggers and not Magnuson held the hostages in the summer of 1970. The activity of the Senate Commerce Committee had, as usual, exceeded that of its cautious House counterpart during the 91st Congress; none of Staggers' bills awaited action in the Senate, while many of Magnuson's had passed the Senate only to accumulate in the House. In fact, one of these Senate-passed bills that Staggers had already stalled was the Bergman-inspired "Poison Prevention Packaging Act," a Magnuson proposal to require "childproof" containers for all toxic household products. The inaction on this bill indicated the momentary lack of tools for bargaining with Staggers.*

Under the circumstances, we couldn't easily propose a "deal" to Staggers. But Magnuson could ask Staggers to introduce the NHSC bill as a personal favor, and leave the Congressman to puzzle out whether the request meant Magnuson wanted compensation for his other legislation that Staggers held in limbo, or whether it contained an implicit offer to reciprocate if Staggers sought a similar favor in the future. Magnuson willingly agreed to this tactic, and wrote Staggers a friendly and informal note—beginning "Dear Harley"—asking him to introduce a House version of S. 4106. "Paul Rogers had intended to introduce the bill," the Senator wrote, "but apparently he was worried about doing it in an election year."

No sooner had Magnuson written to Staggers than we learned that his earlier letter to Yarborough had failed. In fact, the letter never even reached Yarborough, for Forsythe had intercepted it and called Harley Dirks to complain. "I said Maggie would have to *ask* Yarborough, not *write* him," Harley reported Forsythe as saying.

Forsythe's demand seemed unreasonable (especially since he had blocked a letter between two Senators), but also difficult to circumvent. Stan Barer and I discussed the situation with Magnuson, and I admitted uncomfortably that I had no idea what form of satisfaction Yarborough intended (or Forsythe hoped) to exact. Magnuson clearly suspected Yarborough and his aides of setting some sort of trap, and

---

* Staggers' Committee ultimately passed the Poison Prevention Packaging Act, which became law in December 1970.

he trenchantly pointed out that our difficulties in the House might already have extinguished S. 4106's chances in the 91st Congress. Consequently, he declined to commit himself to making the request of Yarborough, although he did acknowledge that without Yarborough's support the bill couldn't pass even the Senate in 1970. Barer and I could add nothing, and left the Senator alone with his decision. No one on the staff mentioned the matter to him again, for we all realized that Magnuson's legislative judgment was not only sufficient, but better than anyone else's in his office.

Nonetheless, I couldn't help taking an unusual interest in Magnuson's activities on the Senate Floor. From the staff couches in the rear of the Chamber, I frequently saw Magnuson and Yarborough pass each other in the aisles, but I could never discern any conversation between them. Back in the office, other staff members took delight in teasing me. "Maggie just talked to Yarborough," they would say, rushing into the room with feigned breathlessness. "Well, what did he *say*?" I inevitably demanded. "Oh, nothing really," would come the nonchalant reply; "they just talked about the weather." And the office would fill with laughter, and my curses.

Then, one afternoon, Magnuson stopped me in the hallway on his way back from the Senate Floor. Considerately, as if it were an everyday part of our relationship, he recounted the afternoon's activities, and then suddenly turned to walk into the office. Just as he opened the door, however, he turned around again as if he had forgotten something. "Oh by the way," he said almost playfully, "I talked to Ralph today." Suppressing a smile, he walked through the door and closed it behind him.

This incident left me nonplussed until the following morning, when Forsythe called. "Well," he said, obviously amused, "you've got yourselves another cosponsor." Forsythe's hilarity surprised me as much as his news; what had happened? I asked. Chuckling, he related the story.

"Yarborough came back to the office last night, and he stood there scratching his head. 'You know,' he said, 'the funniest thing just happened. I was over on the Senate Floor, and Maggie came up to me, like he wanted to talk about something. He started telling me what a good bill his National Health Service Corps is, and then he just mumbled something and walked away.' 'I think [Forsythe reported himself to have said] that he wanted you to cosponsor it.' 'Oh,' Yarborough said, 'is *that* what he wanted? Why, sure, I'll cosponsor it—but why didn't he just come right out and ask me?' "

So Yarborough had finally joined Magnuson on S. 4106, and Forsythe had been vindicated (if only marginally) in insisting that Magnuson ask Yarborough personally about the bill. Perhaps Forsythe or his employer had simply wanted to make certain that Magnuson himself, and not just his staff, felt S. 4106 to be important; that would explain why the letter to Yarborough had never reached him, since on Capitol Hill letters may be written solely on staff initiative and even signed by a secretary or an "auto-pen" machine. In any event, Magnuson had enhanced the NHSC's prospects considerably by deciding to comply with Forsythe's demand. Twenty-four cosponsors, including every Democrat on Yarborough's Committee, now graced S. 4106—and in confirmation of Harley Dirks's prediction, four Republicans had joined as cosponsors too.

But this resurgence of our hopes did not last for long. A day or so after Yarborough's decision, one of Congressman Staggers' aides surreptitiously called our office to advise us of his employer's reaction to Magnuson's letter. According to his account, Staggers read the letter once and then threw it down angrily. "If this bill is too hot for Paul Rogers," he said in disgust, "why shouldn't it be too hot for *me*?"

Far from acceding to Magnuson's request, Staggers never even sent him a reply.

4.

The maintenance of sanity on Capitol Hill demands that legislative ambitions be elastic; politics, as we are so often told, is the art of the possible. When Staggers, like Rogers before him, showed no inclination to introduce the NHSC bill in the House, we accepted that the bill would not become law in the 91st Congress and decided that it would be progress enough for one year if Magnuson could persuade the Senate to pass S. 4106 in the few weeks remaining before adjournment. We didn't forget Staggers entirely, of course; Bergman and I often busied ourselves with devising one strategy or another for making a convert of him. But we did so more as a hobby than anything else; there survived in a remote portion of our brains the notion that we could *pester* Congress into passing a law. We devoted our more deliberate efforts to persuading Yarborough to hold hearings on S. 4106, after which, we hoped, his Committee could promptly report the bill (since most of the Committee members had cosponsored it). This would give the Senate an opportunity to pass S. 4106 during the 91st Congress, and make Magnuson's job that much easier when the 92nd Congress convened in 1971: by then, the situation in the House might have improved, and it would be a relatively simple matter to pass the bill again in the Senate.

For some time, I tried to talk with Forsythe about setting up hearings, but when he seemed always too busy to return my phone calls, I accepted Harley Dirks's advice and began making daily visits to Forsythe's office. There, pacified with a magazine and eyed warily by a secretary with the improbable name of Miss Eagle, I waited in vain for Forsythe's private door to open and admit me. After this sit-in had lasted nearly a week, Forsythe finally emerged and granted me a brief audience. He explained that the backlog of Committee business precluded holding hearings on a new bill, especially one with little chance of enactment. Besides, resignations had decimated the Committee staff (Yarborough's appointees had to search for other jobs after his defeat), and the head staff man for the Health Subcommittee had just quit. Forsythe had to do most of the Committee staff work himself, and he already had too many bills to edit, reports to write, and hearing transcripts to correct. His priorities had an ineluctable logic: the legislation he was putting in order was all destined to become law during the 91st Congress; S. 4106 was not.

Helpless, I left Forsythe's office and walked downstairs to talk with Harley Dirks. "Well," he concluded after hearing my story, "I guess Jack and I will just have to sit down over a cup of coffee and have a little chat."

Harley called to report the following afternoon. He had learned that Forsythe was about to leave his post as Chief Counsel and take a job elsewhere, like the rest of Yarborough's staff. He genuinely wanted to clear his desk as soon as possible, and he didn't want to assume new responsibilities—particularly fruitless ones. Moreover, Forsythe didn't want to deal with me if he could avoid it; the misunderstanding during our solicitation of cosponsors still rankled him. But Harley had been gently insistent, and at length Forsythe had agreed to let us work with a staff member named Lee Goldman, whom he had temporarily assigned to the Health Subcommittee. Goldman, who had an extensive background in health affairs, had come to Capitol Hill for a three-month "professional internship." If he was willing to assume the staff work, and if Yarborough would agree to chair the hearing, Forsythe had no objections.

Elated, I thanked Harley and immediately called Lee Goldman. Goldman then thought the matter over for a few days before asking me to have lunch with him on Tuesday, August 25, at the Carroll Arms restaurant. Despite (in my opinion) its mediocre cuisine, slow service, high prices, and wobbly tables,* Senators and their staffs favored the Carroll

---

* Apparently the Carroll Arms's management has changed since mid-1970.

Arms for its proximity to the Senate Office Buildings. Goldman and I had merely to walk across the street, but even before we had been seated he came bluntly to the point: it was impossible, he said, for the Health Subcommittee to hold hearings on S. 4106. He outlined in detail Yarborough's travel plans and the hearings already scheduled on other legislation, demonstrating dispassionately that from the beginning of the following week until the adjournment of the 91st Congress (then slated for late September), not a single day remained free for a hearing on the NHSC. "In fact," he said as we sat down, "the only available day would be this Friday, but that's practically the day after tomorrow, and three days isn't long enough to prepare for a hearing, is it?"

Gloom hit me first, violent and quick, like a bone snapping. Then, unexpectedly, fatigue followed, suffusing every limb and simply anesthetizing thought. The months of hope and disappointment and hard work, falling over one another always toward some end, suddenly had hit a wall: the National Health Service Corps was dead. I wanted to go home to my apartment and sleep. I didn't want to have to tell Stan Barer or Senator Magnuson. I didn't want to call Bergman.

Allowing his pronouncement to penetrate fully, Goldman preoccupied himself for some minutes in slicing up one of the Carroll Arms's garlic pickles. Then he reopened the conversation, as if on a wholly different topic. "How's Maggie coming with the HEW Appropriation?" he asked. "I know there are some specific things Yarborough would really like to see Maggie put in that bill."

Numbly, I understood at last what Goldman was after. Did he think I would do *anything* in return for a hearing on our bill? He apparently did not understand that I couldn't play the game; only Dirks and Barer could influence Magnuson on matters concerning HEW's funds. After he had listed several items of special interest to Yarborough,

I told him rather pointedly that I had nothing to do with the HEW Appropriation more significant than drafting the Chairman's opening statement and proofreading the Report. I also noted that Nixon had vetoed the previous HEW Appropriation, which had exceeded his budget request by only $300 million, and added that Dirks predicted a greater excess this year—even without Yarborough's personal requests. In short, Goldman should talk to Harley Dirks if he wanted a "deal," not to me, and there appeared to be no basis for a "deal" in any event. Although I said this somewhat angrily, Goldman accepted the statement with more equanimity than disappointment, as if he had held no firm expectations in the first place. With the business portion of our lunch evidently concluded, he steered the conversation to small talk and Senate gossip.

In the course of our discussion, however, Goldman mentioned offhandedly that he planned to leave the Hill in October to become chief lobbyist for the Association of American Medical Colleges (AAMC). This remark intrigued me immediately. The focus of the AAMC's lobbying effort is to obtain more Federal money for medical education—and Magnuson controlled that money through the HEW Appropriations Subcommittee.

"Well," I said casually, "if you're going to go lobby for the AAMC, I guess you'll be seeing a lot of Senator Magnuson next year."

For the first time during our luncheon, Goldman's composure seemed to change. We moved on to other topics, but before we parted outside the restaurant, we had more or less agreed that perhaps three days *might* be sufficient to prepare for a hearing.

Twenty minutes later, back in Magnuson's office, I received a call from Goldman.

"I just talked with Senator Yarborough," he informed me. "Hearings on S. 4106 will be held this Friday."

VI

A SENATE HEARING

1.

"The Subcommittee on Health of the Labor and Public Welfare Committee will come to order, and hearings will proceed on S. 4106, a bill to amend Title III of the Public Health Service Act for the establishment of a National Health Service Corps . . ."

The washtub-melodic voice of Chairman Ralph Yarborough swelled through the hearing room. The milling spectators were suddenly silent, and what had been a disordered crowd hurriedly resolved itself into long rows of attentive seated figures. The time was 10 A.M., Friday, August 28—less than seventy-two hours after Goldman and I had lunched at the Carroll Arms. Now Goldman sat next to Yarborough on the horseshoe-shaped dais. His eyes followed the text of the Chairman's opening statement, which I had written only hours earlier. In front of him, he had a list of the morning's witnesses—a list that Bergman and I had compiled in three hectic days. It was highly unusual that we, rather than Goldman, had orchestrated this hearing, but then, the Health Subcommittee did not often hold hearings on legislation whose author was not a Subcommittee member, especially with the adjournment of Congress only a month away. Special treatment has a special price; in this case, Goldman had decreed explicitly that it was up to us to prepare Yarborough's statement, the witness list, and all the other details of the hearing. "I'll make sure the Chairman is there," Goldman had said. "You guys take care of the rest."

"The need for this legislation lies in the problem of maldistribution of health professionals in the United States. Isolated communities, and areas of urban or rural poverty, are notoriously deficient in health manpower and facilities . . ."

Senator Yarborough warmed to his text. Sitting erect behind the Chairman's microphone, speaking emphatically and departing freely from the prepared statement to make his points more clearly, he sounded like a man who would always be Chairman, not one who would soon leave the Senate forever. He did not sound like an old man, a man whose electoral support had suddenly collapsed beneath him like a flimsy grandstand at a county-fair disaster. With his black hair slicked back, his voice an amalgam of Texas farm towns and Capitol cloisters, he seemed to have little in common with the long-haired mobs of Chicago, the teargassed crowds of Lafayette Park—little in common with the youth-culture stereotypes, Dissent, Permissiveness, Violence, to which his opponent had successfully linked him, at a cost of several million dollars, in the minds of the Texas electorate.

". . . a bill offered primarily by the two distinguished Senators from the State of Washington, Senators Magnuson and Jackson, but with the help of most of us here on the Health Subcommittee . . ."

Yarborough *believed* in the National Health Service Corps; the more he talked, the more he praised the bill, and he praised it in terms far less equivocal than anything I had dared write in his prepared statement. Of course, this new-found advocacy surprised us—but why? In our perplexity at his belated cosponsorship and in our exasperating dealings with his aides, we had lost sight of Yarborough himself, a man almost certain to share the philosophy of S. 4106. Everyone on Capitol Hill knew him as an uncommon Senator, one whose legislative principles were unswerving and consistently liberal (and hence, in Texas, politically fool-hardy). Someone should have reminded us about the thrust of his own health legislation, or about his famous wrestling match with Senator Strom Thurmond, his Southern anti-thesis, when Thurmond had attempted physically to pre-vent him from voting for a civil rights bill. Had I not been so steeped in the Senate's gossip, its petty grudges and petty feuds and petty conventions, I might have realized much earlier that Yarborough himself would obviously support S. 4106, regardless of what his aides alleged about Magnuson having slighted him years ago. Now I wondered if the seaminess of interstaff rivalries had not created an unwar-ranted cynicism in all of us, if it had not led us to demean the genuine fineness in the men for whom we worked. Or did the Senate's division of labor allow only Senators them-selves the scope for magnanimity, while compelling staff members to develop more rapacious qualities?

"The distinguished Senator, the principal author, is entering the room now, and Senator Magnuson, if you will have a chair I will finish my opening statement and you will be the first witness . . ."

Magnuson had a busy schedule this morning. At 9:30 he had testified before an Appropriations Subcommittee to ask for more funds to implement land reform in Vietnam, and now he would have to rush through his appearance here in order to attend a simultaneous hearing on the supersonic transport (SST), the "Big Bird"—the great issue in Washington State (now that the nerve gas had been stopped), and the political albatross from which neither Magnuson nor his coauthor of S. 4106 could disentangle himself. Magnuson looked as if he felt hard pressed, but if he had steeled himself for an unenthusiastic reception from Yarborough, at least the Chairman's now spontaneous statement would reassure him.

"Unfortunately, the Administration has declined this Committee's invitation to present testimony on this important health bill. They have been invited, and we sought to provide them with a bill that would be satisfactory to them today. They didn't see fit to come. The Congress in general, this Committee, and the author of this bill, who is here with us, grow increasingly weary of an Administration which, after almost two years in office, still finds itself unable to take forthright positions on vital domestic health issues.

"Unquestionably, the vexing crisis which besets the Nation worsens while the Administration continues to 'study the problem,' conducts various studies, and vetoes hospital-construction bills and health appropriations. Bookshelves are full of studies. We now need effective action. In the future, this Committee would hope to have the benefit of the Administration's views with regard to health legislation. It is now time for this Administration to put aside its studies and its rhetoric and to begin to deal with real problems. Anything less than that amounts to an abdication of the trust which was temporarily placed in the Administration in November 1968."

Yarborough, his prepared statement abandoned, looked squarely at the audience as he excoriated the Administration. One of the HSMHA bureaucrats from our May 26 meeting fidgeted uneasily in a front-row seat. Although he represented the Administration, the HSMHA bureaucrat would not testify today. He would not have a chance to

profess publicly, for the record, the views he had expressed
on May 26—the same views he had reaffirmed hastily outside the hearing room in the tumultuous minutes before
Yarborough had first rapped his gavel. "We wanted to
help," the bureaucrat had told me; "we wanted to help very
much, but we ran into opposition at HEW, and finally the
word came down from the White House to 'stay away from
Magnuson's bill.'" The HSMHA bureaucrat had come to
the hearing merely as an observer; even so, he would not
have a pleasant time.

Congressional committees always invite the Administration to testify on legislation. HEW had demurred in the
case of S. 4106; too little time to prepare a position, the
Department said. Actually, HEW had two positions—
contradictory ones—and that was the real reason no Administration witness would testify. Throughout the Department, men like Dr. Egeberg, Surgeon General Jesse Steinfeld, the three HSMHA bureaucrats, Larry Platt, and
Harley Frankel all hoped to see a doctor corps established.
But they faced a potent (if motley) opposition: men who
opposed government intervention in the sacrosanct system
of private practice, men who hoped to abolish the Public
Health Service, men who could not countenance the pre-
sumptuousness of Democrats like Magnuson who introduced their own legislation instead of waiting for the
Republican Administration to act—men, in short, like Dr.
Glen Wegner, HEW's chief lobbyist on Capitol Hill.

Glen Wegner had first visited our office immediately
after Magnuson introduced S. 4106; he claimed he had
come only to pick up an official copy of the bill. We found
this explanation unconvincing: HEW must have had dozens of copies of S. 4106, and it was also printed in the
Congressional Record, freely available to any member of
the public. I surmised that Wegner really wanted a chance
to "size up the opposition"; to ascertain, perhaps, whether
we could be dissuaded from pushing the legislation seri-

ously (if *our* fantasy was that we might pester Congress into passing the law, HEW's was that Magnuson would suddenly desist, and that the whole NHSC issue would miraculously disappear). He must have been encouraged to find such a young and inexperienced staff man working on the bill.

Wegner was a doctor by training (a pediatrician, someone said), in his mid-thirties, and with Seattle roots, but still I found him disagreeable and somehow sinister—perhaps because of a certain shiftiness in his bearing, or because he sneered derisively when I spoke. He hated Magnuson's bill (which explained part of my distaste for him), but he hated it with a curious excess of passion, a pure hatred that transcended rationality. This made him seem alternately dangerous and pathetic; there was something sad and incongruous in his vehemence, something out of place in his railing against a bill with so little chance of passage (Rogers had just refused to introduce it when Wegner first appeared). He dismissed disdainfully those justifications I attempted, perhaps foolishly, to offer, and in parting he contemptuously advised me to "tell Magnuson to forget about this ridiculous bill."

Ironically, I had one reason—then and later—to respect Wegner: he alone of S. 4106's opponents seemed to grasp the significance of *Magnuson* sponsoring the bill. HEW had so far treated Magnuson as if he were just another Senator, and the bill itself as if it were a necessarily futile effort. Wegner knew better; Capitol Hill was his beat, and the Pacific Northwest his home. I felt certain that he must have protested HEW's decision not to testify at the hearing; his instinct would be to kill S. 4106 early, to expose it as "ridiculous" right away—before its ponderous legislative pace could begin to accelerate. But if Wegner had in fact made such an argument, his views had not prevailed. For whatever reason, HEW had chosen not to testify at all, apparently discounting the possibility that Chairman Yarborough might embrace the bill in retaliation.

Nor had HEW taken steps to avert a ploy it could have foreseen: that in the absence of Departmental testimony, Magnuson himself would present "evidence" of Administration support for the bill. During his own hearings on the HEW Appropriation, Magnuson had carefully developed a useful and official transcript in questioning the Surgeon General, Dr. Jesse Steinfeld:

> THE CHAIRMAN. Because of the lack of physicians, and the problem of distribution of physicians, we introduced a bill the other day, Senator Jackson and I, to see if we couldn't use Commissioned Officers of the Public Health Service in direct medical services to the urban poor and to rural areas. Dr. Steinfeld, do you think this is a good idea?
>
> DR. STEINFELD. I think it is excellent.
>
> THE CHAIRMAN. Thank you.

Magnuson would quote this exchange in his testimony to Yarborough; it would become part of the hearing record, and it would represent the only official HEW testimony on the subject of S. 4106 during the entire course of the Senate's deliberations. Magnuson did not have to point out— since Yarborough and everyone else present already knew —that Steinfeld had unique reasons for supporting S. 4106: the bill would grant the Surgeon General more authority than he had enjoyed in years, and provide a new role for the failing PHS and its Commissioned Corps. Nor would Magnuson mention that while Dr. Steinfeld had pronounced the bill "excellent," his superior—Dr. Egeberg— had sat beside the Surgeon General at the witness table and remained studiously silent. Magnuson's one question to Dr. Steinfeld and Steinfeld's five-word response hardly matched the elaborate Magnuson-Egeberg dialogue we had planned so hopefully at Egeberg's office in April. But if HEW chose to confine its official testimony to five words, these five were perfect.

"With that, we can proceed with our first witness, the distinguished Senator from Washington, Mr. Magnuson, the Chairman of the Appropriations Subcommittee dealing with health. He has also served with distinction for many years as the Chairman of the Commerce Committee. It was my privilege to serve on that Committee under his chairmanship for seven years, and I saw there his interest in the health of the people by the care that he gave to bills for consumer protection laws, including the protection of children from flammable fabrics, and in many other measures.

"He has sponsored great bills before that Committee, so it has been a great benefit to the country that he has become Chairman of the Appropriations Subcommittee dealing with questions of health.

"Senator, it has been a great privilege to work with you here for more than 13 years, and especially for the 7 years I served on your Committee under your Chairmanship."

Gamely (for flattery makes him uneasy), Magnuson endured the formalities, including a long and equally deferential welcome from Senator Jacob Javits of New York, the ranking Republican on Yarborough's Committee and another cosponsor of S. 4106. Then he spoke very briefly, announcing that rather than take up the time of the Subcommittee by reading his testimony aloud, he would simply submit it, along with Senator Jackson's, for inclusion in the hearing record. "Since you and eight other members of the Subcommittee have cosponsored this legislation," Magnuson told Yarborough, "and since the Subcommittee has had a distinguished record under your leadership in health matters of all kinds, I don't think I need to try to convince the Chairman and others on the Subcommittee of the bill's merits." Magnuson could have done very little else; everyone in the hearing room had read his introductory speech for S. 4106 (from which his testimony was drawn), and they all knew the rationale that his speech and Jackson's offered in conjunction. So he simply thanked Yarborough, handed his prepared statement and Jackson's to the clerk, and rose to depart. He wanted to leave quickly, for he knew he had kept the SST hearing waiting—Chairman John Stennis, a courteous Mississippian, would not begin without the Senator from Washington. Magnuson had almost reached the door when Yarborough began to speak, bringing him to a quick halt.

"Senator," Yarborough called, "we all know serving here that very often when we have a beneficial measure in the closing days of Congress, we try to get hearings on it and set it up as a prelude to succeeding Congresses—but that is not my object in calling these hearings. I intend to get this bill out of the Subcommittee and the full Committee and onto the Floor of the Senate, and I am sure the Leadership of the Senate will cooperate. I would like to see it passed this year. We can't speak for the House; we hope to have the same cooperation.

"It is my intention," Yarborough repeated firmly, "not just to set something up for next year, but to try to pass the bill *this year.*"

Magnuson had turned at a point near the exit; without returning to the witness table, he stood and replied to Yarborough. The audience stared as this impromptu and wholly unorthodox dialogue between the two Chairmen developed into a roving discussion of Federal health-care policies. Both men seemed oblivious of the decorum of the hearing—Yarborough intent on Magnuson, Magnuson intent on leaving. Yarborough deplored the decline of the Public Health Service, the closure of the PHS hospitals and clinics, and he told Magnuson that S. 4106 was "a landmark bill in helping to bring back, revitalize, and extend the PHS system." "Yes," Magnuson replied, "they tell me that the introduction of the bill itself built up morale in the Public Health Service."

Yarborough, as Chairman, was entitled to the last word. He used it judiciously, clarifying once and for all his reason for advocating the NHSC so forcefully. "Morale in the PHS is going down," he began, "because the Administration is closing the Public Health Service hospitals and trying to destroy the Service." With unsuppressed anger, Yarborough then added a solemn declaration:

"I want to assure the Senator—and I seldom make this statement publicly—that I intend to push this bill with every resource I have."

Everyone in the hearing room realized that Yarborough had just flung a defiant challenge at the Nixon Administration. He would fight to save the Public Health Service during his few remaining weeks as a Senator, and that meant fighting for the passage of S. 4106. The NHSC issue, as Yarborough framed it, was not the essentially bogus one of government health care vs. private health care. It was a much more real issue: would the Nixon Administration abolish one of the oldest and proudest agencies of the U.S. Government, or would Congress save that agency by giving it a new purpose? Ironically, chance alone had linked the PHS and the National Health Service Corps; had it not been for the draft law, S. 4106 would never have mentioned the PHS. And whereas our office had become interested in saving the PHS in order to establish the NHSC, Yarborough now wanted to establish the NHSC in order to save the PHS. The Administration might reassure itself with the knowledge that S. 4106 was still far from enactment, and that Yarborough was, after all, only a lame-duck Chairman, but nonetheless the emerging controversy could not please the Administration. The National Health Service Corps, once an insignificant proposal, was now becoming an issue.

Having made his intentions clear, Yarborough at last excused Magnuson, then perfunctorily accepted written testimony on several other bills designed to deal with the "physician maldistribution" problem. Theoretically, the hearing concerned these bills as much as it did S. 4106, and unlike Magnuson's legislation, these had all been written by Health Subcommittee members. Yet Yarborough disposed of them in less than a minute; whatever their merits, they did not involve the PHS. Instead, they sought to lure private practitioners to needy areas through various financial incentives, some quite intricate. Yarborough had no time for them; at the moment he cared only about the PHS, and S. 4106.

"Now we come to the professional witnesses, and the first witness is Dr. Abraham B. Bergman . . ."

Although Bergman had often testified on Capitol Hill before, Yarborough's animated enthusiasm obviously infected him as he sat down at the witness table. He began his statement by praising Yarborough for his role "in virtually all programs of the past decade launched to improve the health of the American people." He then described briefly three doctorless towns in Washington State and Alaska (officially, Bergman testified for the Washington/Alaska Regional Medical Program and the Washington State Society of Pediatrics). Wary of potential opposition from conservatives, Bergman stressed the medical plight of small rural communities such as those in the Pacific Northwest, virtually ignoring discussion of corresponding needs in the ghetto. Although S. 4106 declared that "priority . . . shall be given to those urban and rural areas . . . where poverty conditions exist," we didn't want to emphasize the NHSC's role in the cities just yet. Senate liberals had already cosponsored S. 4106; Senate conservatives might kill it (just as Rogers' conservative colleagues on the Health Subcommittee had preemptively killed the House version). Consequently, Bergman also stressed that S. 4106 would not permit the government to force doctors onto unwilling communities: the doctors could be sent only in response to local requests, and only if full cooperation from the community—including existing physicians, if any—was assured.

Then Bergman reiterated briefly the tripartite justification for the NHSC that Magnuson had first elaborated in his Senate speech. The Corps, he said, would bring medical care to the needy, and it would attempt to transplant doctors into "physician deficient areas" rather than create permanent dependence on the government. Second, it would "revitalize" the Public Health Service and "rejuvenate" the PHS's Commissioned Officer Corps (at Bergman's insistence, Magnuson's Senate speech had argued that the PHS must not be allowed to "wither on the vine," and already this somewhat trite phrase had become an indispensable part of the NHSC litany). Finally, the NHSC would provide an opportunity to harness for social ends the professed idealism of the "new generation of young health professionals." In conclusion, Bergman added, "I can't conceive of any *justified* opposition to this bill."

Now Yarborough began to interrogate Bergman; but since we had written the questions ourselves, Bergman was well prepared. In a neatly executed give-and-take, he and Yarborough established—to their own satisfaction, at least—that the local-initiative provisions of S. 4106 would preclude dissatisfaction within the medical community, that the much-discussed abolition of the "doctor draft" or the passage of national health insurance would not render the NHSC obsolete ("the NHSC provides an *organizational framework* within which young doctors will want to work"), and that passage of S. 4106 would not hinder the development of other schemes to attract doctors to needy areas ("We must have a variety of programs; there can be no one answer"). Yarborough had finished with Bergman, and thanked him, all within ten minutes.

"The next witness is Dr. Amos Johnson of Garland, North Carolina, the past President of the American Academy of General Practice . . ."

We had planned Dr. Amos Johnson as a pleasant surprise for Yarborough early in the schedule of witnesses, and the

Chairman's face showed his delight even as he read the elderly physician's name. Johnson and Yarborough were longtime friends; the doctor had inspired S. 3418, Yarborough's "Family Practice Act" (a bill to train more family practitioners) in much the same way that Bergman had inspired S. 4106. Because of this special relationship with Yarborough, Bergman had exulted when Johnson agreed to testify about S. 4106 on such short notice. Had Yarborough been indifferent to the bill, or even openly hostile, Johnson might have persuaded him to change his mind; now he would certainly reinforce the Chairman's enthusiasm. Yarborough beamed as Johnson approached the witness table. "I think," he said, "that the people of the country know how much they owe you—or they ought to know—for your efforts to get medical care to the farming and rural areas of our land."

We hadn't known precisely what Dr. Johnson would say about S. 4106, but as he began his testimony ("I want to be recorded as being in support of this bill in its entirety"), we immediately sensed that his would be the most effective statement of the day. For Johnson *spoke* like Yarborough, in simple, homey phrases, and as with Yarborough, the resonance of his voice suggested a life divided between professional meetings in the nation's Capital and relaxed personal dealings with rural Southerners. Like Yarborough too, Johnson did not seem wholly at ease in a staid Congressional hearing room, but he knew—perhaps better than any other resident of Garland, North Carolina—that what happens in Congressional hearing rooms can directly affect the way many Americans live.

Johnson focused on two aspects of S. 4106: its avowedly experimental nature, and its use of PHS doctors. He quoted approvingly from Magnuson's speech—" 'The NHSC is, frankly, an experimental concept, and one that may lead to many different conclusions about the nature of health care in the future' "—and pointed out that Magnuson himself had said that at the $5,000,000 funding level, fewer than 75 doctors and 150 supporting health professionals would be able to staff the NHSC in its early years. "And yet," Johnson added, "if this concept with its relatively insignificant funding is implemented, and carefully nurtured as it grows by the competent health professionals who even yet exist in our Public Health Service, it may well come to be our most productive health-care-delivery-system experiment of recent times."

Then Johnson described starkly the decline of the PHS during the 1960's, and catalogued with equal simplicity all the reasons the PHS should be restored. S. 4106, he predicted, "will prove to be the proper motivating impetus to start the return of the PHS to its proper stature of leadership among the health-affiliated Federal agencies."

Had the hearing's sole purpose been to persuade Yarborough of S. 4106's merits, it could have adjourned after Dr. Johnson finished. The only question Yarborough put strenuously to his old friend was whether he had time to come by the office and chat before heading back to Garland. Johnson said he would be happy to do just that, and three smiles responded—Yarborough's, Bergman's, and mine.

"*Our next witness will be Dr. James R. Kimmey, Executive Director of the American Public Health Association . . .*"

We had selected the remaining witnesses just as carefully. The American Public Health Association (APHA), for example, had 28,000 members—mostly state and local public-health officials—and the most respected voice of any professional group in the crowded public-health field. Dr. Kimmey, the APHA's newly elected head, submitted a written statement and then used his time at the witness table to give a highly personal account of the decline and demoralization of the PHS, which he had joined in 1963 and quit five years later. With barely controlled emotion, Kimmey told why he had given up his hope of a PHS career.

Yarborough listened intently, and so did the two men in the audience who had arranged Kimmey's appearance: Bob Barclay and Noble Swearingen, the APHA's Washington lawyers.

Barclay and Swearingen had advised Bergman and me about the NHSC almost from the beginning. Few men in Washington knew the nuances and personalities of health politics better, for few other men make their living at it. Barclay had spent most of his professional life on Capitol Hill; he had sat, in fact, where Lee Goldman now sat, next to the Chairman of the Health Subcommittee, but in those days the legendary Lister Hill had held the gavel. Hill had monopolized Senate health affairs, for he had simultaneously filled the chairmanships Yarborough and Magnuson now held, and in his failing years—or so rumor had it—Barclay had kept Hill going, devotedly helping him to make crucial legislative decisions, or maybe even making those decisions himself ("I don't say Barclay actually *ran* the Health Subcommittee," one veteran health lobbyist once told me, "but I do say that no staff man except Barclay ever sat *at the table* when the House and Senate Subcommittees met in conference").

Like Yarborough, Barclay had taken an interest in Magnuson's bill primarily because it might rescue the Public Health Service. Service on Capitol Hill, especially for Democrats, leads quite naturally to support for the PHS— for two reasons. Historically, the PHS has always been something of a renegade within Executive ranks, cooperating with Congress and relying on Congress for support during the long years (especially Eisenhower's and Nixon's) when the President and his budget officers have tried to cut back on health funding. Secondly, the PHS—in contrast to the rest of HEW—has always conceived of its role as an active, interventionist one; it has rarely been complacent about the adequacy of the private-practice system in meeting the many health needs of the nation. If Nixon abolished the PHS, Congress would lose both a firm ally and the hope of greater Federal involvement in health care (to its opponents, of course, the demise of the PHS would eliminate an "unnecessary" bureaucracy and a large portion of the "socialized medicine" threat).

Barclay's professional interests now that he had left Capitol Hill strengthened his philosophical commitment to the PHS. He and Swearingen represented not only the APHA, the professional analogue of the PHS, but also the Maritime Council of the AFL-CIO—i.e., the merchant seamen of America, the one population group other than "wards" of the Federal government to receive medical care from the PHS. Opponents of the PHS argued that the rationale for using government doctors to treat merchant seamen and their families had weakened considerably in the twentieth century, and that the PHS should not be kept alive merely to perpetuate the mercantilist philosophy of the 1790's, the era in which Congress had established the PHS's predecessor agency. Friends of the PHS (and of the merchant seamen) realized that such logic would in fact destroy the Service sooner or later, and that consequently the PHS needed a new function too. This explained some of Barclay's enthusiasm for S. 4106, and also indicated that he would help the bill in more ways than simply presenting Dr. Kimmey as a witness at Yarborough's hearing.

"Our next witness is Mr. William Lucca, Executive Director of the Commissioned Officers Association of the U.S. Public Health Service . . ."

The Commissioned Officers Association (COA) does not match the APHA in size, but its 4,600 members include 87 percent of the active-duty PHS Commissioned Corps. Bill Lucca therefore spoke not only as an individual, and as the representative of a private organization, but also as the spokesman for the PHS and its medical personnel, the people who would staff the NHSC if it became law.

Yarborough understood this, and spoke to Lucca as if he

were addressing the Commissioned Corps itself: "I have instructed the staff, Mr. Lucca, while this hearing is going on, to put this bill as a crash program at the top of the legislative calendar for health." Lee Goldman, sitting stolidly at Yarborough's side, showed no emotion. But his recent gambit—that Yarborough would consider S. 4106 only if Magnuson granted certain "favors" in the HEW Appropriation—had been exposed as fraudulent, and he certainly knew it. Yarborough wanted to see S. 4106 passed, period.

"Our next witness is Dr. Robert L. Nolan, Chairman of the Department of Preventive Medicine at the University of West Virginia Medical School in Morgantown, West Virginia . . ."

Dr. Nolan had volunteered to testify in behalf of the NHSC; we had never heard of him until he called Magnuson's office to offer his services. Nolan soon arrived in Washington and proved himself to be the one person who could match Bergman's zeal for S. 4106; most important, he came from the same state as Congressman Staggers. When Staggers received a copy of the Senate hearing transcript (which we would be careful to send him, with a paper clip on the first page of Nolan's statement), he would find some stark statistics on the doctor shortage in West Virginia. He might not realize that Nolan had been addressing him, rather than Yarborough, but at least he would know that the NHSC had not escaped notice among his constituents. Our elastic legislative ambitions began to stretch a bit again.

"The next witness is Dr. Robert Shannon, Vice President of the Student American Medical Association . . ."

Bob Shannon was a fourth-year medical student at the University of Maryland. The Student American Medical Association (SAMA), despite its name, had no official connection with the AMA—in fact, the students were considering changing the name in order to clarify their independence. With 24,000 medical students and 36,000 interns and residents, SAMA was only a third of the AMA's size, but the "new generation of young health professionals" would have to provide the manpower for the NHSC if it became law. And, as Shannon immediately pointed out to Yarborough, fully 90 percent of the delegates at a recent SAMA national convention had voted to support the concept of a national health-service corps.

Shannon's testimony signified something more than just support for the NHSC from the men and women who would have to staff it. It showed that SAMA, after years in the customary student haven of slogans and resolutions, had decided to descend into the morally suspect world of "practical politics." This unprecedented development intrigued Yarborough, who couldn't resist digressing to learn why SAMA had suddenly become "involved":

> THE CHAIRMAN. In your statement you say:
> "For many years, the concept of a National Health Service Corps has received wide support from young professionals in medicine."
> I am wondering why I never heard that before. I have been on this Subcommittee for nearly 13 years.
> DR. SHANNON. Unfortunately, Senator, the young medical students are just beginning to understand power in Washington, and the places and methods to get particular ideas out front. I think our presentation today is an indication of that. . . .

What Shannon's statement did not indicate was the full extent of SAMA's sacrifice to pragmatism in supporting S. 4106. A few weeks earlier, SAMA had proposed its own NHSC plan, and almost succeeded in persuading a member of the Senate Health Subcommittee to introduce it. Until this news reached Magnuson's office, I had not even known of SAMA's existence; more important, I had complacently assumed that the threat of a rival bill had vanished when Senator Nelson's office agreed to support Magnuson's. Having learned by chance of SAMA and its plans, I immediately met with Jeff Harris, a UCLA medical student who had drafted SAMA's proposal. Slightly panicked, I tried to explain why we thought only Magnuson's NHSC plan could pass in the 91st Congress; the SAMA scheme, I pointed out, would require a change in the draft law, and that just wasn't possible politically. Harris seemed unconvinced (and indeed, I didn't even have a draft of our bill yet to show him), but he nonetheless agreed to delay action on the SAMA plan temporarily if I would meet with other SAMA officials to discuss the legislative situation. And so, on a Saturday afternoon when I had hoped to escape from Washington, I found myself instead in a classroom of a local college that SAMA had taken over for its "Summer Workshop."

The occasion had its preposterous aspects: college classrooms are inherently undramatic places, especially in midsummer, and crucial legislative decisions are rarely made in a meeting of young medical students with an even younger Senate staff man. Nonetheless, the stakes were quite high, particularly in the realm of student politics. Unless the SAMA officials, who obviously distrusted me, agreed to support Magnuson's bill, they would revert to their own plans and inevitably complicate—if not vitiate entirely—our legislative effort. They listened quietly while I carefully outlined Magnuson's proposal on the blackboard, but then they attacked it angrily. It was too limited, they said, and worse yet, it relied on the PHS, the symbol to young medical students of everything old, tired, stodgy, and unimaginative in the Federal government. The SAMA proposal, they insisted, was much better.

Unhappily, I had no defense except the one I had relied upon since meeting Harley Frankel: political reality. I explained why a bill seeking a draft-law change could not pass in the 91st Congress, and why its mere introduction might kill Magnuson's bill as well. But if support coalesced behind Magnuson's bill, I insisted, it just might pass: it enjoyed a useful "low profile" (in the popular jargon of the Nixon era) and a uniquely influential Senate sponsor. The

NHSC's legislative prospects, I concluded somewhat di-
dactically, could be summarized with an old adage: "the
Best is often the enemy of the Good."

Grudgingly, perhaps worried they'd been "co-opted," the
SAMA officials at last gave in. Pleased and very much relieved, I rose to depart, but one of them stopped me with a
blunt warning. "We'll support Magnuson's bill for one reason," he said evenly, "and that is that you say it is the best
that can be passed in this session of Congress. But if you're
wrong, if it *doesn't* pass, then we will have made a mistake.
Because if we're going to lose this year anyway, we should
lose fighting for the best bill of all. That way we're more
likely to get the best bill passed in the future. So you had
better be right."

I did not forget these words; they haunted me every time
we suffered a setback, every time someone like Congressman Rogers balked at performing some crucial function.
These young medical students were my real contempo-
raries, members of the same much-discussed generation.
Though their trust and my assurances had both been tentative, I didn't want to be responsible for that trust being
misplaced. Now, on August 28, when Yarborough promised
publicly to do everything possible for S. 4106, and when he
praised it explicitly because it *was* "realistically modest"
and relied on the PHS, I felt for the first time that SAMA
might realize how sensible its maiden legislative effort had
been. And since the expressed willingness of young doctors
to join the NHSC was crucial to S. 4106's passage, I felt
very grateful to SAMA, too.

*"A roll call is going on on the Floor, and the hearing
must be adjourned . . ."*

Senator Yarborough disposed of the final witness just as
the roll-call buzzer began to buzz insistently and the roll-
call lights lit up orange on the face of the hearing-room
clock. Banging his gavel for adjournment, he rushed off to
catch the subway for the Capitol and the Senate Chamber.
The audience, suddenly loosed, relaxed again into its nat-

ural state of noisy, jostling confusion. Reporters came up to ask for more information; witnesses sought reassurances about the quality of their testimony. "Would this bill have the effect . . ." "Don't you think he liked what I said about . . ." The hearing room was a bobbing, enjoyable happening, through which, feeling mellow and rather pleased with ourselves, we joked and waved and moved erratically toward the exit and lunch.

2.

Across the street at the Carroll Arms, we savored the sensation of a well-planned and thoroughly successful hearing—half an hour after the event. We needed a large table: the party included Abe Bergman and Judy, his distractingly beautiful wife, Barclay and Swearingen, Bill Lucca, and Jerry Brazda (the editor of *Washington Report on Medicine and Health.*) To the other diners, we must have sounded like part of a baseball team that had just won a pennant.

The morning's events justified our elation. SAMA had supported Magnuson's contention that the NHSC would attract adequate manpower, the APHA and COA had agreed that S. 4106 would "revitalize" the Public Health Service, and almost all the witnesses had produced examples and statistics to verify the need for a doctor corps. On every point, and with complete unanimity, the testimony had borne out Magnuson's tripartite justification for the NHSC.*

* We had invited the Student National Medical Association (SNMA), a black students' organization, to testify at the hearing, but unfortunately its witness was struck by a car as he crossed the street, and taken to a hospital. His injuries were not serious; and SNMA's testimony did appear in the printed hearing record.

Of course, neither the Administration nor the AMA had testified—a fact that rendered the consensus in the hearing room somewhat artificial. But the Administration had had its chance, and it was hardly our responsibility to argue that health care ought to be left to private doctors, that the PHS was wasteful and inefficient, or that the Commissioned Officer Corps had outlived its usefulness in a Civil-Service-dominated Department of Health, Education and Welfare. Until the Administration chose to refute it, the only official HEW position on S. 4106 would be the Surgeon General's: "I think it is excellent." Similarly, the testimony of so many medical organizations (including those who had sent written statements instead of witnesses) offset to some extent the conspicuous absence of the AMA. At the very least, the AMA could no longer purport to be the sole voice of American medicine (particularly when it kept silent)—American medicine had become a complex, many-faceted, and competitive field.

Yarborough's sudden passion for the bill, we all agreed, had surprised us more than any other development at the hearing. But why had he taken so long to cosponsor it? We could guess only that he had delayed reading the bill when we sent it to him—or else that his aides had not been fully candid with us. Whatever the explanation, we could now rely on Yarborough for positive assistance, when initially we had dared hope for little more than his benevolent neutrality. In the Carroll Arms, and probably in Dr. Glen Wegner's office at HEW, it was apparent that S. 4106 had begun to move.

3.

On September 2, a few days after the hearing, Yarborough wrote Magnuson and Jackson a short letter. The letter had a formal appearance, typed on the official stationery of Yarborough's Committee and addressed to the "Honorable Chairmen" of the Commerce and Interior Committees. Yarborough might not have written it himself, but somehow I couldn't imagine that Forsythe or Goldman had produced it; the style (and the sentiments) seemed to be Yarborough's own.

Dear Messrs. Chairmen:

I completed hearings on your National Health Service Corps Act of 1970, S. 4106, last Friday morning, August 28, leaving the record open until today, September 2, for further documents. I am attempting to get the Health Subcommittee to report this measure out so that we might attempt to get it before the Full Committee on the 8th, the 9th, or the 11th of this month. If I cannot get it before the Committee this week, I will try the following week, beginning September the 14th.

You have a good bill, a badly needed bill, and I am honored to co-sponsor it. Wisely, you put only a little money in it. It is so hard to get money, but the principle is big. I am convinced that this is one of the worst-needed medical bills of any right now. We need to write this principle into the law right now, then you distinguished Senatorial leaders can get the money needed to make it the great viable piece of legislation it ought to be, when you return next year.

With gratitude for your great leadership and the privilege of having worked with you here for more than 13 years,

Sincerely your friend,
Ralph W. Yarborough

I sat contemplating the awkward but moving letter for some time. Then I took it to Senator Magnuson at his desk, along with several newspaper articles about the hearing. The clippings all pointed out that it was probably too late in the session for the bill to become law, but Magnuson hardly noticed them. Instead, he studied Yarborough's letter in silence. After some moments, he looked up.

"Our problem isn't that it's too late in the session," he

said firmly. "Our problem is right there in the first paragraph of Ralph's letter, right there where he says what he is
'attempting' to do, and that he will 'try' to get the bill
before the Full Committee this week or the next. *Our* problem is that Yarborough can't get a quorum in his Committee."

This unexpected declaration startled me. A Chairman is
omnipotent, I thought; a Chairman can *always* get a
quorum. Had some deep-seated opposition to S. 4106 suddenly arisen without my knowing it?

"No," Magnuson laughed, and then explained, "this
thing doesn't have anything to do with our bill. The problem is that the Republicans are boycotting Yarborough's
Committee meetings to prevent him from reporting out the
'Occupational Health and Safety' bill. And if blocking that
one bill means blocking every other bill before the Committee, the Republicans will do it.

"Yup," Magnuson concluded, "the National Health Service Corps may never make it out of Committee, and all
because the President is opposed to some other bill."

I had brought Yarborough's letter to Magnuson thinking
that it presaged Senate passage of the NHSC. I took it back
again wondering whether it would become the final document in our S. 4106 file.

VII

DECISION IN THE SENATE

1.

In the weeks between the August 28 hearing and mid-September, Yarborough's Committee did not meet once. As Magnuson had warned, Yarborough couldn't get a quorum, despite almost daily summonses. With no cessation of the Republican boycott in sight, and with adjournment no more than a month away, S. 4106 seemed destined for a somewhat anticlimactic end.

The stalemate irritated us in Senator Magnuson's office, but it infuriated Senator Yarborough and his aides, who had more than S. 4106 to consider. Yarborough had planned a spate of legislative victories for his last weeks in the Senate, and now the boycott not only frustrated his intentions but rudely exposed his lame-duck status to his colleagues and the press. Yarborough's electoral defeat had heightened rather than diminished the intense loyalty of his staff, and this final humiliation made their attempts to break the boycott desperate. So desperate, in fact, that Lee Goldman finally consented—with obvious reluctance—to my offer to use Magnuson's influence to help produce the needed quorum.

Even with Goldman's permission, I didn't intend to act too overtly; meddling in committee politics is never safe, and Forsythe's testiness in previous weeks had schooled me in the special hazards of the Labor and Public Welfare Committee. If an outsider like Magnuson called Yarborough's colleagues and urged them to attend Committee meetings, they would resent it as undue interference, notwithstanding Magnuson's great popularity, and my calling the aides to these Senators would have been similarly provocative and much less persuasive. I suspected, though, that Yarborough and his aides had pridefully refused to ask for help from key Committee members, and my first exploratory call—to Carey Parker in Senator Kennedy's office —soon confirmed this. Although Kennedy would probably become the next Chairman of the Health Subcommittee, Yarborough had not enlisted his support in overcoming the Republicans' intransigence. Carey Parker sympathized with the Chairman's plight, however, and he also liked S. 4106—he had persuaded Kennedy to cosponsor the bill, and written the Senator's statements for both the hearing and the bill's introduction. When I asked him, he willingly agreed to talk with Kennedy about helping break the boycott.

Then, since the onus of the boycott lay on the Republicans, I called Jay Cutler, the Minority Counsel of the Health Subcommittee and a top aide to Senator Jacob Javits. Cutler good-naturedly agreed that S. 4106 should be saved, since Javits had cosponsored it, and he promised to talk to the other Republicans about suspending the boycott long enough to consider our bill.

Hoping that Parker and Cutler could successfully supplement Yarborough's efforts to piece together a quorum, I turned to the other tasks that had to be performed before the Senate could vote on the bill. I had already corrected the acronym-abundant hearing transcript for the printers, and now, on Goldman's instructions, I had to draft the Committee Report to accompany S. 4106. A committee files a report with every bill it favorably considers, and the reports serve a variety of purposes. The courts, for example, use the report as a reference document whenever a legal question arises about the "legislative intent" of a law (so does the Executive Branch, at least in theory, but in practice "legislative intent" often plays an indiscernible role in public administration). Within the Senate itself, reports are important chiefly because many Senators read nothing else before deciding how to vote on a particular bill. A good report, therefore, does more than explain—it also persuades.

Like most legislative assistants, I had read many reports, but I had never written one. Consequently, I sought advice from the more experienced members of Magnuson's Commerce Committee staff. Dan O'Neal, the Surface Transportation Counsel, searched his files and proudly presented me with a report he had written on a Magnuson bill dealing with boxcar shortages in the Pacific Northwest. "In all modesty," Dan said with obvious immodesty, "I have to admit that the 'boxcar report' is a model of clarity, simplicity, and style." Armed with this minor classic in Senate literature, I began writing the "Committee on Labor and Public Welfare Report to accompany S. 4106, The National Health Service Corps Act of 1970." That the Committee had still not met to consider S. 4106, and that I did not even belong to the Committee staff, struck me as richly ironic.

In addition to the "report language," Goldman had told me to make a list of any changes we wanted in the text of the bill itself. Our original draft had not been perfect. Witnesses at the hearing had pointed out several necessary wording changes, and I compiled these for Goldman so that the Committee could report the bill in a form consistent with the argot of Public Health Service law (we found, for example, that PHS doctors would have to be "assigned" to communities, rather than "detailed"). But the bill's wording, in some sections, involved political issues as well as technical ones.

The most pressing of these political issues was whether or not the Surgeon General ought to have a role in administering the proposed NHSC. To the layman, the mere articulation of such an "issue" might induce a yawn, but in health circles it was like asking modern Greeks whether the King should be brought back to share power with the Colonels. The Surgeon General had once been the chief health officer of the United States, but bitter HEW infighting had gradually circumscribed his position until finally, in 1968, he had been reduced to a mere figurehead, a pathetic shadow of authority who traveled around the country lecturing high school students on the hazards of smoking. Yet the entire PHS system and its medical personnel (the Commissioned Officer Corps) remained stubbornly loyal to their former leader long after HEW had severed the traditional chain of command, for like him they were outnumbered by civil servants in HEW and scheduled for elimination by "rational" administrators and cost-conscious budget officials. Like its predecessor, the Nixon Administration apparently planned to put the Surgeon General and his frail PHS allies out of their misery, but for the time being at least, HEW's *ancien régime* plotted its return to power just as strenuously as its bureaucratic rivals plotted its demise.

Magnuson's introduction of S. 4106 had exacerbated this conflict, just as the PHS officer had warned us months before. Like Senator Yarborough, both the pro- and the anti-PHS forces decided that the bill's "true" significance lay in its provisions to strengthen the PHS and the Commissioned Corps, and to restore the Surgeon General to a portion of his former domain and authority. The bill would make the Surgeon General responsible for the operation of the NHSC, and create as his subordinate a post of "NHSC Director." Ironically, Bergman and I had devoted little attention to this section while drafting S. 4106; we had given the Surgeon General such prominence largely inadvertently.

Since S. 4106 had little chance of becoming law, however, we assumed that the anti-PHS forces at HEW would continue to ignore it, although we suspected Glen Wegner would play a spoiler's role if he could. We were surprised, therefore, when in the wake of Yarborough's hearing we received a call from HEW's second-ranking health official —Dr. Vernon Wilson, the newly appointed Administrator of HSMHA. Wilson was already somewhat notorious in Washington, for like Egeberg, he had displayed maverick tendencies within weeks of taking office. He had become controversial when the press obtained a private memorandum he had written in which he had suggested that the Nixon Administration consider—and perhaps even support —Senator Kennedy's national-health-insurance bill. The furor had not subsided for months: the Administration regarded Kennedy as a pariah, and his health-insurance proposal as an anathema, and yet a leading Nixon appointee had looked favorably on both. The incident had obviously embarrassed Wilson, and probably diminished his standing with the White House, but on Capitol Hill he became a minor hero, and no one—I least of all—would refuse to talk with him if he called.

I soon learned that Wilson's unfortunate experience had not chastened him appreciably, or made him less independent of Administration views. He told me immediately that he supported Magnuson's idea for an NHSC, and that he would like to help us pass the bill. It was, he said, almost an ideal piece of legislation, except for the role we'd assigned the Surgeon General. As the head of HSMHA, which the 1968 Reorganization had created over the Surgeon General's administratively dead body, Wilson explained that he supervised all health programs in HEW, and that we would have to make the NHSC part of his "shop" if we wanted it to be compatible with existing HEW structure and tolerable to the Administration. If we simply substituted "the Secretary of Health, Education and Welfare" for "the Surgeon General" everywhere in S. 4106, he pointed out, the bill would follow the normal pattern for health legislation —and the Secretary would delegate responsibility for the NHSC to him. Everyone recognized, Wilson said, that in the short run the draft law made it necessary to use PHS doctors to staff the NHSC; the further step of involving the Surgeon General, however, would make the bill wholly unacceptable to the Administration. If we deleted the Surgeon General, Wilson concluded, he might possibly persuade the Administration to support S. 4106 actively.

We couldn't dismiss Wilson's proposition lightly. His professed sincerity in supporting the NHSC concept squared with his reputation for forthright dealing, and he made no attempt to disguise his ulterior motive of purging the Surgeon General from the bill. That purge had no point unless Wilson genuinely hoped—or feared—that the bill would become law, and fear was out of the question: S. 4106 was stalled in the Senate, nonexistent in the House, and adjournment-prone in any event (and if it passed despite these obstacles, the President could veto it). Moreover, Wilson admitted his superiors had not authorized his offer, and he seemed clearly nervous lest word of his actions "leak" ("You'll forgive me," he said, "for discussing this by phone—I try not to write too many memoranda anymore").

If Wilson could obtain Administration support for a modified S. 4106, the House might act swiftly, and the bill might still become law. But could he succeed? And could we agree to his conditions? Eliminating the Surgeon General from S. 4106 now would precipitate a crisis among the bill's supporters, and we couldn't forget that the Surgeon Gen-

eral himself had been the one HEW official to testify that
the bill was "excellent." One of the reasons enthusiasm was
building for Magnuson's bill was that it would, as the Senator promised, "revitalize" the PHS (*Modern Medicine*
magazine had hailed it editorially as "a vitamin pill for the
Public Health Service"), and few of the bill's partisans
could distinguish between the fate of the PHS and the fate
of its former head. Wilson's offer consequently posed a difficult choice: should Magnuson jeopardize the firm backing
of a relatively weak group (the Surgeon General and his
allies) in a gamble for the potential support of a much
more crucial group (HEW and perhaps even the White
House)?

We decided not to make that choice. Instead, as so often
happens in politics, we compromised. Wilson had asked
that we change every mention of "the Surgeon General" to
"the Secretary"; we finally mentioned them both. In my
memorandum to Lee Goldman, I asked that the Committee
amend the relevant section of the bill to read (new words
italicized):

> The Corps shall be headed by a Director, who shall be ap-
> pointed by *the Secretary, in consultation with the Surgeon
> General of the United States Public Health Service*. It shall
> be the responsibility of the Director to direct the operations
> of the Corps, subject to the supervision and control of the
> Surgeon General *and the Secretary*.

That, we concluded, would be suitably ambiguous. On the
one hand, the authority granted the Surgeon General in the
original bill would be diminished, but no one could say by
how much. On the other hand, the Surgeon General would
still have more authority than he did in HEW at that time,
and more than he could ever hope to have if the bill failed
to become law. As to the "legislative intent" behind this
queer delineation of authority, we decided the report accompanying the bill should remain inscrutably silent.

Why had we "sold out" the Surgeon General by even this

much? Because our aim, after all, was to bring doctors to needy people, not to fight the Surgeon General's battle. Successive Surgeons General had been losing that battle for nearly twenty years, and a single bill could hardly deflect the forces of history altogether—particularly if it failed to become law. If S. 4106 passed, even as amended, it would represent the greatest victory for the Surgeon General and his former palace guard since the Truman Administration.

Why then had we not gone further and acceded completely to Wilson's request? Could the Surgeon General and his allies really help us in the future? The answer could be an elaborate one, but in fact it would have been hard to make a political case for not abandoning the Surgeon General entirely at this point. Yet a quaint sense of loyalty deterred us; as a Texas football coach replied when advised to shuffle his lineup, "We'll dance with who we brung."

2.

In the House, meanwhile, neither the transcript of Dr. Nolan's testimony nor a second letter from Magnuson, this one under the significant Senate Commerce Committee letterhead, had yet persuaded Congressman Staggers to introduce a companion bill to S. 4106. Unfortunately, we couldn't wait to see whether the new wording in the Senate bill would satisfy Dr. Wilson; we needed Staggers to introduce the House bill immediately, and then to call hearings on it himself if his Health Subcommittee leader, Paul Rogers, failed to take the hint. Since Staggers did not respond to Magnuson's letters, we decided to undertake a somewhat more intensive lobbying effort.

The first help came from Mike Gorman, the nation's foremost health lobbyist and a colorful figure on Capitol Hill. Like his employer, Mary (Mrs. Albert D.) Lasker, Gorman is largely unknown to the public, but observers in

Washington, D.C., universally acknowledge that he more
than any other individual has shaped the development of
American health policy over the past generation. He has
done so by tirelessly cultivating and educating solons, writing their speeches and their legislation; under Democratic
Administrations, he has enjoyed easy access to the White
House, too, as well as to the Secretary of Health, Education
and Welfare. In the years when Senator Hill and Congressman Fogarty dominated health news stories, Capitol Hill
nonetheless spoke privately of a "troika" when discussing
the formulation of any new health bill. Gorman wrote
much of President Truman's historic health message; he
and Mrs. Lasker and their allies built the National Institutes of Health into what President Johnson called "a
billion-dollar success story"; and in 1970 Gorman remained
the single most influential figure in what had become a very
complex environment for health legislation.

The son of a Tammany Hall politician, red-haired as
well as Irish, and never seen without a Phi Beta Kappa key
dangling across his vest, Gorman is ostentatious both by
nature and inclination, but his success lies in the staff-
like anonymity of his work, and he eschews publicity as
fervently as others in Washington seek it. When, in 1968,
The Atlantic Monthly published a somewhat catty article
about his and Mrs. Lasker's activities—entitled "The
Health Syndicate: Washington's Noble Conspirators"—the
vague criticism of the "Syndicate's" priorities merely dis-
comfited Gorman (there had been no suggestion, or not
much, of any improprieties), but he was terrified that the
publicity might undermine his key asset: a friendly, first-
name relationship with several hundred (*The Atlantic*
noted) Congressmen and Senators. (He also feared the
public might misunderstand some of Mrs. Lasker's philan-
thropy: her modest campaign contributions to "friends of
health" in both parties).

Gorman had patiently tutored me in the politics of

health ever since the NHSC's inception—partly because he liked the bill, partly because any increase in Magnuson's health role pleased him, but primarily, I think, because he felt very fond of Magnuson himself, with whom he had worked for more years than any member of the Senator's immediate staff. For my part, I found Gorman easily the most fascinating and flamboyant personality I'd met in Washington, and I looked up to him with an uncritical admiration that in higher-placed individuals (who had to deal with his importunities) had often dwindled to grudging respect. Although he was preoccupied with more substantial health bills, I regularly called him (and Harley Dirks) for advice on S. 4106, if for no other reason than that he and Harley somehow dignified the bill merely by discussing it.

When Congressman Staggers proved unresponsive, however, I asked Gorman for help rather than advice, and he generously agreed to talk with Staggers personally about the bill. He also told me that Staggers' daughter and son-in-law were both West Virginia doctors; why not send them a copy of S. 4106 and see if they'd be willing to discuss it with Staggers too? I passed this suggestion on to Dr. Nolan, home in West Virginia after testifying at Yarborough's hearing, and a few days later he called to say Staggers' relatives would gladly help.

At the same time, Bob Barclay arranged a meeting between Staggers and Hoyt Haddock, the head of the Maritime Council of the AFL-CIO. Haddock told Staggers that far from viewing S. 4106 as a threat to their own medical care by PHS doctors, the merchant seamen welcomed the bill. Unless the PHS was assigned a new and broader mission, Haddock argued, the Administration would soon dismantle it altogether and leave health care for merchant seamen and their families to the expensive private-practice system.

But Dr. Nolan, canvassing among Staggers' constituents,

devised on his own initiative the most thorough lobbying effort of all. He organized a large group of West Virginia doctors and medical-school faculty members to press Staggers for action on the bill, bolstering the effort with a number of medical students whom he and SAMA had alerted. When Staggers made a campaign speech in Circleville, West Virginia, on September 12, he found Nolan and his entire delegation in the audience. Staggers discussed the bill with them (having already spoken with his daughter and son-in-law), and Nolan publicized the event by sending a press release to all the local newspapers.

Bergman, for his part, wrote to Dr. Amos Johnson in Garland, North Carolina. Thanking him for his help with Senator Yarborough, Bergman asked hopefully, "Can you use some of the same old 'Southern Magic' on Harley Staggers?"

Whether Staggers responded to "Southern Magic" or whether, in the Border State of West Virginia, more tangible forms of persuasion had had the decisive influence, the Congressman at last told Gorman privately that he would act on the requests. On September 16 (with a relieved co-sponsor in the person of Representative Brock Adams), Staggers introduced H.R. 19246, "The National Health Service Corps Act of 1970."

And on the same morning, thanks probably to Jay Cutler and Carey Parker rather than to magic in any form, Senator Yarborough found a surprise when he walked into his Committee meeting room: a quorum.

3.

By custom, Senate Committees do not admit "outside" staff members to their meetings, so although I had written the Labor and Public Welfare Committee's Report on S. 4106, I could not watch the Committee's deliberations on the bill itself. Lee Goldman, who might have recounted the meeting in detail, chose instead to tell me only the results: the Committee had approved the bill, raised the authorized level of funding substantially, and added as cosponsors—at their own request—all but one of the Committee Republicans. Although gratifying, this information stimulated my curiosity more than it satisfied it. Goldman refused to divulge anything further, but fortunately Jay Cutler proved less taciturn and more sympathetic.

As Cutler described the meeting, Yarborough first announced that the Health Subcommittee was in session. After the assembled Senators had approved the bill in their Subcommittee capacity, the Chairman announced—without anyone leaving his place at the table—that the full Committee would now come to order. Sitting as the full Committee, the Senators then ratified the decision most of them had just made as Health Subcommittee members, and so, in an absolutely minimal amount of time, Yarborough had deftly cleared S. 4106 for the Senate Floor.

At some point in this speedy process, discussion and amendment of the bill took place. The Committee duly accepted the wording changes we'd requested, including the cryptic ones pertaining to the Surgeon General. Then Peter Dominick, an archconservative from Colorado and the ranking Republican on the Health Subcommittee, offered an amendment to delete from the bill a section creating a "National Advisory Council on the Health Service Corps." This Council proposal had attracted much favorable comment at the hearing, and we had included it out of an idealistic desire to provide NHSC doctors and patients a high degree of participation in the program's administration. But Dominick argued that HEW programs already had too many councils, and that none of them did anything besides waste time and the taxpayers' money. So the Committee adopted the Dominick Amendment and eliminated the proposed Council from the bill.

At another juncture, the Republicans made a halfhearted

effort to amend the bill more substantially by adding to it
the substance of a bill that California's George Murphy and
several other Health Subcommittee Republicans had introduced in August. The Murphy bill, embodying a concept
known as "loan forgiveness," would have allowed the government to pay back the educational loans of any medical
student who agreed to practice for a few years in a "medically underserved area." Although a number of states had
tried "loan forgiveness" schemes without success, the Republicans evidently liked this free-enterprise alternative to
the NHSC and hoped to aid Murphy, who was then in the
process of losing his reelection campaign. We could easily
have accepted this amendment, for we still believed the
"doctor distribution" problem required a variety of policies, but Yarborough apparently reminded his colleagues
that passing Magnuson's bill intact might give them more
leverage with the Chairman of the HEW Appropriations
Subcommittee. So the Committee rejected the Murphy
Amendment.

Yarborough himself offered the final amendment. Magnuson's version of S. 4106 provided a funding level of $5
million per year; Yarborough insisted on $10 million in the
first year and annual additions of $5 million until the pro-
gram reached $25 million in the fourth year. This proposal
jolted Dominick, who offered a substitute amendment re-
stricting the NHSC to a much slower growth rate. In the
end, the Committee reached a "compromise" and set the
funding ceiling at $5 million in the first year, $10 million
in the second, $12 million in the third and $15 million in
the fourth. These figures demonstrated Yarborough's sagac-
ity, although on close inspection the progression itself
seemed perplexing (why should the increase in the second
and fourth years exceed that in the third?). Not only had
Yarborough more than tripled the potential size of the
NHSC, but he had skillfully created the impression for the
Republicans that Dominick had scored a victory in averting

still larger increases. Those Republicans who had not already cosponsored S. 4106 (except Senator Saxbe of Ohio, who was absent) expressed their satisfaction by adding their names to the bill now, bringing the total number of cosponsors to twenty-seven—more than one quarter of the Senate.

Yet S. 4106 had not progressed entirely without mishap. By accident, the Committee had eliminated a subtle but politically important feature of the bill: the criteria for deciding which communities should receive NHSC doctors. We had drafted these "assignment criteria" more carefully than any other section of S. 4106, for we had to strike a delicate balance between "local control" on the one hand and Federal discretion on the other. We wanted to assure communities that NHSC doctors would not be "forced" upon them, and we wanted organized medicine to know that the government would not place NHSC doctors in areas where they would compete with other physicians already practicing. But we did not want to give any community or medical group an absolute "veto power" over NHSC assignments; we could too easily imagine stubborn local officials or reactionary medical societies excluding NHSC doctors from a needy but powerless poor community, especially if the community were black. In order to preserve the freedom to assign doctors to such communities, while at the same time signaling the intention to cooperate with local government and local physicians, we included as general criteria for NHSC assignments the "willingness" of the community and the "recommendations" of the nearby medical groups. Unfortunately, however, we had listed these "local control provisions" in the section of the bill pertaining to the National Advisory Council—and Dominick's amendment had stricken this entire section.

Despite the political importance of the "local control" provisions, and the fact that Dominick and his fellow Republicans would certainly have favored retaining them in the bill, we now had no way to restore the inadvertent deletions. Calling S. 4106 back to Committee would delay its Senate passage indefinitely, and we dared not risk a Floor amendment; the bill would almost certainly pass as it stood, but prolonged debate might jeopardize it. So, as an unhappy substitute, we decided to insert the "local control" provisions in the Committee Report, thus making clear the "legislative intent" of the bill, if not the bill itself. Goldman agreed to this last-minute change, and when the Report appeared on September 17, it contained (besides the invisible skeleton of the "boxcar report") a special section labeled "Qualitative Criteria for the Corps' Activities." We hoped this would suffice if criticism arose; and we hoped, too, that the Senate would not wait long before bringing S. 4106 to a vote.

4.

But it was not in Washington, D.C., alone that S. 4106 was being considered. Three thousand miles away, in Portland, Oregon, the Legislative Council of the American Medical Association met to decide what position the AMA should adopt on the NHSC and other health bills. The meeting took place on September 19, three days after Staggers had introduced the bill in the House and Yarborough's Committee had approved it in the Senate. Since the nineteenth was a Saturday, Bergman had planned to see the University of Washington football game, but he knew the Portland meeting might decide the bill's fate. Reluctantly, he gave up his seats in Husky Stadium, obtained permission from the Washington State Medical Society to serve as its "representative" (although he did not even belong to the AMA), and flew south to Oregon.

So far, the AMA had shown remarkably schizoid reactions to the concept of a doctor corps in general and to

Magnuson's bill in particular. Many months earlier, for example, the AMA Board of Trustees had approved the idea of letting doctors practice in needy areas as an alternative to military service, but the AMA House of Delegates had thunderously rejected the proposal—for the ironic reason, apparently, that the younger delegates thought the resolution in question implied support for continuation of the doctor draft. After Magnuson introduced S. 4106, Bergman had taken a copy to the AMA's Washington lobbyists. They said they liked the bill, but couldn't act without instructions from AMA headquarters in Chicago. At Jerry Brazda's suggestion, I then called the second-ranking AMA functionary in Chicago, Dr. Richard Wilbur, reputedly the most "progressive" official in the AMA's top echelons. Dr. Wilbur had not seen the bill, but he liked the sound of it, so I sent him a copy. A week later, I called him back, and this time he thoroughly denounced S. 4106. Despite this unsettling incident, two AMA councils (on education and rural health) had subsequently endorsed S. 4106, while the council on private practice opposed it.

Bergman had oscillated between frustration and amusement as the AMA's fretful indecisiveness wore on, but by the time he flew to Portland he had begun to fear, intuitively, that the AMA would suddenly intervene with forceful opposition to Magnuson's bill. The Portland meeting dispelled this fear completely. Bergman found, to his astonishment, that the AMA Legislative Council solemnly intended to pronounce upon every health bill still pending in the 91st Congress—as if Congress could not adjourn until the AMA had spoken. Each Council member had been supplied with a thick file containing all the bills, and no priorities had been set: the Council would consider each bill in turn, whether it was poised for passage or had been forgotten even by its sponsor. While notable for its egalitarianism, this system allowed little time for discussion of any particular bill. When S. 4106 came up in the morning session, the Council listened to Bergman and Robert Shannon (the SAMA Vice President who had testified at the Senate hearing), then debated the bill hurriedly. When the debate failed to yield a quick consensus, the Council simply set the bill aside rather than spend all morning on it; they had many other bills to consider. The AMA would have to survive without an official position on S. 4106—and Congress would have to muddle through without the AMA's advice.

The decline of the AMA as a political force is often discussed in Washington, D.C., but as Bergman flew home (arriving, happily, just in time for the kickoff at Husky Stadium), he knew he had found an explanation other observers hadn't noted. The AMA has lost prestige and power for many reasons: its irresponsible and scandal-ridden fight against Medicare has not been forgotten on Capitol Hill; its membership has declined substantially; its legislative efforts have degenerated into predictable rearguard actions to slow the pace of reform. But as the Portland meeting vividly demonstrated, the AMA has become inept as well as out of touch; not only have its organizational arteries hardened, but its reflexes have slowed pathetically.

After Portland, we stopped worrying about the AMA, except to wonder whether some high-ranking official might visit the White House in the event S. 4106 reached the President's desk. And one phenomenon we noted seemed significant far beyond the immediate context of our bill: in the entire course of Congressional consideration of S. 4106, not one Congressman or Senator ever asked us what position the AMA had taken on the legislation.

5.

On Monday, September 21—two days after the AMA meeting in Portland—I was at lunch with other members of Magnuson's staff in the Carroll Arms when I unexpectedly heard my name over the restaurant's public-address system. At the front desk, I found Jack Forsythe waiting. "You'd better get on over to the Floor," he said drily, "because your bill is coming up for a vote right now, and Yarborough is out of town." This news stunned me: we hadn't expected the Senate to act so soon, five days after Yarborough's Committee reported the bill, and we certainly hadn't known Yarborough would be away. As Chairman of the relevant committee, Yarborough would ordinarily have been the bill's Floor Manager during the Senate debate; Magnuson might indeed have replaced him, but ironically, Magnuson had not yet returned from a weekend trip to Seattle.

"Well," Forsythe said with unconcern, "if Maggie's not here and Yarborough's not here, that's all the more reason for you to hustle over there and find a Senator to manage your bill." Forsythe was letting me know that he would make no effort to help, even though technically it was his responsibility—not mine—to find a substitute for Senator Yarborough.

Apologizing hastily to my companions, and abandoning a half-eaten lunch, I ran to the office for the S. 4106 file, then hurried through the crowded underground passage to the Capitol. The moment I had my Floor pass and stepped into the Senate Chamber, an aide to the Majority Leader rushed up. "Where's Maggie?" he asked urgently, his voice pushing me to near panic. "Yarborough isn't here to manage the bill, and it's up *right now!*" Magnuson was gone too, I said; "we need a delay." The aide rushed away again, searched through some papers on his desk, and breathlessly handed the Presiding Officer a bill to consider before S. 4106.

Briefly reprieved, I found a telephone in the corridor and called Senator Jackson's office; he was now the logical choice for Floor Manager, even though we'd failed to keep him up to date on the bill's progress. Jackson was on his way to the Senate already, the secretary said; I hung up and waited for him anxiously. Moments later, he strode through the east doors of the Chamber, and I quickly intercepted him. He winced when I told him our dilemma. He explained he had a meeting and could come to the Floor only to vote. "Get another Democrat from the Committee," he advised, "and try to get a roll call, not just a voice vote."

The roll call was agreed to; the problem of a Floor Manager remained. The only Democrats on the Floor from Yarborough's Committee were the type Spiro Agnew had just called "radic-libs"—Kennedy, Hughes, Cranston, Nelson. They could manage the bill, but they might alienate potential votes from conservatives (Senators often know nothing about "minor" bills before voting; they come in, look around, ask a friend, and vote). Our bill wouldn't lose, but we wanted every possible vote—we had to impress the House that S. 4106 was "safe."

Then Jay Cutler appeared. He heard my story, looked around the Chamber, then turned to me with a smile and said: "Dominick." Dominick! Cutler laughed as I stared incredulously; conservatives didn't just trust Dominick—they lionized him. "Of course it's crazy, but why not?" Cutler insisted. "He's the top Republican on the Health Subcommittee, he's a cosponsor, and he amended the bill in Committee—so at least he should know something about it." Cutler laughed again, then walked jauntily to Dominick's desk. The Senator bent down to hear, stood up again, shrugged his shoulders, and smiled. Cutler looked at me and grinned. Dominick would manage the bill.

Cutler had transformed the day's nightmare into a happy fantasy. I relaxed at once, even though I could hardly believe our luck. Since Dominick needed a speech, Cutler simply handed him the one I had prepared for Yarborough (fortunately, it bore no such inscription), as if it didn't matter that Dominick and Yarborough stood at opposite ends of the Senate's political spectrum. Could this be real? I asked myself again. The ranking Republican on the Health

Subcommittee, a man who wrote columns for right-wing magazines, was about to Floor-manage a "socialized medicine" bill, a bill to rescue the PHS from the policies of a Republican Administration? In delight and disbelief, I sat down on the tawny-colored staff couch and watched the improbable spectacle begin.

At first, everything went smoothly. Dominick articulated splendidly the case for Magnuson's bill. He did not follow the text of the prepared speech slavishly, but rather deleted and added ideas adeptly as he spoke, making his remarks conform much more closely to his own views. He finished within a few minutes, asked unanimous consent to have printed in the *Record* statements I had prepared for Magnuson, Jackson, and Yarborough (the last was simply an expanded version of the speech Dominick held in his hand), and then yielded the Floor. Senator Winston Prouty of Vermont, another Republican cosponsor, spoke first, and urged his colleagues to vote for the bill. But then something unexpected happened: Senator John Sherman Cooper of Kentucky rose to speak.

Senator Cooper, a Republican, had not cosponsored S. 4106, and the tone of his voice indicated immediately that he had deep misgivings about it. Admitting almost apologetically that he had just read the bill for the first time, Cooper objected that it contained no guidelines, no "local control" provisions—nothing at all, in fact, to prevent the government from sending doctors into a community even if local physicians or the community itself objected. He was absolutely right, of course, for he had just discovered the accidental damage the Dominick Amendment had caused in Yarborough's Committee. Cooper's perceptiveness impressed me greatly; he had noticed the absence of assignment criteria immediately, whereas the bill's cosponsors had not noticed the *presence* of those same criteria during the Committee meeting devoted to the bill. Yet I wished Cooper had never read the bill at all. I dreaded that he would try to amend it, and that as a result the state and district medical societies—the grass roots of organized medicine—would acquire the "veto power" over NHSC assignments that we had tried so carefully to deny them. Even as this anxiety took shape in my thoughts, Cooper articulated it: "I shall offer an amendment to that effect. . . ."

Instantly, the staff couch erupted. Cutler streaked to Dominick's desk; Bill Miller (Cooper's legislative aide) dashed to the Kentuckian. I grabbed the Majority Leader's assistant, who grabbed the Majority Leader, who interrupted Cooper to "suggest the absence of a quorum" (the Senate's standard delaying tactic). While the clerk called the roll at a leaden pace, a hasty conference took place on the Senate Floor. Cutler explained to Dominick, for the first time, that his amendment in Committee had eliminated the "local control" provisions along with the National Advisory Council, adding that the provisions had been printed in the Report and that Dominick himself had just repeated them in his speech—all to emphasize the "legislative intent" to make the provisions a corollary of the bill itself. I explained this simultaneously to Bill Miller (whom Cooper's spontaneous action had also surprised), and he promptly clarified the situation for his employer. Assuming this explanation had satisfied Cooper, Cutler and Miller and I all returned to the staff couch in relief. The quorum call was suspended, and business resumed.

Dominick explained, this time for the *Record*, that the Committee had inadvertently stricken the "local control" provisions from the bill and had consequently printed them prominently in the Report in order to make the "legislative intent" clear. But then, inexplicably, Cooper insisted that he *still* wanted to amend the bill. Once again Senate business halted, and this time Dominick as well as Cutler and Miller descended upon Cooper. Straining to see from the back of the chamber (I would have been an interloper in this Republican council), I noticed Miller pointing out to

Cooper something in the Report. Then everyone returned to his appointed place—Dominick to his desk, and Cutler and Miller to the staff couch. And Cooper offered his amendment: to restore the original "local control" provisions to the bill.

Cutler and Miller laughed as my surprise turned to wan relief and then elation. Another near disaster had been averted, and S. 4106 would now resume its original form (except, of course, for the National Advisory Council itself). And the result had been accidental; I would never have dared seek it. Dominick graciously accepted the Cooper Amendment for the Republicans, and Senator Hughes—noting with heavy irony that he, the lowest-ranking Democrat on Yarborough's Committee, was nonetheless the only one then present—accepted the amendment for the majority, and the roll call began on S. 4106 itself.

Now came the test. S. 4106 would pass, but by how large a margin? Dominick had helped, I knew; conservatives would feel less inclined to oppose it. The clerk called the names rapidly, and "Aye" after "Aye" echoed through the chamber; near the end of the roll, not a single "No" had been reported. Then—and many heads turned—Senator John Williams of Delaware strode purposefully onto the Floor. Williams, a Republican, styled himself as the Senate's fiscal conservative, the "Treasury's watchdog"; he voted against new programs on principle, to save money—the government had too many programs already. And since he habitually voted "No," Williams had little need to read the bill under consideration; he probably couldn't even decipher the acronym "NHSC." But this time Williams looked squarely at Dominick, who nodded and smiled ingratiatingly, and he apparently decided that any bill Dominick agreed to manage couldn't be very expensive. Williams voted "Aye," and Cutler and Miller began to laugh aloud.

Two Senators who had not voted when their names were first called now approached Dominick. Both were Republicans. One of them, a Southerner, shook his head and said with chagrin, "If this bill will help Maggie and Scoop, I'll vote for it. But you'd better be able to promise me that there will never be any money appropriated for this hare-brained scheme." The second Senator, a junior member of the Appropriations Committee, replied with mock solemnity, "I think I can give you certain assurances in that regard." Dominick only chuckled ambiguously, and his two colleagues then turned toward the clerk and added their "Ayes." Dominick had managed S. 4106 superbly.

The roll call had ended. While the Senate bustled in preparation for the next item on the agenda, the clerk tallied the votes. Then Senator J. Caleb Boggs, sitting temporarily as the Presiding Officer, announced the result: sixty-six "Yeas," no "Nays." S. 4106 had passed unanimously.

Dazed with happiness, exhausted from suddenly relieved tension, I walked out of the Senate beside a mirthful Jay Cutler. "Feels good, doesn't it?" he asked laughingly. Still incoherent, I stammered out my thanks to Cutler for all his help. "Don't thank me," he insisted, "thank Yarborough. He's the one who held the Committee's feet to the fire, telling them about all the goodies Maggie would put in the HEW Appropriation for us."

Outside the Chamber, we paused at a clerk's desk to surrender our Floor passes. Cutler looked through the doorway, gave me a friendly prod with his elbow, and said, "Hey, guess who's waiting in the Reception Room? Glen Wegner!"

I hadn't seen Wegner for weeks, not since the day he had come to Magnuson's office to denounce S. 4106 and belittle its legislative prospects. Now, as Cutler and I approached him where he sat in the ornate Senate Reception Room, his calm expression indicated clearly that he had no idea what had just happened. Apparently he had simply come to see Cutler on some ordinary business in his capacity as HEW's

Congressional liaison. The prospect of breaking the news to him miraculously restored my speech.

"Guess what?" I asked, with ill-concealed glee. "The Senate just passed the National Health Service Corps—unanimously!"

Wegner's jaw dropped; I had to continue. "And guess who managed the bill? Peter Dominick!"

Now Wegner began to mumble, and the mumble quickly grew to a near shout. "Dominick!" he retorted furiously. "What happened to Yarborough? What happened to Magnuson?"

"Yarborough was out of town," I responded, as nonchalantly as possible; "and so was Magnuson."

By now Wegner had become livid. "Magnuson will rue the day he introduced this bill," he declared hotly, as if pronouncing a curse. "It will turn out to be one of the biggest mistakes of his career. You know what will happen, don't you, if this thing ever becomes law? The PHS will seize upon it to justify their own existence, and they'll ruin it like they've ruined every other program they've ever been in charge of. You just don't realize how bad the PHS is. They'll appoint as Director some member of the 'Old Guard,' someone about sixty-five years old, and he'll totally mismanage the program."

"But Glen," I replied with cheerful familiarity, "just because the Senate passes the bill unanimously doesn't mean it's going to become law. We still have plenty of problems in the House, you know. They haven't even *begun* to act on it over there."

Then I turned to go, thinking Wegner would stay behind to fume with Cutler, for I wanted to get back to Magnuson's office with the good news. But Wegner followed me in anger for a few strides, obviously not finished yet.

"And another thing—Magnuson ought to get rid of that crazy little pediatrician from Seattle, that Bergman." He spat out the name contemptuously. "Do you know that he's so bad his colleagues at the University of Washington won't even *talk* to him?"

I could only smile and keep walking. The sun was out, and I decided to walk back to the office outdoors, avoiding the Capitol subway. I'll have to *ask* Bergman about that, I thought with amusement. As I descended the bright Capitol steps, savoring the victory and Wegner's fulminations, I came to a curious knot of men and women gathered on a landing. They had clustered around a Republican Senator, a man who had not cosponsored S. 4106 but who did happen to be running for reelection. The Senator was looking earnestly into a hastily erected television camera and describing eloquently the "landmark bill" he had just "helped to pass" in the Senate, the National Health Service Corps Act of 1970.

The day complete now, I must have puzzled some tourists with my happy and no longer restrained laughter as I made my way through the crowd.

VIII

LOOSE ENDS

1.

The Senate passed S. 4106 only two weeks before I was due to leave Senator Magnuson's staff and go to study in England. I felt particularly unhappy—and oddly uneasy—about saying goodbye with the NHSC issue still unresolved. My colleagues in the office tried to reassure me, for although none of them thought the bill would become law in 1970 (it was simply too late for the House to act), they all felt the 66–0 Senate vote had fittingly capped Magnuson's NHSC effort in the 91st Congress. Final passage, they predicted, would come early in 1971, during the first months of the new Congress. In the face of these optimistic assessments from my more experienced co-workers, my own disquiet seemed irrational, and yet it persisted.

At least I could understand why deferring S. 4106 until the 92nd Congress did not trouble the other members of Magnuson's staff. They could set the bill aside for the time being because they felt confident of winning—winning, no matter how long it took, simply because Magnuson had set his mind to it, and because Magnuson was the nearest thing to an irresistible legislative force in the entire U.S. Senate. They viewed our success in the 91st Congress, the unanimous Senate passage, as a prelude rather than a climax, with ultimate victory perhaps less than a year away. Even though I lacked their experience, lacked the knowledge of what it was to fight a legislative battle from one Congress to the next, I could certainly comprehend their perspective, and even share it in the abstract. But no matter how hard I tried to think of the NHSC as a certain "winner" in the 92nd Congress, I could not escape a host of nagging and interrelated doubts.

These doubts, I knew, might reflect nothing more than my own selfishness, for I could never fully recoup my emotional investment in the bill if it became law after I'd left. Certainly, too, my association with Bergman had colored my thinking, for his time horizon never extended beyond the immediate; to Bergman, winning meant winning *now*. Unlike Magnuson's top aides, the cool professionals and legislative masters, Bergman could not enjoy an intermediate victory, could not savor the delights of the Senate's unanimous vote or find satisfaction in the promise it held for the future. If I succumbed to Bergman's vision, his insatiability, I might lose the respect of my staff colleagues, the men with whom I identified; yet I could not repeat their complacent predictions to Bergman without infuriating him.

But beyond these perhaps irrational considerations lay other, more convincing reasons for questioning the theory that Magnuson could simply pick up the legislative thread of the NHSC again in the 92nd Congress. Yarborough would be gone, for one thing, and to date no one knew precisely who would succeed him as Chairman of the Health Subcommittee or the full Committee on Labor and

Public Welfare; we might easily find ourselves with a less sympathetic man in either post. It was even conceivable (indeed, many observers thought it highly likely) that the Republicans would win enough new Senate seats in November to wrest the majority from the Democrats after nearly twenty years; Nixon and Agnew were waging an intense campaign all across the country with precisely this aim in mind. A Republican majority in the Senate would mean Republican, not Democratic, committee chairmen: Magnuson would lose the chairmanships of both the HEW Appropriations Subcommittee and the Commerce Committee, which had not been irrelevant resources for him in his effort to pass S. 4106.

Even if the Democratic majority survived the election intact, the New Year might not find the Administration (or the AMA) so confused and indecisive about Magnuson's bill. Top HEW officials had already announced that Nixon would present Congress with a "sweeping" health program (a "Health Package," they called it) early in 1971. If, as HEW had recently hinted, the "Package" included proposals to deal with the "doctor distribution" problem, then Magnuson's bill would quickly lose its Republican cosponsors, who were supporting Democratic health bills in 1970 at least partly because they had no alternative: the elections were approaching, and the Administration had provided them with no health programs of its own. In 1971, things would have changed; at the very least, the fortuitous circumstances that had made Peter Dominick the Floor Manager of S. 4106 were unlikely to recur.

In addition, of course, the Nixon Administration intended to abolish the Public Health Service, and might succeed before Magnuson could pass his bill in the 92nd Congress—in fact, the PHS might be dead by the time the 92nd Congress convened in January. With the PHS gone and the Commissioned Officer Corps disbanded, the Magnuson bill would become anachronistic; only a change in

the draft law could then create a doctor corps, and that
would make the NHSC a wholly different (and almost
hopeless) legislative task. The present support for the
NHSC—predicated in large part on the assumption that it
would help save the PHS—would certainly diminish once
the PHS was defunct.

When I catalogued these fears in a conversation with
Stan Barer a few days after the Senate vote, he agreed that I
should keep working on S. 4106 until I left. Besides, he now
had reason to suspect that the situation in the House was
not as bleak as it had earlier appeared. Quite unexpectedly,
he had received a phone call from Congressman Rogers.
Rogers hadn't mentioned the NHSC; he wanted Magnuson
to introduce a Senate companion to a water-quality-stan-
dards bill he had just introduced in the House. Graciously,
Barer had promised to ask Magnuson, who promptly introduced the bill—without asking a favor of Rogers in return.
"Sometimes," Barer said, smiling, "the best trump card is
one you never play at all."

2.

By September 23, at least six versions of Magnuson's
NHSC bill had found their way to the House Commerce
Committee. S. 4106, the latest arrival, had come over that
morning from the Senate, two days after its passage. H.R.
19246, the bill Staggers had introduced a week before, embodied the proposal in its original form. The remaining
bills were permutations, mostly replicas of S. 4106 as Yarborough's Committee had approved it; a few enterprising
Congressmen had introduced NHSC bills "spontaneously"
the day the Committee Report came out. Yet despite the
variety of NHSC bills to choose from, on September 23 the
House Commerce Committee had, as far as we knew, no
plans to act on any of them.

We had hoped, of course, that the 66–0 Senate vote and the sudden flurry of NHSC bills in the House would goad Congressman Rogers to action in the Health Subcommittee. But he seemed indifferent to the Senate events, the encroachment of his colleagues on his own legislative territory, and even the fact that he himself had helped write the bill that Staggers, his Chairman, had introduced. Nor did Rogers betray the slightest apprehension that Senator Magnuson might play the "trump card" he now held. Instead, when I called his aide, Bob Maher, I obtained only the by now gratuitous advice not to count on Rogers for anything.

So our only hope was to have Staggers call hearings himself. He had promised Mike Gorman, in fact, that he would, but neither he nor his staff had said anything at all to us. We realized that persuading him to call hearings might prove more difficult than our earlier task (which had been difficult enough) of persuading him to introduce the bill, and consequently we discounted still further Staggers' alleged "promise" to Gorman. He had already done Magnuson one favor, with H.R. 19246; it was hardly his fault that Rogers had failed to take the hint. Staggers could not conduct his own NHSC hearings without interfering, highhandedly and perhaps unprecedentedly, with Rogers' Health Subcommittee—and why should he risk making enemies of his colleagues just to please a Senator? The fact that Staggers had introduced an NHSC bill did not necessarily imply that he cared what happened to it; he might simply have given in to the combined pressures of Magnuson, various health lobbyists, and the constituents Dr. Nolan had organized. But if he thought he could escape further lobbying merely by introducing H.R. 19246, Staggers had miscalculated. For although we took little pleasure in subjecting Staggers to still greater pressures, Rogers' recalcitrance had left us no other choice—and after all, it had worked once before.

Senator Magnuson, for one, thought Staggers could be

persuaded to act on the NHSC. He was quite impressed that his House counterpart had introduced the bill at all, and the fact that Staggers had delayed for many weeks did not diminish Magnuson's appreciation. After the Senate passed S. 4106, the Senator wrote Staggers again, thanking him for introducing H.R. 19246 and asking him now to push the bill to passage in the House. Magnuson discussed the bill's politics reassuringly in his letter, stressing particularly the unanimous and bipartisan support the bill had enjoyed in the Senate. Leaving no doubt that he wanted to see the NHSC enacted in the 91st Congress, despite the short time remaining, Magnuson emphasized that "minimal hearings and a brief report may well be sufficient to deal with this legislation in [your] Committee."

Magnuson had to treat with Staggers directly, for the Congressman had surrounded himself with a phalanx of enigmatic and protective aides who precluded negotiations between the two offices at the staff level. Staggers' Administrative Assistant, the sphinxlike Marguerite Furfari, possessed a truly remarkable ability to engage in a lengthy phone conversation without providing the slightest clue as to Staggers' plans, thoughts, or disposition. The Chief Clerk of Staggers' Commerce Committee, W. E. ("Ed") Williamson, was similarly uninformative, although in a distinctly less voluble manner. When I called Williamson after the Senate vote and emphasized how noncontroversial the bill had been, he dismissed me with a simple comment. "Hell," he said, "you know as well as I do that just because a bill is noncontroversial in the Senate doesn't mean it's going to be noncontroversial in the *House*."

Experience (not always pleasant) had already taught me that the Senate was a far more intricate and subtle legislative labyrinth than the institution my college textbooks had described. Now Staggers' staff taught me a parallel lesson about the House of Representatives. I had anticipated that the House might consider itself the legislative equal of the

Senate, despite the condescending habit of Senators of referring to it as "the lower body." Yet I soon learned that
the House really considers itself the Senate's superior;
superior in wisdom, in behavior, and (not least) in virtue.
Congressmen and their staffs, in fact, cherish a fine disdain
for the Senate and Senators, whom they regard as "hot-
heads" writing ill-considered, poorly drafted, and generally
irresponsible legislation. A young Congressman might consider the Senate a political utopia: progressive, democratic,
and with plenty of power for all. But to House careerists—
and to the career staffs of the House committees—the Senate
is an unseemly, anarchic, and almost dissolute body. Congressmen of real importance, and their staffs, do not attach
great significance to suggestions or legislation that emanate
from the opposite side of Capitol Hill.

Bergman and I had received our first blunt lesson in
House attitudes on August 28, the day of Yarborough's
hearings, when we paid an afternoon visit to Jim Menger,
one of Staggers' lieutenants. Like Harley Dirks, Menger
had an innocuous title: officially, he was a "professional
staff member" of the House Commerce Committee. As with
Dirks, however, Menger's title understated his true importance, for his authority derived directly from the Chairman,
and to a great extent he controlled, along with Williamson,
the Committee's legislative efforts. We had been warned
that Menger was "conservative," unlikely to favor the
NHSC, and we wanted to discuss the bill and its politics
with him immediately after Yarborough's hearing, for we
thought the testimony might win his cooperation in the
House.

Menger greeted us cordially enough, although this minor
deputation from the Senate hardly awed him. Gallantly, he
invited Judy Bergman to join us during our meeting, and
he displayed no more than appropriate interest in her red
velvet miniskirt. To our surprise, Menger made no effort to
dispose of us quickly, but instead prefaced our discussion by

screening some antidrug television messages on his private videotape machine. He spoke enthusiastically about this new approach to combating the drug problem in America, and predicted great success for the short tapes, which the Federal Narcotics Bureau or some such agency had prepared. I began to wonder about the "equal time" implications of this proposed television campaign, but decided not to raise the question. Already I had begun to doubt, as the private telecast dragged on, whether Menger knew why we had come.

He knew. When the protagonist of the final message had resolutely pushed aside a proffered "joint," Menger switched off the set, folded his hands on the desk, and arched his eyebrows in a classic "What can I do for you?" expression. Briefly, we summarized the morning's hearings in the Senate and then asked him to help us pass the bill in the 91st Congress. We offered to answer any questions he might have about the NHSC, but Menger only sighed, pushed himself back from the desk, and walked slowly to a nearby filing cabinet. He returned with a detailed chart showing the number of hours the Commerce Committee had met during the 91st Congress, the number of hearings it had held, the number of reports it had filed, and the number of bills it had considered. "You can see," he said in a melancholy voice, "that our work load is way up this year—just compare these figures with last year's." Translation: I've got enough to do without worrying about your little bill.

Of course we expressed due wonderment and appreciation at the Committee's work load. Then, as tactfully as possible, I suggested that if the Senate experience with S. 4106 was any guide, the Committee could nonetheless consider the bill briefly and simply—it needn't add significantly to Menger's burdens.

But I had not been tactful enough. Menger glared at me, and then asked hotly, "Son, how long have you been on

Capitol Hill?" I replied warily that I'd been working for Magnuson for two years.

"Well," Menger announced triumphantly, stretching himself to his full height, "I've been here for *eighteen* years, and when you've been here as long as I have, then I'll listen to your advice about how much work it takes to hold a hearing and pass a bill in this Committee!

"Besides," he added, reverting to a convivial grin, "it's not *me* you have to convince—it's the members of the Committee." With that, we recognized, the interview had ended.

Outside Menger's office, waiting for the elevator, Bergman was dejected and his wife incredulous at Menger's performance. My face still burned with humiliation. "You know, Abe," I vowed melodramatically, "we're going to win—we're going to *beat* that man!" Bergman laughed, justifiably, and spared me further humiliation by not mentioning the incident again.

We hadn't contacted Menger since that August 28 meeting, but we had come to realize that he had correctly identified our task. We didn't have to convince him; we had to convince Staggers. Apparently our initial efforts had succeeded, too, since Staggers had introduced the bill in mid-September. Magnuson's letter after the Senate vote represented the first step in persuading the Congressman to go one step further and hold hearings. Playfully (for we had told him of our meeting with Menger), Magnuson added a special postscript before mailing the letter: "Please let me know if I or my staff can help in any way, as I know the Committee has a heavy work load . . ."

Characteristically, Staggers did not reply to Magnuson's letter, but even before it reached him S. 4106's prospects had brightened. The harassed Congressional Leadership, after several times postponing the adjournment date of the 91st Congress, finally announced that adjournment was impossible before mid-October at the earliest. If Congress could still not overcome the legislative backlog (a direct consequence of Nixon's agenda-destroying invasion of Cambodia), the Leadership warned that a postelection session would be necessary. Although a postelection session appeared initially as a mere threat, one that would never materialize, at least the delayed adjournment meant Staggers had several more weeks in which to act on the NHSC —if he could be coaxed into doing so.

The significance of the Leadership's announcement did not escape the indefatigable Dr. Nolan in West Virginia. Nolan promptly produced letters from 222 West Virginia doctors, dentists, and medical students, all urging Staggers to take advantage of the delay to hold hearings on *his* NHSC bill (for Nolan was clever). Nolan issued another press release on the day the 222 letters were mailed to Staggers, and this time an even greater number of West Virginia papers ran the story. He also wrote to the newspapers directly, describing the bill and its potential significance for the state, and urging readers to write Staggers themselves. In these letters to the editor, Nolan invariably quoted a statement by the President of the West Virginia University chapter of SAMA: "If the National Health Service Corps Act is passed, more young physicians would stay in West Virginia to practice after graduation."

On the same day Nolan issued his press release and sent the 222 letters to Staggers, the *Charleston Gazette* ran an editorial Nolan had obviously inspired. Reiterating the legislation's importance to West Virginia, and repeating the SAMA President's prediction about the NHSC's potential impact, the *Gazette* concluded with an outright appeal to Staggers:

> The need is critical. The Senate action is encouraging. We would urge Rep. Staggers to do everything in his power to assure favorable action in the House before Congress adjourns.

The editorial appeared at just the right moment. One of
S. 4106's most prominent Senate cosponsors was West Virginia's Jennings Randolph; whether through chance or a
special insight of Nolan's, the *Gazette* editorial referred to
S. 4106 as the "Randolph-Magnuson bill." This nomenclature elated Randolph's legislative assistant, Phil McGance,
who had been trying for some time to devise a stratagem
through which Randolph could publicly prod Staggers on
the bill. McGance now wrote a Senate speech, which Randolph delivered on October 6, extolling the "Randolph-
Magnuson bill" and pointedly inserting in the *Congressional Record* the text of the editorial, with its praise for
Randolph and its blunt message for Staggers. In fact, Mc-
Gance cheerfully reported, Randolph liked the editorial so
much that he had even called Staggers personally to discuss
it.

The *Gazette*'s unique appellation for S. 4106 did not
offend Senator Magnuson; in fact, it pleased him immensely. "Instead of hogging the credit," Magnuson had
often said, "we have to make everyone think of this as *his*
bill." Certainly Yarborough saw the bill this way, and now
Randolph did too. Mike Gorman suggested still another
opportunity to garner support by handing out laurels. The
late Walter Reuther, he said, had repeatedly advocated a
"National Health Corps" during his career as head of the
United Auto Workers; why not have Magnuson write to
Reuther's successor, Leonard Woodcock, and enlist his aid
in persuading Staggers to take action in the House? Magnuson liked the idea, and immediately wrote Woodcock a
long personal letter, enclosing copies of the bill, the report,
and the hearing transcript. "Dear Leonard," Magnuson's
letter began,

> Just a note to let you know that the Senate recently
> passed unanimously my National Health Service Corps bill,
> which was a concept advanced many years ago by Walter
> Reuther. It has taken us a long time to bring the idea of a

national health service corps this far, but Walter's idea has clearly found widespread support . . .

While we ·were fortunate in the Senate . . . you well realize that measures such as this have a more difficult time in the House. Congressman Harley Staggers . . . has introduced a companion measure in the House (H.R. 19246) but no hearings have been scheduled. Time is growing very short, and any assistance you might be able to provide in the House would be deeply appreciated. . . .

The UAW President soon responded to Magnuson's suggestion; in a short time, Woodcock publicly "demanded" passage of the NHSC, "on behalf of more than two million members of the UAW and their families."

The pleas to Staggers from Magnuson, Nolan, the *Charleston Gazette*, Randolph, and Woodcock all reached him within the same two-week period, and by early October we decided anything further would only anger him. The recess would begin on October 10, anyway. If Staggers decided to act, it would have to be in November, during the postelection special session (which had become inevitable by now). In the meantime, he had plenty to think about, and of course he could hardly hope to elude Dr. Nolan when he went home to campaign. In fact, we were a little worried that we might have pushed Staggers too hard already, and that Nolan's relentlessness might backfire. As if to confirm these fears, Marguerite Furfari called me on the phone, abandoning for once her cryptic word-screen, and told me angrily, "We've got a problem down in West Virginia at the moment—and his name begins with 'N.' "

It surprised me a little that Staggers' staff thought our office could control the phenomenon of Nolanism, for we certainly had no such delusions ourselves. Nevertheless, I called Nolan and conveyed the message. Then Harley Dirks and I decided the time had come to turn the lobbying effort on a different target: the Department of Health, Education and Welfare.

3.

The Department had still not announced an official position on S. 4106, but that had not prevented various individuals within HEW from working actively for or against the bill's passage. HEW is such a loose, unstable, disjointed agglomeration of people and programs that the notion of a uniform and identifiable "Departmental" policy on any given piece of legislation is nonsensical. We could not treat HEW as we had Congressman Staggers, a single point of resistance that our lobbying effort had to convert or overwhelm. Instead, we thought about each relevant HEW official in turn, tried to determine his personal views on the bill, and then attempted to construct a rough calculus by which to predict what action on S. 4106 might be taken in the Department's name.

Glen Wegner, for example, had already expressed his opinion of the bill clearly, first with his acerbic visit to our office and then with his outburst in the Reception Room on the day of the Senate vote. In conversations with individual Congressmen, Wegner might purport to speak for the Department, but we doubted his opinion mattered much within HEW and we knew his superiors could silence him if they chose. Surgeon General Steinfeld, on the other hand, still liked S. 4106 despite the textual changes we had made in the bill; but unfortunately, the Surgeon General had almost no voice in HEW policy-making. Keeping the Surgeon General in S. 4106 had also cost us the outright support of the Department's second-ranking health official, Dr. Vernon Wilson of HSMHA, who had reacted with ill humor to the ambiguous new compromise language of the bill. Yet Wilson appeared to have retained his negotiating instinct and his interest in health-corps legislation. He had obviously spoken frankly to *Washington Report on Medicine and Health*, which confided that a "top health official" had said HEW would like to support the bill if the Surgeon General were removed from its text.

Given this diverse set of views within HEW's middle echelons, and assuming (as we did) that the new Health and Welfare Secretary, Elliot Richardson, had not yet become involved in Departmental discussions of S. 4106, the logical person to talk to about the bill was again Dr. Egeberg, the Assistant Secretary for Health and Scientific Affairs. His chief subordinates (Wilson and Steinfeld) seemed to favor the bill, the Senate Republicans obviously supported it, and every medical organization that had taken a public position on S. 4106 had urged Congress to pass it. Although Egeberg's top staff aide, Dr. John Zapp, had complicated our efforts earlier, and although the Administration's forthcoming "Health Package" might conflict with Magnuson's NHSC plan, Egeberg himself had told us in April that he liked the concept and would help us establish the new program. We needed to know whether he still held these views now, in early October, despite his six-month silence, and the only way to find out was to pay him another visit.

Bergman, unfortunately, had returned to Seattle, so Harley Dirks and I went to see Egeberg by ourselves. When we arrived at the appointed time, however, the door to his private office was closed, and throughout a long afternoon of coffee, old magazines, and gazing out the window at the first signs of autumn in Washington, Harley and I waited in vain for the door to open. Flustered, Egeberg's embarrassed secretary finally suggested that the Assistant Secretary's meeting elsewhere in HEW must have taken longer than expected; could we possibly come back at the same time the next day?

Somewhat annoyed, we returned to Egeberg's office the following afternoon. While we were waiting this time, the phone rang, and the secretary told Harley the call was for him. Harley took the phone and found that Senator Norris

Cotton of New Hampshire, the ranking Republican on Magnuson's HEW Appropriations Subcommittee, wanted him to come back to Capitol Hill immediately and explain one or two items in the money bill. Dirks made an instant decision and told Cotton he was on his way. Leaving hasty but hardly effusive apologies to be conveyed to Dr. Egeberg, he left at once to catch a cab.

So the audience was a private one when at last it came. Egeberg led me into his personal office, the same office where we had talked in April, and sat me in the same chair, even asking the same secretary to bring coffee. But it was autumn now, and the effect of the intervening months showed as plainly on Dr. Egeberg as on the view from his window. The jaunty yellow BULLSHIT button and the easy jocularity were gone; the atmosphere suggested strain, embarrassment, exasperation, fatigue. Egeberg had been in office only one year, but everything in his manner indicated he would soon be gone.

"Well," he began, a little sheepishly, "I guess I know why you've come." It sounded like a line from a television Western. Ill at ease, he offered congratulations on the Senate vote. "Frankly," he said, "I never thought you'd get this far. I never thought Maggie could pull it off. I guess your boss is a lot more powerful than most of us figured at first."

I asked Egeberg why the help he had promised us had never materialized; why had the Department seemed to fight us instead of cooperating? In theory, any Senator (or Congressman) can get technical assistance from any Department just by asking; I had always thought, I said, that the Department was supposed to help draft legislation for Senators and Congressmen whether or not it approves of the legislation itself. And Magnuson was not just any Senator, nor had Egeberg spoken of the NHSC except in friendly terms. What had happened?

Egeberg shook his head sadly. "We wanted to help, we really did." Pause and a deep sigh. "But our hands were tied. The White House sent down the word that nobody was allowed to help Magnuson with this bill." The HSMHA bureaucrat had offered the same explanation on the morning of Yarborough's hearing, but it still puzzled me. Why did the White House care about our bill? And why would they have cared even before we'd written it? Whatever the explanation, Dr. Egeberg refused to discuss the matter further.

He then volunteered that the bill had no chance of passing in the House. I said I was not so sure. Staggers might still hold hearings in November, after the recess, I hinted. Would Egeberg be willing to help us persuade Staggers that he should?

"I'm sorry, I just don't think that would be possible."

"Well, if Staggers holds hearings anyway, will HEW testify in favor of the bill?"

"No."

"Then could you refrain from testifying at all, the way you did in the Senate? Can HEW remain neutral?"

Egeberg shifted his gigantic mass uneasily in his chair. "No," he replied, "we'd have to testify. If we didn't, Staggers or Rogers would just pillory us the way Yarborough did at the Senate hearings. And besides, if we didn't testify, the only official statement about the bill from a Departmental officer would be that endorsement that the Surgeon General gave Magnuson at the HEW Appropriations hearings. The White House would never stand for that."

Perhaps I should have recognized the finality in Egeberg's voice, but in my desperation my judgment became somewhat distorted, and instead of accepting his pronouncement and leaving, I revealed (or rather, blurted out) the broader significance of S. 4106 to Magnuson's office. I told him, although I hadn't intended to, that Magnuson was thinking of giving up the chairmanship of the HEW Subcommittee in the coming Congress and switching to the chairmanship of the Department of Transportation

(DOT) Appropriations Subcommittee. I explained that
many members of Magnuson's Commerce Committee staff
believed the DOT chairmanship would be better for him:
together with his Commerce Committee position, it might
enable him to realize his dream of reorganizing American
transportation systems and policies, and in any event it
would entail less work for him (since the DOT's budget
was much smaller than HEW's), thus leaving him free to
devote more time to his own legislation instead of the tedi-
ous appropriations process. The DOT chairmanship would
also enhance his control over a project of crucial importance to his constituents: the SST, then being developed
with DOT funds. I added that the same staff members believed the HEW Subcommittee had taken too much of
Magnuson's time and rewarded him with too little publicity and credit. Moreover, they argued, the HEW Subcommittee had not given him the power to pass health
legislation, since health legislation went through the Labor
and Public Welfare Committee, of which he was not a
member.

On the other hand, I said, some of us on Magnuson's staff
(including Harley Dirks, although I did not mention him)
felt strongly that Magnuson should remain as Chairman of
the HEW Subcommittee; despite my enthusiasm for the
National Transportation Act, health still seemed a more
important policy area. We hoped, among other things, that
S. 4106 would demonstrate that Magnuson *could* pass
health legislation, even though he was not a member of
Yarborough's Committee. The HEW Appropriations Subcommittee gave him leverage with Yarborough, and the
Commerce Committee gave him leverage with Congressman Staggers. I added that if S. 4106 passed—a development
that seemed to require HEW's cooperation—Magnuson
might share this reasoning and remain as Chairman of the
HEW Subcommittee; if S. 4106 failed, on the other hand,
he might easily agree with his Commerce Committee aides

and decide that the DOT Subcommittee chairmanship would be a more useful post.

Egeberg readily understood the significance of my frank (although unauthorized) disclosure. If Magnuson gave up the HEW job, the new Chairman would be Senator Robert C. Byrd of West Virginia, an extremely conservative and not wholly congenial power in the Senate. Byrd might not cut back on HEW's health programs, but he would certainly oppose the Department's school-desegregation program—a program many members of HEW still believed in, despite growing resistance from the White House. And if, as Nixon professed to hope, welfare reform were ever enacted, Byrd would undoubtedly resist the new system to the full extent of his "power of the purse."

Despite the fashionable trend toward debunking the vague labels of "liberal" and "conservative," the difference between a Northern liberal chairman and a Southern conservative chairman remains very real for a Department with responsibility for health, education and welfare. Realizing this, Egeberg asked with genuine concern whether he might convey my news to Health and Welfare Secretary Elliot Richardson, and I of course consented—on condition that the story not be leaked to the press. Egeberg promised to respect my wishes, but added that HEW would probably still refuse to support S. 4106; if anything, HEW would respond to the possibility of Magnuson switching chairmanships with other steps aimed at encouraging him to keep his present post.

Abruptly, I realized we had nothing further to say to each other; we had finished our business in a ten-minute conversation. Egeberg walked me to the door, then said goodbye with a small wave of his massive hand. I walked gloomily out of the building, for the last time, and headed for the Senate on foot instead of taking a cab. My ill-considered tactic had not helped S. 4106 at all, I knew, although perhaps it might bring other benefits. The key fact produced by the conversation—that HEW would testify against the bill if Staggers held hearings—depressed me thoroughly. I thought of all the implications as I walked. The fiction that the Surgeon General had spoken for the Administration at Magnuson's hearing would be destroyed. Emboldened, the AMA might then decide to oppose the bill outright. Republicans and other conservatives in the House might organize to block it, or simply delay it long enough to kill it. So much for the "noncontroversial" facade. Staggers might not even hold hearings once he learned of HEW's plans. Even if he did, and even if he pushed the bill through the House, if the Administration really opposed the bill, the President would probably veto it. If HEW actively opposed S. 4106, in other words, it might not matter whether we persuaded Staggers to act or not.

The significance of Egeberg's words was too stark, and my mind too tired. As I walked up Capitol Hill toward the Old Senate Office Building, my thoughts strayed to Egeberg himself, and what I'd learned of him. He remained a somewhat enigmatic figure for me, but perhaps less so than after our first meeting. I had considered him a villain for the past four or five months—the result of my own too great expectations and the weeks of broken promises. He had said he would help us, hadn't he, and that the resources and expertise of HEW were at our disposal? Yet HEW had only hindered us. Egeberg was the Department's top health official; it appeared he must have dealt with us in bad faith.

But now I reached a somewhat different conclusion. Egeberg was not a devious man, I decided, not someone who would deliberately "double-cross" us. Instead, he lived in an organizational nightmare, with no real control over health policy—despite his official position as the number one health policy-maker in the country. The explanation, but only part of it, lay in the fact that the White House was making health policy these days, that Egeberg—as Harley Dirks had put it—was kept on "a very short leash." But no Department had a long leash in the Nixon Administration. Some, like the State Department, were probably more tightly tethered than HEW. Although Egeberg complained that the White House had "sent down the word" not to help Magnuson with the bill, I guessed that more intimate associates, his nominal subalterns at HEW, had really hamstrung him. Some of Egeberg's lieutenants undoubtedly supported him, but others pursued their own ends, their own policy goals, not only within HEW but on Capitol Hill too. These men might have acted like Harley Dirks, or Bob Maher, passionately loyal to their chief, always protecting his interests. But instead they apparently circumvented him when they could, conspired against him when they wanted to, and contributed more than incidentally to the Washington gossip that Egeberg would soon quit, or be fired. Egeberg's subordinates were dissimilar in their views, their cunning, and their intellect. But many showed a common bureaucratic trait: they were all "free lancers."

No, I concluded, Egeberg was not a villain. Enticed into government service after a distinguished career in medicine, he found himself in a Department that resembled a Hobbesian state of nature more than its own organizational chart. Trained as a doctor, not as a politician or a public administrator, he had neither the energy of youth nor the self-confidence of experience to curb the disloyalty and insubordination that surrounded him. He couldn't even get in to see the man who had appointed him. But he still had too much pride—or too little—to admit defeat and get out.

I realized, as I reached the Senate, that Egeberg's case was sad, perhaps tragic, but that it meant only one thing for S. 4106: if HEW ever decided to support the bill, it would do so for reasons having little or nothing to do with the Assistant Secretary for Health. We would simply have to apply our techniques of persuasion elsewhere, not against a man who was little more than a captive, unhappy, and probably bewildered prince.

4.

I had visited Egeberg during my last few days in Washington, and consequently it was too late for me to take part in any new planning for overcoming HEW's resistance. The frustrations of dealing with the Administration were simply a legacy, like the S. 4106 file, that I would have to leave behind for my able colleagues on Magnuson's staff. Before leaving, though, I did want to ensure the smoothest possible functioning of "our team" (as Bergman and I called the NHSC coalition). So when Mike Gorman requested Magnuson's help on another health bill, I became involved in my final legislative task.

The bill that interested Gorman was Senator Kennedy's "Health Security Act," a comprehensive national-health-insurance proposal written by a panel of experts. Kennedy had introduced the bill very late in the session, even later than S. 4106, and neither he nor Gorman supposed it would pass without many years of struggle in Congress (twenty years of similar struggle already lay behind it). But Yarborough had agreed to help call the legislation to the public's attention, and in early October he had convened one last set of hearings, perhaps in part because national health insurance was a classic liberal issue, a fitting theme for his legislative swan song. Yet the Health Security Act had very few influential cosponsors, and this only added to the impression that the hearings were utterly quixotic, mere "grandstanding." Moreover, the Nixon Administration had produced some rough (although questionable) cost calculations, suggesting Kennedy's plan would cost almost as much to operate as the Department of Defense.

Under the circumstances, Gorman earnestly sought Magnuson's cosponsorship of Kennedy's bill. The Chairman of the HEW Appropriations Subcommittee, and the fifth-ranking member of the Senate, would prevent the pundits from accepting too readily the notion that the hearings were a mere gesture and the bill itself irresponsibly expensive. Magnuson had declined to cosponsor the bill originally not because he opposed national health insurance, but because he had advocated it so strenuously for so many years that he had become something of a Congressional patriarch on the issue, and felt that properly he ought to introduce his own bill rather than merely cosponsor someone else's in the final weeks of the session. Now that Yarborough had called hearings, however, and the Nixon Administration had publicly attacked the whole concept of comprehensive national health insurance, the situation had changed. Stan Barer and I talked with Magnuson about it, and he decided to cosponsor Kennedy's bill while at the same time indicating that he intended to introduce health-insurance proposals of his own in the 92nd Congress. Magnuson explained this in a letter to Kennedy, and fortunately it became my task to deliver it. I took it to Carey Parker, Kennedy's aide, and on the second day of the hearings Kennedy and Yarborough read the letter aloud, stressing its importance to the assembled reporters and television crews.

As a result, Magnuson received a great deal of highly favorable and well-deserved publicity—plus the gratitude of Kennedy, Yarborough, and Mike Gorman. Thanks to Carey Parker, Kennedy even made a Senate speech about the significance of Magnuson's cosponsorship, and called attention to Magnuson's leadership in health affairs generally; happily (and not entirely by accident), he emphasized particularly the importance of the National Health Service Corps. Even Bergman, who didn't like some features of Kennedy's bill, had to admit that everyone had benefited from the episode, and that indirectly it had strengthened "our team."

Finally, on my last day in Magnuson's office, I went to lunch with Bob Barclay, Bill Lucca (of the Commissioned

Officers Association), and Norm Dicks, Magnuson's legislative counsel. Instead of the Carroll Arms, we went to the Rotunda, a restaurant on the House side of Capitol Hill with considerably better food. The lunch was not a going-away party, but rather an opportunity for Dicks to meet some members of the "team," for he would now have to add S. 4106 to his many other duties as Magnuson's top legislative aide. In addition, it turned out, Barclay had also invited someone without telling us: Bob Maher, Congressman Rogers' assistant. For some minutes, it seemed that Maher wouldn't arrive, and when he did appear he seemed even more taciturn than usual. He listened intently, but without comment, throughout the lunch, grinning occasionally when his presence forced us to discuss the bill's political situation in the House in somewhat euphemistic terms. But when we left the Rotunda after lunch, Maher quietly took me aside, out of earshot of our companions.

"Look," he said firmly, "this bill is going to become law. Rogers will definitely act on it once Congress comes back into session in November."

I shot Maher a skeptical glance. "That postelection session won't last long; there won't be much time," I said doubtfully.

Maher had obviously anticipated my remark. He smiled, and clapped my shoulder as if to reassure me that he knew what he was doing. "There'll be time enough," he said simply, then bade me bon voyage and walked away.

Lucca had brought his car around from the parking lot, and I climbed in with Barclay and Dicks. As we drove toward the Senate, I related what Maher had told me. My companions dismissed his remarks somewhat contemptuously. "Forget about Rogers," they said. "Staggers is the key now."

We drove on, passing between the Rayburn and Longworth House Office Buildings. I looked out the rear window and watched Maher walking back to work. Staggers might indeed be the key, I thought, but no member of Staggers' staff had ever given us any assurances. Since I was leaving now, finishing up with my brief Senate staff career, lunches at the Rotunda, and the National Health Service Corps, I had to find hope in any assurances we could get. Maher had virtually made a promise—he *had* made a promise—and he sounded as if he knew he could keep it. The last thing I could do for S. 4106 before leaving was to hope that he was right.

IX

INTERLUDE

1.

Suddenly, literally overnight, Washington, D.C., was far away and Oxford was imposed, inescapably, in its place. Like the Connecticut Yankee, I was too dazed by the swift and unprepared-for transition to comprehend fully my new surroundings. A Magdalen College servant, seeing me helpless at the front gate, gathered up my bags and led me patiently through a maze of cloisters, covered passageways, and garden paths to my rooms. The rooms—one for sleeping, one for reading—were on the top floor of the "New Building" (erected 1733) and did not adjoin. In the bedroom, a tiny unheated garret, a bare forty-watt bulb glowed dimly, its socket the only electric outlet in the room. Through the leaded windowpanes I could see nothing except the back of a stone parapet, two feet away. My roommate, I soon learned, was the wind, blowing freely through the floor, the windows, and even the keyhole, merrily making clear to me its rights as prior occupant. Glumly, wondering for one ungrateful and travel-weary moment whether a Rhodes Scholarship was privilege or punishment, I hung my suits and ties—the trappings of another life—far back in the damp closet. On the back of the door I hung the one piece of relevant attire: a black academic gown.

The bed had five blankets; it needed at least ten. In the morning, my "scout" appeared, "knocking me up" at precisely 8 o'clock, opening my curtains to the still-dark parapet, and handing me, as I lay in bed watching my breath, a sheaf of papers addressed to "E. Redman, Esq." I got out of bed and walked down the icy corridor to the toilets, little stalls open to the elements, and then down the corridor in the opposite direction to the sinks. The showers, I found, were down four flights of well-worn wooden stairs, and they dribbled forth in the futile manner of modern fittings grafted onto ancient plumbing. Wet but not warm, I bundled up in sweaters and gloves to walk across the courtyard to breakfast in Hall: fried bread, baked beans, and tea from heavy earthenware pots. It was the first breakfast I'd ever eaten in a room with stained-glass windows.

And so a new, wholly novel daily routine began. Soon it became exciting, and less lonely. Gowned, I met my tutors, one of whom walked me around and around Addison's Walk until I agreed, on the site of a Civil War gun emplacement, to "read" Politics and Economics rather than Law. I discovered the delights of Blackwell's, buying my books and carrying them home to my sitting room. There, in front of a hopelessly inadequate electric "fire," I began to study for the first time in almost a year. Befriended by an electric kettle and a battery of briar pipes, I renewed my acquaintance with the equations and academic terminology of undergraduate days. I moved my bed into the sitting room to be near the "fire," relinquishing the bedroom to the wind.

Before long I was rowing for my college crew, running down to the boathouse through the mud and mist of Christ

Church meadow. My body, completely flaccid after a year in Washington, responded again to the pleasant strain of physical exertion, and my mind, once wholly preoccupied with politics, began to fasten on such phenomena as the sudden, solitary applause of a swan taking flight on the river. At the end of the day, the Magdalen College Tower stood out against the sky in massive silhouette, conjuring up visions of Charles I atop it, watching Cromwell's troops slowly tightening their ring around him.

At first, I thought little about the Senate or Magnuson, except to measure the features of my daily existence against those I had so recently known. I had Oxford to think about, and the fact that I'd become engaged just before my plane left for England. Washington, D.C., was not much in my thoughts, an experience better pondered in the future.

After a few days, however, I received a telegram from Magnuson's office: WORLD ENVIRONMENTAL INSTITUTE RESOLUTION PASSED SENATE UNANIMOUSLY TODAY. Lucky boy, I thought to myself: all three of the major bills on which I'd worked—the World Environmental Institute, the National Transportation Act, and the National Health Service Corps—had passed the Senate without a dissenting vote; but then they would have passed anyway, even if I'd never heard of them. The explanation of this legislative "hat trick" lay solely in the unique power, and the unique personality, of Senator Magnuson. Slowly, I began to think about Washington again, and when I did, my thoughts always made their way back to that same remarkable man— Warren G. Magnuson.

2.

Magnuson's early life almost caricatured a Horatio Alger story, but the Senator himself never calls attention to this fact. Unlike so many self-made men, Magnuson refuses to regale associates with tales of youthful privation; he has a nostalgic streak, but it stops short of the intensely private world of boyhood pain and boyhood devotion to benefactors. Against his wishes, one senses, Magnuson's early political aides once seized upon his background as a political asset, and it is from decades-old campaign literature that present-day staff members and journalists have gleaned what little they know of his early years. It is enough, perhaps, that he was born in 1905 and orphaned at the age of three weeks, then raised by a family of Norwegian immigrants who lived first in Moorhead, Minnesota, and later across the river in Fargo, North Dakota. Magnuson's high school chums and high school teammates can still be glimpsed in tattered photographs he keeps out of sight in his office, but little else about his youth is clear until, at age nineteen, he rode the boxcars west to Seattle. There he entered the University of Washington, playing third-string football on a Rose Bowl team and working his way through school by pushing an ice wagon around the city's better neighborhoods in that age of Prohibition. By 1929, he was a college graduate and a lawyer.

Whether Magnuson had long had political aspirations, or whether—as his old friends insist—the decision was simply a spur-of-the-moment one, he first ran for office in 1932, at age twenty-seven, and rode the Democratic landslide into the State Legislature. Thanks to Washington's Progressive tradition, the Legislature had no seniority rule, and he became chairman of a key committee as soon as he arrived in Olympia. Under the tutelage of the newly elected U.S. Senator Homer T. Bone (who was carrying out a parallel maneuver at the Federal level), Magnuson quickly secured the passage of public-power enabling legislation, making possible the harnessing of the Columbia River. Yet his most vivid memory of the legislative session was forged when the jobless and hungry citizens of the state marched to Olympia and, in a desperate attempt to get aid from the lawmakers, erected a pathetic tent city on the Capitol grounds. In response, Magnuson introduced what became, reputedly, the nation's first unemployment-compensation law. (He also introduced, although unsuccessfully, a bill to lower the voting age to eighteen.)

Before he'd completed his term in the Legislature, Magnuson ran for and was elected to another post, that of King County Prosecutor. King County, the most populous in Washington State, centers around Seattle, and it was in that racket-ridden city where he himself had once pushed an ice wagon that Magnuson first established his credentials as a public official. Yet Seattle was still a small town in those days, and there was nothing glamorous about stalking recalcitrant witnesses on foot through the woods (of what is now the city's industrial area) in order to serve them with warrants and subpoenas. More important, perhaps, the life of a prosecutor was not all racket-busting; it consisted primarily of prosecuting hapless petty criminals, and Magnuson soon found he had no stomach for such work. After witnessing the hanging of a murderer he had successfully prosecuted, Magnuson refused to ask the death penalty of trial juries, and his popularity as Prosecutor was bound to decline. By the end of his term, despite the pleadings of friends, he had decided to abandon the Prosecutor's office and run for Congress against the colorful but deranged Democratic incumbent, Marion Zionchek.

Before this decision became known, however, Zionchek penned a suicide note and jumped to his death from the window of a Seattle office building. Hearing a commotion while prosecuting another murder trial in the courthouse across the street, Magnuson rushed outside, pushed through a crowd of immobilized onlookers, and found the Congressman's broken body lying on the pavement. Suddenly, and not at all as he would have liked it, Magnuson found his path to Congress unobstructed; in January 1937, as a thirty-one-year-old bachelor, he took the oath of office in the House of Representatives.

In the House, Magnuson and another freshman Congressman, Lyndon B. Johnson of Texas, formed a close personal friendship and political alliance that endured without a rift for nearly thirty years. Together they served on the House Naval Affairs Committee, propping up (or so Johnson later said) the aging chairman, and together they went off to serve in the Navy itself when war came. Magnuson became a lieutenant commander aboard the aircraft carrier *Enterprise*, and saw action in the Pacific until Roosevelt (deciding, no doubt, that they'd impressed their constituents sufficiently) ordered Magnuson, Johnson, and the other Democratic Congressmen back to Washington. There Magnuson served several additional terms in the House, and began to wonder whether he should run for a Senate seat in 1946.

In 1944, however, fate intervened once again. Senator Bone, opening his campaign for reelection, broke his leg in a fall, and the leg was slow to mend. "I'll be damned if I'm going to campaign on crutches," Bone announced, and so the immensely popular Senator persuaded Roosevelt to appoint him to the Federal bench. With the President's blessing, Bone offered Magnuson—whom he regarded as a personal protégé—the opportunity to run in his stead, and Magnuson quickly accepted. When Magnuson was elected overwhelmingly, Bone performed an important final favor for him: he clung tenaciously to both his Senate seat and his judicial robes (causing an uproar, and talk of impeachment, among the colleagues who had just confirmed him) until Washington's Republican Governor Arthur B. Langlie reluctantly agreed to appoint the Senator-elect to fill the unexpired few weeks of Bone's term. Sworn in during December 1944, instead of January 1945, Magnuson gained an important margin of seniority over other Senators (like William Fulbright and Wayne Morse) elected at the same time—a fact Governor Langlie lived to rue when he later ran against Magnuson in 1956.

Magnuson's early Senate career consisted largely (al-

though by no means exclusively) of a quest for Federal
dollars to aid the development of Washington State, and by
any standard it must be reckoned one of the most needed
and most successful such quests of all time. Except for some
small industrial enclaves around Puget Sound, Washington
in the mid-1940's was essentially an underdeveloped area.
The western portion of the state depended largely on log-
ging, and the arid eastern portion, in the words of a New
York Congressman at the time, was "an area fit only for
coyotes and sagebrush." Senator Bone and his Northwest
colleagues had been able to induce a trickle of Federal investment in the region even while Magnuson was still in
the House, but Magnuson's appointment to the Senate
Appropriations Committee opened the fiscal spigot fully.
Dams, irrigation works, locks, harbor developments, ship-
yards, a World's Fair, and entire new cities sprang up all
around Washington State. In eastern Washington, the de-
sert was made to bloom abundantly, and a prosperous "In-
land Empire" soon displaced most of the coyotes and sagebrush. By 1962, when Magnuson ran for his fourth full
term, one out of every six Federal public-works dollars was
flowing into Washington State.

But by 1962, Magnuson had a number of political problems. His dollar-getting had been almost too successful:
polls showed that some voters considered him a "pork-
barrel politician" and a "wheeler-dealer"—a dangerous
image for any Senator in the charisma-conscious heyday of
Camelot and the New Frontier. Magnuson was still a bachelor, and his well-publicized interest in beautiful women was
winning him little support among Washington's conservative immigrant population (he is said to have been the
model for Senator Lafe Smith in *Advise and Consent*). Always a liberal, frequently far ahead of the times—he called
for recognition of Red China in 1956, for example—he had
earned the enmity of the still-potent right wing; Senators
Barry Goldwater and Jack Miller, reverting to Joseph

McCarthy's 1950 tactics, came to Washington State to denounce Magnuson as a threat to American security, while
Edgar Eisenhower of Tacoma, a reactionary brother of the
former President, devoted his name, energies, and fortune
to Magnuson's defeat.* Another of the Senator's difficulties
contained an element of grim humor: for ten years he had
carried on his coattails a Seattle Congressman named Don
Magnuson, and by 1962, "No Relation" Magnuson had
thoroughly sullied the good name with his own unfortunate
personal problems.

The Senator might have withstood these various threats
if the voter turnout had been heavy—he always does well in
heavy turnouts—but in 1962, in a rainy off-year election,
the turnout was the lowest in nearly thirty years. Running
against a political nobody, a Lutheran minister named
Richard Christensen, Magnuson barely won reelection. He
received less than 53 percent of the vote, and lost a majority
of Washington's thirty-nine counties.

The 1962 election formed the watershed of Magnuson's
career, even though that career was already thirty years old
and the Senator in his late fifties. Had he been defeated, or
simply reelected without difficulty, he might have been
remembered almost solely for billions of dollars' worth of
capital improvements in Washington State, a handful of
major bills like the National Cancer Institute and the National Science Foundation, and an important but arcane
mass of transportation legislation he had moved through his
Commerce Committee. From the ashes of near defeat, however, Magnuson's career rose in what can only be termed a
phoenixlike transformation. It was not that he stopped
bringing Federal dollars home to Washington State, or that
he backed away from expressing his liberal views. He simply began to use his accumulated power systematically in

* Billy Graham also campaigned against Magnuson, while Richard M.
Nixon warned Washingtonians of the Senator's "dangerous left-wing
views."

behalf of more social legislation with national significance. With a new staff of young lawyers, headed by Jerry Grinstein, he began to produce consumer-protection legislation —first in a trickle, then in a torrent. The Senate Commerce Committee, once the staid guardian of business interests, changed almost overnight into the "consumer's panel" on Capitol Hill (it was as if the Armed Services Committee were suddenly to take up the citizen's cause against the Pentagon). Old cronies and lobbyists spluttered in disbelief, Ralph Nader had easy access to the Senator's office, reporters wrote of a "rekindled" Magnuson, and back home, Republican officials with eyes on a Senate seat became more and more dispirited as Magnuson's image began to change. In 1964, at age fifty-nine, Magnuson married the strikingly lovely Jermaine Elliott Peralta (with President Johnson as the best man), and his constituents rejoiced with an ardor reserved for prodigal sons.

The "New" Magnuson, unlike the "New" Nixon, was not the product of Madison Avenue, although eventually Madison Avenue was invoked to convey the significance and extent of the change to his pleasantly surprised constituents. The transformation was really the result of a fundamental recognition: that the voters not only were willing to accept, but were eager for, the type of legislative leadership Magnuson, with his considerable power and humanitarian bent, could provide. No longer confined by a simple notion of "service" to his constituents, Magnuson grew more assertive, more independent. In 1967, he broke with his old friend and best man (and just as significantly, with his junior colleague, "Scoop" Jackson) to call for a unilateral bombing halt over North Vietnam, even though the position was not popular back home and the antiwar "leaders," like Eugene McCarthy, were still equivocating. In 1968, despite the fact that he was running for reelection, he cosponsored the toughest gun-control bill before the Senate, and didn't waver when the Washington State sportsmen, like the corporate lobbyists before them, turned on him with passionate hatred. During the campaign, he took the offensive, and talked proudly about the record of his past term. Washington responded by electing him as its first five-term Senator—an honor accorded only a dozen or so Americans in the history of direct Senatorial elections—and his 65 percent of the vote made 1968 the biggest victory of his career.

Pleased, Magnuson began his fifth term with a flurry of legislative activity, ranging from an expanded consumer-protection program to environmental-protection legislation to major transportation bills to health care—including, of course, S. 4106, the NHSC. Someone entering Magnuson's office for the first time, and finding himself in the midst of great activity and enthusiasm, might think he was observing the beginning of a legislative career rather than the celebration of its prime.

But the existence of a past, of roots, and of the exceptional time span of Magnuson's public life can be glimpsed in the memorabilia about his office: the wooden paperweight, for example, cut from the flight deck of the *Enterprise*, or the oil painting on the wall, commissioned by a Congressman who killed himself back in 1936. On the mantel stands a silver model of a biplane, the Wright Brothers Award, presented to Magnuson as the Senate's leader in the field of aviation: Chairman of the Aviation Subcommittee, champion (for better or worse) of the supersonic transport, author of the Airport-Airways Development Act, past chairman of NASA's appropriations subcommittee. Near the Wright Brothers Award hangs a small American flag that traveled to the Sea of Storms and back with the Apollo astronauts. Between that silver biplane and that American flag, Magnuson's career stretches. And it says something about him (as well as about aviation) that the boy who was born soon after the Wright brothers took to the air at Kitty Hawk grew up to be a man whose career was still climbing even after other men had left his name on the surface of the moon.

3.

Such is the standard biographical approach to Magnuson —or rather, to Magnuson's career. Over the years it has appeared, anecdotally invariant, in a host of publications as diverse as *The Wall Street Journal* and the *Walla Walla Union-Bulletin*. If you were writing the story properly, however, you'd want to do it with a book—a book in which you could reproduce some of the photographs hanging on Magnuson's office walls or tucked away in one of his closets. Like the football coach in team photographs from twenty-five successive seasons, Magnuson could be seen changing almost imperceptibly from year to year, and the slow transition from state legislator to ranking Senator could be measured in added pounds, lengthened hair, and deepening Senatorial countenance. Routine photographs, the posed shots with Presidents back to Roosevelt, would serve nicely for such a compilation, but the informal pictures would be more colorful: the sleek freshman Congressman, clad in gym shorts and boxing gloves, muscles showing as he slugs a punching bag ("The Ladies Call Him Boudoir Eyes," reads the incongruous caption headline from the 1937 Washington, D.C., *Evening Star*), or the trim, mustachioed lieutenant commander on the deck of the *Enterprise*—"Off Tokyo," according to his own penned inscription. A standard biography of Magnuson could be quite a book, in fact, but the danger would be in illuminating the unusual career without shedding any light whatsoever on the complex and fascinating man himself.

What makes Magnuson real, after all, is not the length of his career, or all that it embraces. Particularly for young

staff members, who were born too late to observe more than
a fraction of his exploits, Magnuson's mind and character
are what elicit laughter, loyalty, and respect. Yet to describe
Magnuson by his qualities requires more than a memory
for dates and election statistics, and consequently the im-
pressions of those who have known him will probably never
be widely heard, much less widely accepted. I first discovered my own inability to "sum up" Magnuson convincingly
when a young Seattle lawyer offered me his condolences on
learning that I was a member of the Senator's staff. On
another occasion, I tried in vain to talk about Magnuson
with former classmates of mine who had left his office disil-
lusioned because he wouldn't—or couldn't—discuss the
"moral" aspects of the war in Vietnam (the fact that he
voted against the war did not satisfy them). From one brief
encounter, the visitor to Magnuson's office may take away
the memory of a portly old man who speaks gruffly, invariably garbles his syntax, and often takes a devil's-advo-
cate position on almost any issue the visitor mentions. Even
leaving aside image-conscious young people, for whom
Magnuson can be something of a shock, there are plenty of
older adults who are simply not going to be persuaded that
a cigar-smoking back-room politician has miraculously
transformed himself into an aggressive champion of broad
social causes (particularly when he persists in smoking
cigars from time to time). For a Magnuson staff member, it
can be frustrating indeed to be thoroughly captivated by
and devoted to a man who outsiders may agree is powerful,
fascinating, even a major force for Good—but *lovable?*

The explanation lies in the fact that Magnuson, for all
his booming voice and bullish behavior with a gavel in his
hand, is really an intensely shy, self-conscious, and unself-
confident person. Like many self-deprecatory and somewhat
insecure people, he protects himself from strangers by
adopting a seemingly fierce bearing. He walks through the
Senate Office Building with eyes downcast, and his unre-

sponsiveness to greetings is sometimes taken as a sign of arrogance, but in fact he is simply embarrassed by his inability to remember names, and inexpert at the glad-handing and instant smiles that his colleagues produce so easily. Far from being consumed by ambition, he seems determined not to follow the Peter Principle and rise to his level of incompetence; at various stages of his career, the Vice Presidency, the Majority Leadership of the Senate, and even a seat on the Supreme Court have been dangled before his eyes, but unlike Caesar, he knows how to refuse a proffered crown convincingly.

Magnuson earns the respect of his staff not only through his private humility, which they soon learn to understand, but also through changing their preconceived notions about the Senate and individual Senators. It is tacitly suggested to the new staff man, who soon reaches the conclusion firmly, that the well-known Senators—particularly the young Presidential aspirants—are in fact rarely deserving of the deference shown them; too often they are really lazy, unpragmatic, egotistical and wholly ineffectual. Reporters and cameramen may dote on such Senators while ignoring the Magnusons, and their names may be household words, but the staff man soon speaks of them only with disdain. Slowly, resisting because the ethic seems conservative, the staff man finds himself drawn into agreement with the statement Senators Carl Hayden and Lyndon Johnson were so fond of making to journalists and freshmen colleagues: "There are two kinds of men in the Senate—show horses and workhorses."

The Hayden-Johnson dichotomy is a bit simplistic (is Ted Kennedy a show horse or a workhorse?), but it unquestionably defines a category into which Magnuson fits proudly. He draws his own dichotomy in somewhat different imagery. "In the Senate," he tells constituents, "there are back-porch philosophers and there are workers in the kitchen—and I'm one of those guys in the kitchen, trying to

make sure the work gets done." Political scientists, scrupu-
lously fair and needing to find a function for everyone,
would probably object even to Magnuson's statement, since
it suggests the Senate has only one legitimate function and
that only some Senators help perform it. In political science
jargon, therefore, the "show horses" and "back-porch philosophers" have become "publicizers" and "interest-articu-
lators"—men with an important role after all, despite what
a few years on a Senate staff might lead one to think. Moreover, a political scientist might point out, the seniority
system of the Senate distributes power so unevenly among
its members that some of them understandably feel the
need to "grandstand" on occasion, or to contemplate the
Presidency as an office in which they could *really* be effective (it's all a question of whether the philosophers are on
the back porch because they like it, or because they aren't
admitted to the kitchen). Yet Magnuson's dichotomy does
some injustice to himself, too, and to Senators like him, for
their legislative initiatives are not wholly lacking in gran-
deur, or divorced from the same philosophical principles
about which some of their colleagues merely make speeches.

In any event, neither Magnuson nor his staff would be so
petty as to taunt junior Senators for their relative lack of
power. At issue really is the work ethic, the willingness to
legislate pragmatically and with a sense of the possible,
even though kudos and headlines can be won from the news
media much more easily through flamboyant rhetoric and
quixotic tilting at windmills. When Magnuson introduces a
bill, he intends it to become law, or at least he sees it as a
useful tactic for furthering some other, definite legislative
purpose. What disgusts him, and what his staff soon learns
to disrespect, is a "show horse"—be he a freshman Senator
or one steeped in seniority—who gets vast publicity merely
for introducing a bill which, on even a cursory reading,
proves hopelessly impractical or even sloppily drafted.
Every Senator has the resources to produce sound, well-

thought-out legislation. If Magnuson and his staff occasionally look down their noses at other Senate offices, then, it is because of the difference in legislative self-discipline, not the disparity in relative legislative power.

Magnuson's conception of a Senator's job, soon adopted by his staff, inspires their respect, but the satisfaction of working for Magnuson stems largely from his consistent, no-nonsense brand of liberalism. "Maggie is never wrong on the big ones," his staff asserts, and he continually gratifies them by deviating from his Senate peer group, his popular junior colleague, or the likely views of his relatively conservative constituency to vote (for example) against the ABM, in favor of gun control, and in favor of the so-called "Amendment to End the War" (McGovern-Hatfield Amendment). One senses that his principles were forged in the New Deal, perhaps during that jobless-and-hungry march on the State Legislature; there is something instinctive, unmodern, almost quaint about them. When informed of a strike at a plant he was scheduled to visit, for example, he cancelled the appearance even though the workmen had voted to allow his tour. "I've never crossed a picket line in my life," he declared flatly, "and I'm not going to start now." On another occasion, I handed him a reply I had drafted to a constituent who had written to express views on the subject of an excess-profits tax for corporations. Drawing on my college economics, I had suggested cautiously in the reply that such a tax might prove ineffectual or inappropriate today. Magnuson looked over what I'd written, then handed it back. "It's a nice letter," he said, "but I'm in favor of that tax. And that's what the letter has to say."

Magnuson's liberalism dovetails with his commitment to the Democratic Party, and although he usually operates in a low-keyed, almost nonpartisan fashion in the Senate itself, on the campaign trail he often puts loyalty to the Democratic ticket ahead of his own self-interest. During the 1968 campaign, I watched him debate some angry trade-union members who intended to vote for him but also for George Wallace; he needn't have mentioned the Presidential campaign at all. A few weeks later, he caused his nervous campaign staff even greater disquiet. He had been scheduled to dedicate the last of the great Columbia River dams he had won from the Federal government, but at the last moment, Vice President Humphrey called. He was making a campaign trip through the Northwest; could he dedicate the dam instead of Magnuson? Without complaint, Magnuson granted the request, then rose at 5 in the morning to fly from Seattle to the damsite to introduce Humphrey rather than make the key speech himself. And when his aides told him of a scheduled meeting after the dedication that would make it impossible for him to accompany Humphrey back to voter-thick Seattle, Magnuson would have none of it. The staff implored him to think of his own campaign; Humphrey stood lower in the Washington State opinion polls than had Goldwater at any point in 1964. To appear with Humphrey along the sparsely populated banks of the Columbia River was one thing, but Seattle would be wholly different. Even Senator Jackson, who did not have to face the voters for another two years, had discreetly slipped off to meet a "long-standing" commitment in remote Wenatchee. But Magnuson could not be swayed. Ordering a special plane, which took off from a cow pasture, he flew home to Seattle and defied the worst hecklers of Humphrey's campaign in order to introduce him again ("Don't waste time howling me down tonight," he told the noise-makers; "you can howl me down anytime"). He later performed the same service for Muskie, and on Election Day, Washington was the only state in the continental West to give its electoral votes to the Humphrey-Muskie ticket.

Although such incidents illustrate Magnuson's independence from his staff, some of his detractors insinuate that his liberalism has become more vocal as his staff has become more youthful. The notion that Magnuson is a "tool" of his staff can be based only on a misunderstanding of how his office works,* or on ignorance of the Senator himself. Of course the staff makes an effort to influence his thinking, but more often than not the effort is superfluous, a mere outlet for staff anxiety over an impending vote of major importance. Staff, after all, have a psychological need to be doing *some*thing.

The best example of this occurred in 1969 with the Senate amendment to block deployment of the controversial ABM. Senator Jackson was leading the fight to save the missile, and he had ample opportunity to persuade Magnuson of its merits during several round-trip flights between Seattle and the Capital. Like most of the Senate, Magnuson had voted in favor of the missile the previous year, and in the preliminary "head counts" of 1969 the anti-ABM forces assumed him to be a lost cause. "Scoop can have Maggie's vote if he needs it" was the common judgment. Magnuson's staff, on the other hand, had heard the arguments on both sides and believed he should vote against the ABM; but the issue created so much tension and dragged on without a vote for so many weeks that Grinstein, still Magnuson's Administrative Assistant at the time, simply prohibited any staff member from mentioning it in the Senator's presence. Finally, when the press still listed only a handful of Senators as "undecided," Magnuson emerged from his office and told Grinstein, "Jerry, I'm going to vote against the ABM. I made up my mind a long time ago, but I didn't want to embarrass Scoop by coming out against him right at the beginning." Relieved, Grinstein simply replied, "Senator, I want you to know that every member of your staff thinks you're doing the right thing." Magnuson looked startled. "Really?" he asked, in pleasant surprise. Thanks to Grinstein's prohibition, Mag-

---

* See the following section (4).

nuson had not known what his staff thought on the issue.

Immediately afterward, Grinstein told me to draft an
ABM speech for Magnuson; I filled it with lofty rhetoric
and imitation Sorensen sentence structure. Magnuson
handed it back to me almost immediately. "I don't want to
hurt your feelings, Ric," he said. "It's a very good speech. I
just think that on an issue as important as this one, I ought
to write my own." He then locked himself in his office on
two successive days, and on the third day he summoned us
all in so that he could read aloud the speech he had written.
On his desk lay a pile of press clippings, magazine articles,
and volumes of Senate hearings—the materials with which
he had schooled himself over the weeks, sequestered from
his staff, and the information on which he had based his
difficult decision.

Of course, Magnuson votes "wrong" occasionally—not
just by ADA or ACA standards, impossible to satisfy, but
"wrong" from the standpoint even of the imaginary "reasonable man." A "bad" vote by his employer is one of the
staff man's most painful experiences, and one of the satis-
factions of working for Magnuson is that such experiences
are rare. More important, perhaps, when Magnuson does
vote "wrong," he obviously feels guilty about it. In the
summer of 1969, he voted against an amendment designed
to give Congress more information on defense contracts by
requiring an annual report on such contracts from the General Accounting Office (GAO), Congress' fiscal watchdog
agency. What made Magnuson's vote inexplicable was the
fact that he had made precisely the same request of the
GAO only a few weeks earlier, in a public letter·to the
GAO head, Comptroller General Elmer Staats. When I
heard that Magnuson had voted against the amendment, a
mere formalization of his own request, I rushed into his
office with a look of complete consternation and (I am
afraid) even reproach on my face. Magnuson, who was
lighting a cigar, almost flinched when he looked at me, and

immediately began to defend himself before I could say a
word. "My vote didn't make any difference in the outcome," he offered, as if to dismiss the subject before I raised
it. Not quite satisfied with his own logic, he retreated into
the bathroom hallway for a moment, out of my sight. Cigar
smoke wafted back into the office in short, furious puffs.
Suddenly he reemerged. "Muskie voted against it too, you
know? We waited right until the end, when we could be
sure our votes didn't matter, before we voted no." At a loss
for words, I said nothing (I was only a minor aide, and
despite my concern over the vote, I suddenly felt ridicu-
lously presumptuous). Magnuson strode back out of sight.
A few seconds later, he charged back into the room, waving
the cigar smoke angrily from his path. "I can't vote against
the Pentagon *all* the time," he boomed. "I'm voting against
them on every single big issue, and I want them to know
I'm serious about it, not just some knee-jerk." Before I
could answer, he turned and walked away again, then reappeared in a rush. "Staats called me after he got my letter,
you know. He told me he just doesn't have the manpower
to compile all that data. Congress can't just order him to
produce a report—we've got to give him the manpower
first." The Senator retreated a final time. Then he stormed
back into the room, brushed past me, and headed straight
for the door. "*Hell*," he said with disgust, "I'm going back
over to the Floor for a while."

Fallibility alone is not all that makes Magnuson human.
It is also regrettably true that he and the English language
have never reached a mutual accord; he occasionally abuses
it brutally, and it retaliates by dragging red herrings across
his conversation unpredictably. In spontaneous speech, he
succeeds simply by booming out key sentences and phrases
at intervals, filling in the gaps with not altogether intel-
ligible mumbling. He makes his meaning perfectly clear to
most listeners, but someone reading a transcript of his
words might be thoroughly confused (which explains the

frequency with which his staff corrects his remarks in the *Congressional Record* before publication—a privilege many other offices rely upon too).

Names give Magnuson the most trouble. He produced looks of stunned disbelief at a hearing, for example, when he introduced President Avery Brundage of the International Olympic Committee as "Average Brundy." The name of the late Secretary General of the United Nations once came out as "Dag Hammershlogg," while the then Premier of France was dubbed "Poopidoo." Shortly after receiving the Wright Brothers Award, Magnuson called Congressman Wilbur Mills to discuss a bill; when the Congressman came on the line, Magnuson said "Hello, Orville?" Perhaps his most unfortunate slip, the result of passion rather than ignorance, came at a hearing on the SST, when he took a witness to task for inveighing too heavily against the notion of progress in general. "We can't *all* go live at Walden Pond," he bellowed. "Even *Walden* only lived there for two years."

Despite these periodic slips, Magnuson's mind is shrewd and acutely perceptive, remarkable for its imagination as well as for the prodigous memory that accompanies it. He detests being "briefed" by his staff, and although he will submit to a briefing if time is short, he prefers a memorandum he can read and memorize. During the 1968 campaign, when his right-wing opponent was assailing him daily for his role in furthering East–West trade, I prepared for Magnuson a detailed memorandum on the actual trade statistics, commodity by commodity and country by country. Less than an hour after I had given it to him (while he was shaving), he amazed me by rattling off the figures verbatim, in tons and dollars, in response to a hostile question at a public appearance.

Two years later, during the Senate debate on his amendment to block the proposed shipment of nerve gas from Okinawa through the Pacific Northwest, I prepared an-

other memorandum cataloguing the arguments he had
marshaled against the shipment and took it to him at his
desk on the Senate Floor. He surveyed the memo cursorily,
then handed it back with an annoyed "No, no, no!" Bewildered, I retreated to the staff couch and waited to hear what
argument he intended to use instead of the familiar ones of
possible sabotage, dangerous sections of track along the proposed route, and populations that would have to be evacu-
ated as a precaution against leakage. When the time came,
he took a wholly novel and ingenious approach. The issue,
he told his colleagues, was not one of the people versus the
Pentagon, as the news media seemed to assume. Instead, it
was another case of the President versus the Senate. The
Senator from West Virginia (Robert C. Byrd) had recently
offered a resolution, which the Senate had passed, stating
that the Senate expected the President to keep it informed
throughout the treaty negotiations with the Japanese government on the subject of Okinawa. The President's sudden decision to move the nerve gas off Okinawa must reflect
some aspect of those treaty negotiations, Magnuson insisted
—and the Senate had not yet been informed of, much less
consented to, any such agreement. To allow the nerve-gas
shipment under such circumstances, he asserted, would be
to abandon the Byrd Resolution and to abdicate the Senate's rightful role in treaty-making generally. The President, Magnuson said, might get the idea that he could
ignore the Senate and its Constitutional prerogatives whenever he wished. Jolted by this reasoning, the Senator from
West Virginia and his Southern colleagues—friends of the
Pentagon almost to a man, but vigilant guardians of the
Senate's Constitutional responsibilities—voted down the
line with Magnuson. The amendment, which had been
doomed a few minutes earlier, passed overwhelmingly.

Perhaps political shrewdness and legislative acumen are
to be expected of a man who has sustained himself in elec-
tive office for four decades. But rather than one particular

characteristic, it is the admixture of so many different qualities that makes Magnuson so fascinating. During the day, he may persuade his quizzical colleagues to enact a major piece of legislation that most of them have never heard of before the vote—as he did with the National Transportation Act, shortly before I left for England—while in the evening he may simply relax with staff members and a cigar, recalling for a captivated audience what it had been like to play poker with Roosevelt ("He always paid his losses with a check, because he knew we'd frame it instead of cash it"), or repeating the words of solace Winston Churchill once offered him with respect to the effeminate nickname "Maggie" ("I attribute my own success," Churchill had confided, "to the fact that I'm known as 'Winnie' in every bar and pub in England").

But the staff can easily overestimate how well they know Magnuson, or how much they understand of the scope and rhythm of his thoughts. There is something out of the ordinary about a politician who suddenly cancels two days of campaign appearances because his dog has died, something reserved and intensely private about a man who chose that same dog as his sole companion in the first hours after President Kennedy's death. Perhaps he thinks about his own mortality from time to time, his inability to go on forever, but if so, he only jokes about it with others. When an elderly judge, a lifelong friend, tried to persuade Magnuson to follow his example and retire at the end of his term, the Senator drily dismissed the topic by contrasting the paltry Senate retirement benefits with those lavished on the judiciary. On another occasion, miserable with the flu, he nonetheless came to the office every day "so that three or four Washington State Congressmen won't have to rush out and start trying on togas yet."

Whatever the problems of the moment, or the thoughts that occupy his mind, he can, when he wishes, turn on a charm that makes any contact with him memorable. My

single most pleasant memory of him is the occasion when he
met for the first time the wife of a particular staff member,
a girl who had grown up in a hotly anti-Magnuson home.
Like Skeffington in *The Last Hurrah*, he simply won her
over by telling her stories she had never heard about her
grandfather and great-uncles, including the time they built
a primitive factory during the Depression to convert cascara
bark into laxatives. A staff maxim has emerged from so
many similar incidents: never underestimate Magnuson.

When I left Magnuson's office, I took with me as a sou-
venir a framed photograph showing the two of us in one of
the most humorous incidents of the 1968 campaign. A very
old woman, seeing the Senator, ran across the street yelling,
"Maggie, Maggie! Drunk or sober, I'm for Labor!" She
threw her arms around his neck and kissed him, while the
flashbulbs popped and I stood there laughing. The press
had the good judgment not to publish the picture, but
Magnuson had it framed and gave it to me, writing at the
bottom, "Dear Ric—You're just jealous!" Sitting alone in
Oxford, with Magnuson and the Senate far away, I *was*
jealous—not of the Senator, but of the lucky twenty-year-old
who stood laughing beside him in the picture, reveling in
the sensation of simply working for an extraordinary man.

4.

Exposure to a personality like Magnuson is one aspect of
Senate life that makes a staff job rewarding, and one reason
why the staff man is likely to miss Washington when he has
moved on to a law practice, his hometown, or (say) Oxford. But though the staff man's world revolves around his
employer, it is still a world of great diversity and one that
satisfies him in many other ways as well.

Essentially, a Senate aide finds himself in a money-power–action nexus, and if he derives enough of the three elements of this nexus, he remains; if not (or if he has no choice), he leaves. The money might surprise an outsider more than anything else: top staff people may earn $25,000 or $30,000 within a year or two of their arrival; some committees have over twenty staff members earning more than $20,000 each. The salary ceiling is lower than in nongovernment employment, of course—no aide can earn more than the $42,500 (the 1970 figure) that Senators and Congressmen receive—but the initial salaries can be breathtaking for someone just out of college or law school. The high initial salaries, in turn, are part of a clever "front-loading" in the pay scale: for the first few years, at least, any aide thinking of quitting Capitol Hill must ordinarily be willing to accept a substantial reduction in his standard of living. In short, money alone can trap young men on Capitol Hill for some time after their arrival (young women, unfortunately, rarely receive a comparable slice of the money–power–action pie, but this is changing). After a time, the aide's value to the outside world of law firms and corporations has increased dramatically by virtue of his experience in the Senate, and then the offers become more tempting. Since there is a limit to the salaries they can offer, Senators may attempt to hold on to their valued staffers by giving in power what they cannot give in dollars.

Distributing power among staff members is a little like distributing land among peasants: it makes them happier, and it increases their productivity. Consequently, a Senator finds it very much in his own interest to allow his staff a great deal of scope for personal initiative and responsibility, since this enables him to hold on to diligent and imaginative aides while at the same time increasing the quality and quantity of his legislative output. Contrary to what one might think, therefore, the "best" Senator is not one who sees to every detail of his legislation at every stage in its development, or who personally studies each issue on which he must vote, or who comes to the office each morning and tells every individual staff member precisely what he or she should be doing that day. Such a strict hierarchy is inefficient, and produces only a demoralized, browbeaten, and unimaginative staff—and a torpid legislative career for the Senator. An efficient office is one in which the Senator devotes his time to tasks that he alone can perform, delegating responsibility for all the preliminaries and details to his aides (who, to be sure, must keep him thoroughly briefed). Such an office is exciting to work in, for ideas flow up as well as down, and everyone has something important to be doing all the time. Provided the Senator is kept fully informed of major steps being taken in his name—and provided he weeds out incapable or disloyal staff members—this type of office can produce a prodigious amount of worthwhile legislation (and very effective service for constituents, too). Like an English barrister who takes up a case only when it is ready to be argued in court, a Senator willing to delegate responsibility and able to retain aides whose judgment he trusts is capable of holding many briefs at once. To an outsider, it might be more useful to think of such Senators not just as individuals, but as organizations.*

There is nonetheless a widespread fear in the Senate that the public would not appreciate the notion of a Senator who does not perform every conceivable legislative task himself, just as the Senate fears that constituents would not appreciate knowing that staff members draft most of the letters Senators sign. The anonymity of Senate staffers is a direct consequence of these fears, for, unwilling to sacrifice the staff assistance that anyone but a superman would re-

---

* Some bills, of course, demand more attention from the Senator personally than do others. S. 4106 required much less day-to-day oversight by Magnuson than most of his legislation, for it did not go through one of his Committees, nor was it a "major" bill. These circumstances make S. 4106 an easier bill for a staff man to write about, but they also make it somewhat atypical.

quire, Senators do their best to give the impression that they are supermen in fact. If they admitted publicly that they did not write each of their letters, a campaign opponent might promise the voters that *he* would. Yet among themselves, Senators agree that anyone who takes the time to answer his mail personally has no time left to perform the other functions his constituents expect of him; it might equally be said that any Senator who does not delegate a single legislative task has almost no time left to legislate at all, nor should he be surprised to discover he soon has an incompetent legislative staff.

Senators have little control over the action aspect of the money–power–action nexus of the staff world—action is simply one of the fringe benefits that make a Senate staff job worthwhile. Many aides who could have more money, perhaps even greater responsibility, and certainly greater recognition if they moved on remain for years in the Senate largely because they would miss the sensation of being at the center of national policy-making. It requires a grandiose imagination to see America's destiny shaped or thwarted in every action taken on the Senate Floor, behind the committee doors, or in the crowded working space of the Senate Office Buildings, but the Senate is still a major part of Washington, and Washington is still the hub, the place where a small movement of policy can translate into significant changes in the lives of Americans many thousands of miles away. This knowledge, this realization—that a small community of men and women on a modest little hill can actually affect how millions of people live—may lead to inflated notions of self-importance in staff men as well as Senators, but it may also break down the isolation and parochialism that inevitably attend any job in any one place. If one wants to see America, know its people, learn its needs, one must simply travel around it; failing that, one can work on Capitol Hill, and also have a chance to participate in the government's response to the people, perhaps even make that response marginally better. Administrative assistants and legislative assistants in particular often assimilate the arguments on all sides of virtually every issue being debated, and learn more of the day-to-day operation of government than they could ever glean from books. For most of them, the Senate is exciting, vital, central; anywhere else seems a backwater by comparison.

The money–power–action nexus is the key to understanding Senate staff members and their behavior. Those who earn little, who are powerless, or whose blood does not race in response to the Senate as an institution tend to leave work promptly at 5 o'clock; those who are more privileged frequently sign out on the night watchman's logbook. Yet money, power, and a glimpse of the action are not bestowed freely upon even the luckiest of staff members; in return, they must pour out their loyalty, their energy, and whatever brains they have in the service of another man and an institution of which they are not full members. In a sense, the Senate exploits young men, for without them its business could not go on and the senior politicians, for all their skill, could not sustain themselves. The staff man's individuality may not be denied him, but he must hold his own ambitions in abeyance; rather than rush out and run for office, as many have dreamed of doing, he must be willing to subordinate his identity and his ego in the career of another man. He becomes, in time, more an extension of that man than a fulfillment of his own aspirations. Small wonder that few staff members join the Senate's pension plan, or that there is such a youthful cast to them. Whether through the need for greater gratification or simply as a result of having burned himself out, the staff man eventually leaves. It is, by its very nature, a transient job.

Yet while he is there, the Senate staff man does more than bolster his bank account, serve the public, and lay in a store of memories for the long years when he will be somewhere remote from Washington. He *learns*, and he is never again comfortable with the popular myths and misconceptions about the Senate he will hear so often. "Lobbyist," for example, no longer strikes him as an inherently dirty word; he has probably met more public-interest lobbyists than he has corporate stereotypes. The piety of the press or the simplifications of the evening news will probably disgust him; if the news media really wanted to "reform" government, to break the power of the "special interests" they decry, they could accomplish much simply by giving credit to the politicians when they do something right. Publicity is the reward politicians seek, and need, in order to base their power directly on the people, but publicity they get only for drama. Good legislation, good hearings are rarely dramatic; if the press covers them at all, it often neglects to name the sponsors, the chairmen (the men who get their names in the paper are the witnesses, who don't need votes, or the Senators who try to pick a fight). Publicity produces votes, and so do big campaign contributions. But what type of Senator gets good publicity? A "show horse." And what type of Senator gets big campaign contributions? Probably a type whom a few headlines might wean from the "special interests"—if only he could get headlines for "kitchen work." In the absence of public credit for acting in the public interest, "special interest" contributions—and all they entail—are more useful.

If a staff man is really lucky, I suppose, he learns not to take all these things or himself too seriously; to write a paragraph like that and then step back a bit, realizing that the Senate, and the nation, do not depend on him for insight into their problems. I remember rushing to the Senate Floor once with three other Magnuson aides, excited and angry about a perceived threat to the jurisdiction of Magnuson's Commerce Committee. We perched tensely on a staff couch, frozen in stern poses as we watched Magnuson go through his paces in debate. Another aide from another staff, walking past our taut tableau, simply shook his head

and smiled at the four of us. "You guys look just like
Mount Rushmore," he said, and laughing made us realize
we were sane. The luckiest Senators are the ones who can
laugh, too. I once saw real enjoyment in the Senate Chamber, during a vote to eliminate the tobacco subsidy: a
Southern Senator, laughing, shouting "Communists! Communists!" each time one of his colleagues voted "Aye." The
Senate may be the center of the world, but it is not the
whole world, nor everything in it.

5.

Self-admonished, I now have no choice but to admit that
S. 4106 was not uppermost in my thoughts when, in early
November, I wrote the Magnuson office from Oxford and
asked if I could return to work for six weeks during my
long Christmas vacation. My fiancée was in New York, and
Washington seemed closer than England. I knew, from
Bergman's letters and the *International Herald Tribune,*
that the special postelection session of Congress would
probably adjourn not later than early December; I could
arrive in Washington no sooner than December 7, so I
probably couldn't help S. 4106 a bit even if I did go back. I
could follow the bill's progress by means of Bergman's letters, but somehow fiancées are more enjoyable in person
than at a distance of 3,000 miles.

Magnuson had told me, "You're not through here; you're
just taking a leave of absence." But could I go back to his
office for such a short time, and after a leave of absence of
only two months? Fortunately, I didn't have to wait long
for an answer. A week after I'd written, my scout handed
me a telegram with the Joycean message YES YES YES. I
skipped a class to buy a plane ticket.

X

DOCTORS IN THE HOUSE

1.

In most election years, Capitol Hill is a somewhat ghostly place between November and January. The staffs of defeated or retiring solons listlessly supervise the packing of files and the crating of pictures, while other aides come to work late, leave early, and spend much of the intervening time in the Capitol cafeterias, rehashing the election results over coffee and doughnuts or making leisurely plans for new legislative battles in the coming Congress. The lawmakers themselves, regardless of how they fared at the polls, usually recuperate from the campaign and the last Congress far from the "corridors of power"—in their home districts, perhaps, or on a Caribbean beach or a Colorado ski slope.

When the 91st Congress reconvened in November 1970, therefore, it became the first Congress to do so in many years. But Congress had not returned for business like the NHSC; it had come back only because it had not yet passed the inescapable legislation of every Congress—the appropriations bills. President Nixon, of course, had excoriated

Congress throughout the campaign for its "dereliction" in not approving the money bills sooner (and for "fueling the fires of inflation" with the increases in those appropriations it *had* passed), but the White House certainly shared responsibility for the delay. Senate Republicans had acted on Nixon's instructions in filibustering for a full six weeks the Church-Cooper Amendment that the invasion of Cambodia had spawned, and the legislative calendar had never fully recovered. Whether they understood this fact or not, the voters apparently paid little attention to Nixon's and Agnew's rather vicious campaign, for they returned solid Democratic majorities to both the House and the Senate.

Ironically, the Democrats' electoral victory dimmed S. 4106's chances of passage, for it ensured Democratic control of the 92nd Congress and thus removed the impetus for immediate action on bills of secondary importance. Congress wanted to adjourn quickly, and the Leadership thought the appropriations bills could be passed by Thanksgiving, or by early December at the latest. Everything else could wait until the 92nd Congress convened in January and the "dance of legislation" began again, as it had ninety-one times before.

Within the first week of the postelection session, however, S. 4106 received national publicity for the first time since Craig Palmer's fateful article in July. Flora Lewis, whom SAMA's Jeff Harris had alerted, had long intended to devote one of her nationally syndicated columns to the NHSC; in fact, she had called me to discuss the bill before I left Magnuson's office in October. Now, more than a month later, the column finally appeared, and Bergman sent me a copy in Oxford:

> Behind-the-scenes machination [the article began] is blocking House consideration of a new health-service bill so obviously wise and useful that it sailed through the Senate by an extraordinary vote of 66-0.

Miss Lewis did not elaborate on the "machination"; in fact, her column never mentioned the House of Representatives again after the first sentence. She did, however, discuss the bill's "wisdom and utility" at length, cataloguing its widespread support among health professionals and citing an example of a community (Fayette, Mississippi) that NHSC doctors might benefit. Moreover, Miss Lewis identified the White House and HEW as the real villains: "[They] are so clearly unenthusiastic about the measure that it may be left to die in the 91st Congress, although HEW has shrewdly avoided any open opposition." Not only did the President and the nefarious Department hope to destroy the Public Health Service, she intimated, but their opposition to the Magnuson bill also represented (somewhat curiously, I thought) a "quiet scheme" to "force out" Dr. Egeberg from his post at HEW. Adapting the jargon of the Apollo moon landings, Miss Lewis concluded her column with a paragraph certain to touch off a minor letter-writing campaign to Congress:

> [S. 4106] is a cautious innovation at a time of drastic need. If anything is wrong with the Magnuson bill, it is that it is but one small step when the country is crying out for giant leaps in the delivery of health care.

Bergman, although pleased with the Lewis article, feared it might have appeared "too late" to help the NHSC. In an ironic sense, he was right. For on November 13, even before some of Miss Lewis' subscribers had printed her column, Congressman Staggers issued a simple press release. The Health Subcommittee of the House Commerce Committee, he said, would hold two days of hearings on S. 4106, H.R. 19246, and "related bills." The sudden announcement surprised everyone but Mike Gorman, to whom Staggers had long ago promised such action. "Staggers," Gorman insisted triumphantly, "is a man of his word."

2.

Bergman flew to Washington on November 19, five days before the hearings. He gamely offered to help Ed Williamson, the Chief Clerk of Staggers' Committee, with the preparations, pointing out that we had put together the Senate hearing and that Menger had mentioned the Committee's already heavy work load. Politely but firmly, Williamson declined; the Commerce Committee staff was quite capable of doing its own work, thank you. "The House," Bergman wrote, "is a different ball game."

Congressman Rogers, on the other hand, welcomed Bergman warmly. Safely reelected, he ushered him into his private office, chattering in a relaxed and happy fashion. Then, completely to Bergman's surprise, he confided another reason for his ebullience: one of the "related bills" at the NHSC hearings would be his own. Rogers explained that he would introduce his bill in a few days, after he had solved some technical problems, and he added confidently that his would be the legislation the House eventually passed. So Bob Maher's promise in October had not been an idle one; and Magnuson had never even played his "trump."

Elated, Bergman offered his assistance, and unlike Williamson, Rogers accepted. He said that he planned several changes in the bill to avoid a repetition of our midsummer fiasco. The name of the program would have to be changed, for one thing; the word "Corps" would reawaken the suspicions of his Health Subcommittee colleagues, and besides, it had become unhealthy through general overuse in the New Deal, the New Frontier, and the Great Society. Similarly, Rogers intended to eliminate any explicit mention of "poverty" from the bill; the "War on Poverty" was too unpopular now, too laden with connotations of administrative foibles and failures and droves of "do-gooders." The program would still serve the poor, Rogers insisted, but the bill itself should use only the euphemistic term "medically deficient areas." Rogers stressed that these were merely wording changes; he wanted to retain the original purpose of the bill, but in a form his colleagues might accept more readily. A rose by any other name . . , Bergman thought, and he assured Rogers that Magnuson would not object.

The technical difficulties bothered Rogers as much as the semantic ones, he confessed. S. 4106 did not deal with such troublesome problems as "licensure" or malpractice insurance for NHSC physicians—somehow the Rogers bill would have to take care of these. And as one tactic in his legislative strategy for the embryonic bill, Rogers contemplated including a "loan forgiveness" provision, similar to the unsuccessful Murphy bill in the Senate, whereby the government would take over a medical student's educational indebtedness in exchange for his promise to practice for a time in a needy community. Senator Murphy's bill, belated and clearly partisan, had never attracted much support, but more than 100 Congressmen had cosponsored a similar bill in the House. Rogers hoped to swing this bloc of support to his bill (the cosponsors represented about half the votes he would need at the time of final passage), and he thought he could succeed if he simply incorporated the "loan forgiveness" bill into his own. Bergman demurred; while inoffensive in itself, the "loan forgiveness" provision might complicate ultimate agreement with the Senate on a single version of the bill to be sent to the President. But the technical questions, he agreed, did require answers, and he promised to help Rogers find someone competent enough to draft the necessary legislative language. (In desperation, Bergman finally sought this assistance from a minor but knowledgeable HEW official, who pledged his support immediately and then—typically—never called back.)

At Rogers' suggestion, Bergman next visited a number of other Congressmen, trying to lobby quietly for the bill before the hearings began. Representative Brock Adams, a cosponsor of Staggers' bill and a member of his Committee (though not the Health Subcommittee), willingly agreed to testify, and Bergman promised to write his statement for him. Then Bergman called on a somewhat more formidable Congressman, Dr. Tim Lee Carter of Kentucky. The second-ranking Republican (and the only M.D.) on the Health Subcommittee, Carter had already thwarted the NHSC once, when he denounced it—on the basis of Craig Palmer's article—in the tempestuous Subcommittee meeting of July 20. Although Bergman found the Kentuckian "polite but reserved" at the beginning of their discussion, Carter warmed discernibly toward the bill when Bergman described it in "populistic" rather than "liberal" rhetoric. "What really turned him on," Bergman wrote me, "was my telling him that this bill would force the bureaucratic PHS doctors out from behind their desks in Washington and into the field to do some real 'doctoring.' " Carter stopped short of promising his support unconditionally, but Bergman left his office confident that he had at least undone the inadvertent damage of the Palmer article. In fact, he suspected Carter might have felt some affinity for "a fellow physician willing to brave the perils of politics." A subsequent visit with Representative Ancher Nelsen of Minnesota, the Subcommittee's ranking Republican, added to Bergman's optimism, yet he knew that private conversations weren't the true test of his persuasiveness or Rogers' shrewdness. That test would be whether the members of the Health Subcommittee supported their de facto leader during the hearings—and afterward.

3.

The hearings began precisely on schedule—at 10 A.M., November 24, almost three months after Yarborough's—but they did not begin auspiciously. Neither Staggers nor

Rogers had appeared by the time Subcommittee Chairman John Jarman listlessly rapped his gavel, nor, for that matter, had any reporters or cameramen. Troubled, Bergman found a seat among reassuringly familiar faces—Bill Lucca of the COA, Dr. James Kimmey of the APHA, Robert Shannon and Jeff Harris of SAMA, and, of course, Dr. Nolan of West Virginia. Apparently anxious to make the hearing as brief as possible, Jarman immediately called the first witness, Representative Jonathan Bingham of New York.

Congressman Bingham had introduced one of the six NHSC bills pending before the Subcommittee, a curious hybrid combining the text of Magnuson's original bill with the funding levels Yarborough's Committee had approved. No great significance attached to his testimony; the Subcommittee heard it as a matter of Congressional courtesy, and Bingham's reputation as a predictable Eastern liberal may not have enhanced the general attentiveness in the hearing room. Bergman, however, did not like the drift of Bingham's statement, and the dandyish Congressman astonished him when he began to discuss the Selective Service aspects of the bill:

> I am particularly anxious . . . to avoid and find some way so that we don't have the appalling situation we have today with Americans, good conscientious Americans, finding that, for reasons of their own conscience, they have to flee the country or go to jail [to avoid the draft]. . . .
>
> These men, in my judgment, are not criminals. I do not agree with them. I hope my son would not do that. . . . I think we should find some way to avoid this situation and some way of giving these men an honorable way to serve their community. . . .

The one label we had feared more than "socialized medicine" was "a draft dodge"; S. 4106 carefully made no mention of military service, for we had written it within the terms of the Selective Service law, and no one had called attention to the draft issue so explicitly as Bingham, much less in such impolitic terms. Bergman anxiously watched the Subcommittee members to see how they would react, but fortunately none of them seemed to be listening to Bingham at all. Jarman, obviously bored, simply dismissed Bingham and accepted testimony from Representative Howard Robison, another New Yorker who had introduced one of the NHSC bills (this one a duplicate of S. 4106 as the Senate had passed it, and consequently superfluous). Jarman accepted Senator Magnuson's familiar testimony with greater courtliness, but with similar dispatch, and then called Dr. Nolan to the witness table.

Staggers' absence must have disappointed Nolan, but while he was reading his statement, Congressman Rogers strode into the hearing room. Pausing to whisper a few words to each of his Subcommittee colleagues, Rogers then stopped beside Chairman Jarman's place on the dais. Jarman, visibly relieved, handed the gavel to Rogers and immediately departed. Taking the Chairman's seat, Rogers encouraged Nolan to continue, then questioned him with friendly enthusiasm. Somewhat surprisingly, Nolan evoked a statement from Congressman Carter, who assured him that the "doctor distribution" problem in Kentucky matched that in West Virginia. And Carter added significantly that he, for one, "would like to do something about it." It was the first statement of support, however tentative, from a Republican member of the Subcommittee.

Bergman followed Nolan, but only after he had given his testimony did Rogers reveal the extent of the Subcommittee's consensus. He announced, almost offhandedly, that he would introduce his own bill in the House that afternoon, and he hinted openly that the Subcommittee would support it unanimously. Rogers added that he would drop the "National Health Service Corps" nomenclature from his bill, and because he had not yet thought of a substitute name for the program, his legislation would simply vest authority for performance of the same function in the Public Health Service generally. He extracted publicly from Bergman (whom he treated as the Senate's representative) the assurance that this change would not harm the legislation, and then asked him what he thought of adding the "loan forgiveness" provision to the new bill. Bergman repeated the answer he had given Rogers in private: "loan forgiveness" might have its virtues, but "I worry terribly that if loan-forgiveness legislation gets hooked onto this bill, it could possibly complicate it and delay passage." Apparently still weighing Bergman's anxieties against the potential support the provision might attract among his colleagues, Rogers called the next witness without stating his precise intentions.

Before long, Rogers had reached the morning's final witness: Robert Shannon of SAMA. Shannon spoke with even greater self-assurance than he had in the Senate, and the unprecedented appearance of a student organization at a Congressional hearing intrigued Rogers as much as it had Yarborough; like Yarborough, Rogers kept Shannon at the witness table for a very long time. Perhaps the most significant item in Shannon's testimony was that SAMA had recently polled medical students on the subject of the National Health Service Corps; fully 1,500 had replied that they would like to serve, thus dispelling any lingering fears that the program might lack for medical manpower.

Rogers adjourned the hearing promptly at noon, reminding the audience that testimony would resume the following morning with a spokesman for the Department of Health, Education and Welfare. Then he descended from the dais and approached Bergman and the other observers still present. The precise wording of the bill still troubled him, he confessed, for he wanted to eliminate the phrase "National Health Service Corps" without running afoul of the draft law, which allowed PHS doctors to fulfill their military obligation only through service in "an office or bureau" of the PHS. How could the bill create a new "office or bureau" without giving it a name? Lee Goldman, present now in his new capacity as the AAMC's lobbyist, provided the answer: why not simply establish the program as a function of "an identifiable administrative unit of the PHS," and leave HEW to puzzle out a name for it if it became law? Goldman's logic and his felicitous phrase pleased Rogers, and within hours he introduced his bill, H.R. 19860, the "Emergency Health Personnel Act of 1970." Bob Maher had evidently conceived the bill's title, and he defended it simply: "What was Rogers going to call it—the 'Identifiable Administrative Unit Act'?"

So the protean NHSC had become the "EHPA." With the exception of the new name, and the elimination of the term "poverty areas," Rogers had virtually reproduced Magnuson's original bill; he had even restored the National Advisory Council, which Dominick's amendment had deleted from S. 4106, and he made no mention of "loan forgiveness." But close inspection of H.R. 19860 revealed two important differences from S. 4106. First, Rogers' bill did not contain the words "Surgeon General" anywhere; the Congressman had simply vested authority for the new program in the Secretary of Health, Education and Welfare (we never learned whether this change reflected Dr. Wilson's influence; neither he nor Rogers cared to discuss it). But as if to soothe Magnuson and the PHS alliance, Rogers had adeptly modified the bill in a second way. In place of the $5 million funding level in the original bill (a figure on which he had once insisted), or even the $5–$10–$12–$15 million progression Yarborough had extracted from his Committee, Rogers boldly provided a funding ceiling of $10 million in the first year, $20 million in the second, and $30 million in the third. The Congressman had been away a long time, but he marked his homecoming with prodigality, not its repentance.

So the nascent doctor corps, while still not the "giant

leap" for which Flora Lewis had hoped, was nonetheless
becoming a larger and larger "small step." And if anyone
doubted that Rogers could move such an ambitious and
belated bill, the EHPA's list of cosponsors suggested that
the Health Subcommittee at least would present no obstacle: seven of the Subcommittee's nine members had
lent their names to Rogers' effort. "We would have had all
nine," Bob Maher complained, "but two were out of
town."

4.

The second day of hearings began at 10 A.M. on November 25. This time Congressman Rogers himself called the
hearing to order, and the number of bills had increased,
too. H.R. 19860, less than a day old, was available to spectators, but only in typewritten form; the Government Printing Office could not move as quickly as the Gentleman from
Florida. Yet despite the new bill's significance, the spectators did not direct their attention to a sheaf of Xeroxed
papers. For Rogers promptly announced the first witness:
Dr. Jesse L. Steinfeld, the Surgeon General of the United
States.

Dr. Steinfeld found himself in a distinctly uncomfortable
and humiliating position this morning, thanks to his enemies within HEW. As the official representative of the Administration, he would be forced to testify *against* S.
4106—a bill he supported ardently, a bill he had publicly
praised as "excellent," a bill designed explicitly to "revitalize" the Public Health Service and to return the Surgeon
General himself to an active role in health affairs. Nor did
these ironies represent the limit of Steinfeld's misfortune.
The story going around was that he had actually volunteered for this assignment, making a special pilgrimage to

Camp David when Secretary Richardson had spent a "working holiday" there. Steinfeld had pleaded with Richardson and finally won his permission to testify at the House hearings, and he had returned believing that he could write his own testimony. But someone else had written Steinfeld's statement, and the testimony represented the diametric opposite of the Surgeon General's personal views. He had protested, bitterly, but his superiors had not allowed him to back out, or to change one word of the statement; they had ordered him to testify, to deliver the statement precisely as written, and to defend the Administration against the inevitable attacks its position would provoke.

Any preface to his testimony or exculpatory remarks would cost Steinfeld his job, and he knew that if he left Washington the Administration might never appoint another Surgeon General to succeed him. So he followed orders and kept silent on the origins of this testimony (so silent, in fact, that we did not learn the story from him). He even accepted stoically the final irony: H.R. 19860, Rogers' bill, offered the Surgeon General no role at all in the proposed program.

Congressman Rogers understood the haplessness of Steinfeld's position even if he didn't know all the details behind his selection as the Administration's witness. He knew that Steinfeld advocated this legislation as forcefully as he did himself, but duty—which had trapped Steinfeld—exerted an inescapable influence on Rogers too. Rogers had to demolish the Administration's opposition to the bill, regardless of who presented it. It was too late in the session to jiggle this bill into law; it would have to be passed in a rush, suddenly and irresistibly. If this meant humiliating the Surgeon General further, Rogers would not enjoy himself, but he would do what he had to do—the Administration had left him no other choice.

Steinfeld himself was not unresourceful. He dutifully

read his testimony (urging that action on S. 4106 be "deferred," a nice euphemism when Congress is about to adjourn), but he read it in such an obviously unenthusiastic monotone that he effectively repudiated each word as he spoke it. Rogers seemed to take this diffident style of delivery into account when he began his questioning, gentle and courteous. He inquired, for example, about the terms of service of PHS doctors; did they not serve, he asked, "subject to the pleasure of the Surgeon General"?

> DR. STEINFELD. Subject to the needs of the Public Health Service. I don't get too many pleasures in this job.

> MR. ROGERS. Well, we are all trying to change that for you.

> DR. STEINFELD. I will do everything I can to help, Mr. Rogers.

> MR. ROGERS. We are trying to give you some more pleasures. (*Laughter*)

The air of complicity did not last long. Slowly, methodically, displaying the skill and cunning of an expert trial lawyer, Rogers cross-examined Steinfeld with a line of questioning designed to force an admission that the Administration had chosen an indefensible position on the legislation. Were there any Federal programs, he asked, "to assure medical service to an area that has none"? Valiantly, Steinfeld tried to deflect Rogers' attack. He catalogued monotonously a great number of Federally funded health-care programs, none of which happened to deal with the "physician maldistribution" problem. Undeterred, Rogers finally lost patience with Steinfeld's dissembling, and with barely controlled anger he stated his questions firmly and succinctly:

> MR. ROGERS. You do not presently have the authority to assign a doctor to a community where there is no health care, and to have him provide all the services for that community, do you?

> DR. STEINFELD. We do not have that authority.

Mr. Rogers. That is what we are talking about—giving you that authority.

Dr. Steinfeld. I think the problem is a large one, and there are many other things we should consider at the same time.

Mr. Rogers. I don't doubt that. There are plenty of problems, so many that the President has said we have a health-care crisis in this country, but I haven't seen any reaction [within the Administration] to that statement.

Dr. Steinfeld. The reaction is in preparation.

Mr. Rogers. It has been in preparation two years, I guess, but the Congress is trying to act now. And some have called this a lame-duck [session of] Congress—I would term it a lame-duck Administration, because they don't expect us to do anything in the time we are here. And we want to do something.

Now here is what I want to go into. What is your solution for a community that says, "We have no doctor"? They look to you, the Surgeon General, the chief health officer of the United States [*sic*], and say, "Get us a doctor here." What can you do?

Dr. Steinfeld. As you have pointed out, we do not now have the authority to assign doctors to communities.

Rogers then listed the alternatives to a health-service corps that had already been tried—including state "loan forgiveness" programs and the AMA's physician-placement service—and extracted from Steinfeld the admission that none of them had worked. "It's fine to talk about these problems, but that is not very meaningful to a community that has no doctor," Rogers said indignantly. "We still have the problem."

After a pause, the Surgeon General quietly agreed. "We still have the problem," he said. But then Steinfeld sought refuge in the one hedge HEW and the White House had left him. "We are studying the problem," he declared.

At this, Rogers—like Yarborough before him—simply exploded. "All I *see* is studying," he said heatedly, and immediately attacked what he regarded as the ultimate villain, the secretive Office of Management and Budget (OMB). Rogers did not pick the OMB as a scapegoat, for although the uninitiated might not understand its relevance, the OMB had become the stronghold of anti-PHS sentiment (since the PHS was "wasteful" and "inefficient"). The Administration's opposition to S. 4106 probably stemmed less from genuine "socialized medicine" fears than from the OMB's belief that the bill would prevent the elimination of the PHS. Steinfeld, however, dutifully tried to rebut Rogers' accusation, and curiously defended the very men who most wanted to see his job abolished:

> DR. STEINFELD. I want to say something in defense of OMB. I think we have a very good system of government. I have traveled recently to other countries, and while our system of health care has problems in it, I think it is a good system. Our problem is to improve it. I think our government is a good system and we ought to improve it. I find it hard to criticize any one particular part of it.

> MR. ROGERS. Well, I would agree with you that we do have a good system of government, or I would not be part of it. I think all of us feel that way. But I am willing to criticize a lot of it, and that is what this committee is going to do until we get some action.
>
> If we are going to sit back and say, "We are going to have studies, and we are going to think, and one of these days we are going to move," we will never move, because you will be out and someone else will be in and he will have to start studying all over again.

> DR. STEINFELD. I will be here for a while.

> MR. ROGERS. We hope so and this committee wants to help you try to stay here and do a good job. But none of us is here for long in a certain way. Certainly Members of Congress are not, and from what I have seen of Surgeons

General and Assistant Secretaries and Secretaries, neither are they.

And so we go through this process of studying everything every time we get a new man in. . . . We are tired of studies. We want action. And the people want delivery of health care in this country.

After this angry broadside, Steinfeld never fully recovered his composure, and Rogers never fully reverted from Implacable Chairman to Courteous Southern Gentleman. He dismissed Steinfeld and his pitiful defense of the Administration's position with a vow every person present knew he intended to keep.

"You are only proposing studying," Rogers said contemptuously, "and here we are, ready to move with the bill and the legislation. What we are going to do, I am sure, is to report out a bill, and I believe the Senate will accept it. The President may veto it on the advice of HEW. I hope not, but if he does, we will start back again next year. Because we have got to have some help in the medical field in this country."

For all practical purposes, the hearing had ended. Rogers heard other witnesses, and accepted written testimony from men like Amos Johnson and Leonard Woodcock. But once Steinfeld had picked up his papers and departed, the outcome of the hearing was apparent. Like Yarborough, Rogers had adopted the bill as his own, and he would devote his energies and his skill to passing it in the House. Only one question remained: would he have enough time?

5.

Bergman flew home to Seattle, tired but optimistic. "Trying to be objective," he wrote, "I now think we are going to win." This assessment reached me just as I was leaving Oxford for the London airport and my flight home. I couldn't know, since the December 4 *International Herald Tribune* had made no mention of it, that the House Commerce Committee had approved Rogers' bill the day before, or that *The New York Times* (prompted by Dr. Nolan) had editorialized in its favor. I only knew that the days of waiting for Bergman's letters, the hasty phone calls from Oxford to the United States, were over now. Soon I would arrive in Washington. I was restless and eager, like the Navy captain my father had once seen, racing his warship through the Panama Canal on the eve of the Japanese surrender. He had to be in the Pacific when the war ended, and I had to be in Washington when the bill became law.

XI

A WAR OF NERVES

1.

Before leaving for England, I had lived in a Capitol Hill apartment, three blocks from the Senate Office Building, and when I returned in December for six weeks, my former landlord generously allowed me back in. The five-minute walk to Magnuson's office was therefore a familiar one on the morning of December 7. Along Constitution Avenue, the World Women's Party headquarters—an ivy-covered brick home where Gallatin had once lived—seemed only a bit more dilapidated, while the shiny modern VFW Headquarters and the Reserve Officers Association building looked even more prosperous and ostentatious than when I left. Had it been autumn, I would have continued down Constitution to the Capitol Plaza, past the starling-infested Corinthian capitals of the stately Old Senate Office Building; but it was December, and cold. So I ducked into the first shelter along my route, the back door of the New

Senate Office Building, and paused to say hello again to Harley Dirks. Then I descended the back stairs to the basement and walked through the underground labyrinth toward the Old SOB, passing the familiar decorated doorway of "Jack the Wrapper," already at work binding Senate packages for the mail. As I approached Magnuson's office, feeling more and more at home, I suddenly encountered someone I had forgotten: Dr. Glen Wegner.

I hadn't seen Wegner since September 21, the day S. 4106 had passed the Senate and provoked his ill-tempered remarks in the Reception Room. He seemed equally surprised to see me.

"I thought you were in Oxford," he said, perplexed, as we shook hands. The remark troubled me—why had he bothered to learn that I had left, or where I had gone?—but I cheerfully replied that I had come home for a six-week working vacation—adding, of course, that I wanted to be in Washington when our bill became law.

"Well," Wegner responded, feigning sympathy, "that's one thing you probably won't see. It looks like the bill won't make it through the House."

This remark bothered me more than the first, even though I knew Wegner was far from impartial. What problems could the bill have encountered so suddenly in the House? Only a few days earlier, Staggers had reported the bill from his Committee and announced publicly that the Committee members supported it "nearly unanimously." But I tried to mask my consternation. In a few minutes, in Magnuson's office, I could learn what substance, if any, lay behind Wegner's disturbing prediction. As if I understood the problems to which he'd alluded, I replied, "Who knows? We thought it was dead plenty of times before."

Wegner only smiled, shrugged, and shook his head. This time it's *really* dead, he seemed to suggest. We said goodbye, a little guardedly, and I quickly climbed the stairs toward the office.

At Magnuson's office, after a two-month absence, I discussed the legislative situation with the other staff members
and with Bergman, by phone, in Seattle. None of us could
find any reason to believe what Wegner had said: Staggers
and Rogers, now ardent members of the "team," would
certainly engineer the bill's passage in the House within a
few days. Our real problem, we agreed, lay not in getting
the bill to the President, but in persuading him to sign it
once it reached his desk.

Had Congress passed the bill earlier in the year, it would
have become law automatically, with or without the President's signature, unless he vetoed it outright. If he *had*
vetoed it, Congress might easily have mustered the two-
thirds majority in each House necessary to override the
veto, the same way Congress had overridden his veto of the
Hill-Burton hospital-construction funds earlier. Now, however, Nixon would have another option: the so-called
"pocket veto." The Constitution grants the President ten
days, excluding Sundays, in which to make his decision on
any bill Congress sends him. If he decides to veto a bill, he
must send it back to Congress, where the veto may be overridden. If, however, Congress has adjourned before the ten
days are up, the President cannot return the bill, and if he
fails to sign it, it simply dies on his desk—this is the "pocket
veto," obviously a slight misnomer (but reflecting the idea
that the President has "pocketed" a bill rather than act
affirmatively on it). Since the 91st Congress was now scheduled to adjourn on December 16 or 17, and since the House
had not yet passed the Emergency Health Personnel Act
(EHPA) on December 7, Nixon would definitely have an
opportunity to "pocket-veto" the bill—which we thought he
might do, since the Administration had opposed the bill
publicly at Rogers' hearings only two weeks earlier.

And so, as Bergman had written in a December 1 memorandum, "strategy must now be geared toward averting a
pocket veto." The strategy itself was easy: Nixon had to be

persuaded to sign the bill. But what could we use as tactics? We decided, first of all, that Magnuson should write Health and Welfare Secretary Richardson (no point in dealing with Dr. Egeberg anymore), asking him to intervene in the bill's behalf. Second, Bergman would attempt another indirect plea to Nixon, this one from Washington's Republican Governor Dan Evans to Presidential advisor John Ehrlichman, a former Seattleite and now Nixon's chief aide for domestic affairs.

Similar tactics suggested themselves over the next few days, but suddenly events compelled a temporary abandonment of the entire strategy. Overnight, the legislative course of the EHPA became a very minor subplot in the December installment of the 91st Congress story. And for quite unrelated reasons, it became a subplot whose resolution seemed more likely to please Glen Wegner than us.

What happened, first of all, was that the Senate unexpectedly became in December what it had earlier been in May: a body dominated by a single issue, and hamstrung by a filibuster. This time, however, the issue was the SST, not the invasion of Cambodia or the war in Indochina, and the leaders of the filibuster were Democrats, not Republicans. Although the issues involved were highly complex, the events leading up to the filibuster had been simple enough. In early December, the Senate voted narrowly to delete all funds for the SST program from the Department of Transportation (DOT) Appropriation. The House, on the other hand, defeated a similar move and approved the SST funds intact. The House-Senate conferees on the DOT bill reached a "compromise" that cut back the SST funds somewhat, but not enough to kill the controversial aircraft outright. Normally, the Senate would have accepted routinely the conferees' decision (embodied in the "conference report"), but when the plane's leading opponent, Senator William Proxmire of Wisconsin, saw that his colleagues were about to permit the SST program to continue, he

decided to filibuster and block action on the conference
report until his demands were met.

Proxmire's filibuster threw the Senate into confusion, for
the tactic was more controversial than the SST itself. Traditionally, the filibuster has been employed almost exclusively by Southerners and/or extreme conservatives, generally for the purpose of blocking civil rights legislation. This
ideological tinge to the tactic (although "liberals" have
sometimes used it too), its blatant antimajoritarian nature,
and its unseemliness—who can forgive the monotonous
reading aloud of Southern cookbooks in "the world's greatest deliberative body"?—have combined to make the filibuster and its obverse, cloture, important issues in their
own right in every Congress of the past three decades. The
Cloture Rule—Rule XXII of the Senate—is the subject of
the first struggle in each new Congress, with Northerners
and liberals trying to reduce the two-thirds vote required
for cloture (i.e., for cutting off "debate") to a simple majority, or even 60 percent. In every debate on the Cloture
Rule, Southerners and conservatives respond by inveighing
against the "gag rule" at such great length that they finally
succeed in filibustering to death the attempt to change the
filibuster. Columnists cite the predictable outcome of this
biennial farce as evidence that the South really did win the
Civil War after all, and the filibuster's opponents (including, in the past, Senator Proxmire) derive nothing from the
fight except legislative bruises and a sense of moral superi-
ority: no self-respecting Senator would ever lead a filibuster.

The filibuster against the DOT Appropriation conference report upset these traditional coalitions. Led by two
Northern Democrats (Proxmire and his Wisconsin colleague, Gaylord Nelson), it survived because Southerners—
who mainly supported the SST—could not, on principle,
vote for cloture. Liberals, on the other hand, hated the
filibuster, but they found themselves in a dilemma because

many of them hated the SST too. Senator Philip Hart of Michigan, for example, a leading SST opponent, agonized for a week before announcing that whereas he considered the SST bad, he held the filibuster to be immoral, and consequently he would reluctantly join sides against Proxmire and Nelson. The Senate Leadership felt the same way, and sought to cut off the filibuster with the help of the SST's chief proponents: Senators Magnuson and Jackson, in whose state the plane was to be built.

The filibuster thus presented many ironies. To me, the subtle irony was that Proxmire's filibuster threatened to keep Congress in session right up to January 2, the eve of its mandatory adjournment—a delay that Magnuson needed for his NHSC bill. For Glen Wegner had been right after all: there was trouble—serious trouble—in the House of Representatives. We needed all the time we could get, and Proxmire was giving it to us.

2.

We had underestimated the potential difficulties in the House because Staggers and Rogers had had such easy successes following the two days of hearings in late November. Rogers had reported his EHPA from the Health Subcommittee on November 27, just two days after the hearings—it was the last health bill reported in the 91st Congress. Staggers had secured the full Commerce Committee's approval less than a week later, on December 3; except for emergency legislation, the bill was also the last that his Committee reported. Glen Wegner had urged Republicans on the Commerce Committee to block the bill, but the Staggers-Rogers team (and the *New York Times* editorial of November 27) had proved more persuasive than HEW's acting Congressional liaison. If HEW or the White House or the OMB wanted to stop this bill, the Committee Republicans seemed to be saying, they could damn well arrange to have the President veto it; why should the Congressmen perform that unpleasant task and risk the ire of their Chairman and the national press? The Republicans had settled for what appeared to be a major modification of the bill—an amendment by Congressman Carter specifying that the Government could send doctors only to communities that state and local medical societies had certified as "needy." Having conferred this "veto power" on organized medicine—something we had successfully resisted in the Senate—the Committee Republicans had been content to let the bill go to the President, absolving themselves of any responsibility for its ultimate fate.

But the legislative process in the House does not parallel the Senate's in all respects, and favorable consideration by Staggers' Committee could not lead directly—as it had in the Senate—to a vote on final passage. The Senate had passed S. 4106 only five days after Yarborough had reported it, but in the House the bill still faced one formidable obstacle: the House Rules Committee. Except under a "suspension of the rules" (a procedure Staggers tried unsuccessfully to invoke), every bill reported by a House committee must then go to the Rules Committee, from which it reaches the Floor for a vote only after it has been approved a second time and granted a "rule." The Rules Committee's actions are neither routine nor predictable; secretive and independent, the Committee moves, like God, in mysterious ways. Despite its "reform" in 1961, the Committee nonetheless manages to stifle numerous bills that enjoy apparently overwhelming support; for this reason, House reformers continue to make the Committee one of their chief targets. In the second week of December, it looked very much as if the Rules Committee would transform the EHPA not into a law, but into another footnote in the annals of legislative history.

The EHPA, H.R. 19860, had two problems in the Rules Committee: opposition and competition. The opposition came from Glen Wegner, who, undeterred by his rebuff from the Commerce Committee, carried to Rules his persistent search for a Republican legislator willing to spearhead an attack on the bill. The competition came from other bills in the same straits—some sixty in all, of which no more than a dozen could possibly get rules. During most of the Congressional session, the Rules Committee can delay legislation but not kill it, yet the approach of adjournment makes delay and death legislatively synonymous. The Committee decides which bills in the "adjournment crush" shall receive the life-giving rule and which shall perish. The Committee does not generally exercise this discretionary power randomly, and Wegner might easily hope to influence the Committee members with his imprecations. Killing any particular bill, when so many had to die, did not appear a very difficult task.

Apparently, however, the Republicans on the Rules Committee wanted guidance on the Administration's wishes from a source more authoritative than Glen Wegner. So they sought, successfully, an audience with President Nixon himself. At the meeting, they presented the President with a list of the five dozen bills pending, awaiting rules, and told him that the Committee could act on only twelve, or perhaps fifteen, within the remaining days of the 91st Congress. If the President would care to declare his priorities, they said solicitously, they would try to help the bills he wanted to sign and block those he opposed, or didn't care about. Surprisingly, Nixon told his visitors that he expected the Committee to act on *all* the bills; he, not they, would decide which bills would become law and which would not. Nonplussed, one of the Congressmen repeated that it was simply not possible for the Rules Committee, much less for the House as a whole, to consider sixty bills in the last few days of the 91st Congress. He respect-

fully reiterated his and his colleagues' willingness to cooperate with the President, if only he would state which of
the bills he wanted to reach his desk. But Nixon was adamant: he wanted all the bills to receive rules, and he
wanted the House to act on each of them. When the bills
reached him, he would decide which to sign. Irritated and
disbelieving, the Rules Committee Republicans returned to
Capitol Hill without any Presidential guidance whatsoever.

To Mike Gorman, watching even more closely than usual
the December deliberations of the Rules Committee, the
President's supercilious position was unexpected and inexplicable, but a godsend nonetheless. Gorman was not concerned solely with our bill; he had written an alcoholism
treatment and prevention bill that the Senate and the
House Commerce Committee had also passed, and that now
reposed along with ours in the Rules Committee. The Administration had not supported the alcoholism bill either,
and both pieces of legislation might easily have expired had
the President simply told the Rules Committee Republicans he did not intend to sign them. Now, however, Gorman thought the Committee might prove more tractable,
and in his practiced and methodical style, he began quietly
to line up the necessary votes. The effort pitted him directly against Glen Wegner, of course, but Wegner was
inexperienced and abrasive, while Gorman's skill and con-
geniality were polished, proven. So he felt somewhat confident, if hardly cocky.

The Rules Committee held its final meeting of the 91st
Congress late in the second week of December, just as the
filibuster began to take shape on the Senate Floor. In tacit
recognition of his stature in health affairs, Gorman was the
one outsider permitted to attend the session; Glen Wegner, if he even bothered to come, could only pace the corridor outside the closed doors. Congressman Staggers, with
whom Gorman had conferred in advance, presented the
case for both the alcoholism bill and the EHPA, but he

encountered instant and vocal opposition from Representative William Springer of Illinois, one of the Committee's leading Republicans. Springer, not noted for his liberalism, attacked both bills at length, and he received unexpected if somewhat tentative support from California's Bernie Sisk, a self-proclaimed liberal who happened to be running for the post of House Majority Leader. The session quickly degenerated into something of a shouting match, but then the timely intervention of Florida's Claude Pepper (a former Senator, longtime liberal, and friend of the Lasker forces) bolstered Staggers' position. Pepper had obviously spoken with Gorman, and probably with his Florida colleague Paul Rogers, before the meeting; together, he and Staggers at last succeeded. With the Republicans in disarray after their meeting with Nixon, the Rules Committee voted by the narrowest of margins to grant rules to both health bills, and to some ten others. The remaining bills—approximately fifty of them—were dead when the meeting adjourned.

So the House could now vote on the alcoholism bill and the EHPA; Staggers and Rogers (and also Gorman) had won. In granting the rules, however, the Committee—which also determines the time allotted for debate on each bill—had set aside two hours for debate of the EHPA, but only one hour for the alcoholism bill. This discrepancy troubled us: why did the House need two hours to debate our bill? Relieved as we were simply to have obtained a rule, the prospect of a two-hour debate unnerved us; suddenly the House seemed alien and impenetrable, and not at all certain to grant us our victory. Gorman listened to these fears with amusement. "Will you amateurs do me one favor?" he asked. "Relax."

3.

Bergman flew to Washington, D.C., soon after the Rules Committee acted. Although the SST filibuster had forced Congress to postpone adjournment again, thus making a pocket veto less likely, we still worried that Nixon might veto the bill outright after the House passed it. So Bergman had come to lobby (as a "private citizen") at both the White House and the OMB, hoping to persuade someone who might be able to persuade the President that he ought to sign the bill. He also wanted to watch the House pass the bill—an event scheduled for Monday, December 14. As soon as Bergman arrived, moreover, we paid a "checkup" call on Congressman Rogers, just to make sure all the preparations were in order. Rogers greeted us happily, exuding confidence and obviously looking forward to managing the bill on the House Floor. "There's nothing to worry about," he assured us. We discussed vaguely the possibility of a Presidential veto, but even that did not impinge on Rogers' mood. "I believe," he said firmly, as we rose to go, "that the principle of this bill makes it the most important piece of health legislation in the 91st Congress." That might not prevent Nixon from vetoing it, I thought, but coming from Rogers, at least the statement underscored the remarkable nature of our bill's legislative odyssey. July, with all its disappointments, was far behind us.

Bergman and I went to the House gallery on December 14 to watch the bill's debate and passage. No sooner had we arrived, however, than events on the Floor took a series of unanticipated turns. First, the House ignored its legislative calendar and plunged into lengthy debate—first on the printing and distribution of a House Internal Security Committee report ("Report of Inquiry Concerning Speakers Honoraria at Colleges and Universities"), then on a District of Columbia revenue bill. And whenever it appeared that the House would break free, accelerating its legislative pace, a legendary Iowa Congressman named H. R. Gross intervened to preserve the virtual standstill.

I had heard of H. R. Gross and his dilatory tactics, but I had never seen him in action. The diminutive Republican is a fiscal conservative who has built his reputation (and his career) on the notion that the best way to save the taxpayers' money is to slow down the proceedings of the House to such a great extent that only a trickle of legislation can pass. During most of the session, Gross represents little more than a nuisance to his colleagues, but his power—like the Rules Committee's—waxes considerably as adjournment approaches and the House tries to act quickly on a great deal of legislation. Employing every conceivable parliamentary trick, Gross requests quorum calls, rises repeatedly on points of personal privilege, and worst of all, demands roll-call votes on each substantive issue instead of permitting the timesaving voice vote. A House roll call takes at least half an hour, and usually twice that long, for the House has 435 members, each of whom must be called a second time if he does not vote on the first reading of his name. More amused than uneasy, Bergman and I watched as Gross helped prolong debate on relatively routine matters for four hours. At quarter to six, exhausted, the House simply adjourned for the day.

We returned to the gallery the following day, December 15, and this time a fretful Mike Gorman accompanied us. Gorman was worried not only about H. R. Gross, but also about the spate of conference reports that had come back to the House for approval. Conference reports, he explained, have priority over other legislation, and the House debates them as soon as they appear. In the last days of the 91st Congress—as in every Congress—literally dozens of bills were in conference between the House and Senate, and new reports were being issued daily. "If our bills don't come up soon," Gorman warned, "they might never come up at all—

there are just too damn many conference reports, and the
number is growing every day." Genuinely concerned now,
we waited all afternoon for our bills to be called up; but
the conference reports continued, while H. R. Gross and
like-minded colleagues tenaciously frustrated all efforts to
dispose of them quickly. To make matters worse, the House
adjourned early—the President had invited Members of
Congress to a White House reception. The House had considered neither health bill when the Speaker rapped his gavel
for the final time of the day.

By Wednesday, December 16, we had become quite worried. The scene on the House Floor became excruciatingly
painful to watch. Jim Menger and Ed Williamson, as well
as the principals in the drama, Staggers and Rogers, paced
irritably back and forth, waiting for a break in the stream
of conference reports and the exasperating tactics of delay. Sitting anxiously in the gallery, Bergman and Gorman and I hardly spoke. Hours later, for the third consecutive day, Speaker John McCormack adjourned the House
without any action on the alcoholism bill or the EHPA.
Had it not been for the SST filibuster, we reflected ruefully, the two bills would have died that day, for the Congressional leadership had planned December 16 as the date
for adjournment.

On Thursday, December 17, our frustration reached a
peak. Miraculously, the House had no conference reports to
consider, H. R. Gross sat inexplicably silent, and for the
first time all week the House was ready to proceed with the
items on its calendar—the two health bills. But at precisely
this moment, Staggers was called away to preside over a
hastily convened session of the Commerce Committee,
which suddenly had to wrestle with emergency legislation
to prevent the collapse of the Penn Central Railroad. By
the time Staggers had extricated himself and returned to
the Floor, the opportunity had passed: a batch of new conference reports had come in, and H. R. Gross had revived.

Once again, the House adjourned without acting on either bill.

Hours later, our alarm increased still further. One of our NHSC allies, "a man in a position to know," called me and agitatedly reported that a "reliable source" had told him a plot had been devised in the House to prevent either of the two health bills from coming up for a vote. Since my informant refused to name his source, and since he pleaded that I not use his name either, I had no way of knowing how to treat his report. I quickly called Gorman and told him that "someone who ought to know" had claimed a plot existed to block our bills. Gorman thought the story too bizarre to believe, but he called the office of Majority Leader Carl Albert to make sure the two bills still headed the legislative calendar. I made the same call myself, and soon Gorman and I compared the assurances Albert's staff had provided us.

Superstitiously, perhaps, I made another call in the early evening, this one to the recorded message that advises Congressmen of the House's legislative calendar for the following day. I naturally expected to hear the two health bills at the top of the list, but instead, to my surprise, the impersonal taped voice announced that the "International Coffee Agreement" had become the first order of House business. Suddenly the notion of a plot did not seem at all improbable.

Gorman exploded when I told him of the International Coffee Agreement's new status. He rushed to the Majority Leader's office and asked to speak to Carl Albert himself. After Albert emerged and reassured him, Gorman nonetheless went to see Staggers, who also told him that the bills would come up the moment that conference reports and H. R. Gross permitted. Somewhat gratuitously (but I couldn't just sit around doing *nothing*), I called Albert's staff and warned them as solemnly as possible that if any further problems arose, Senator Magnuson would free himself from the SST filibuster fight long enough to have a few words of his own with the House Majority Leader.

In the midst of this frenetic activity, however, Bergman began to lose heart. He could no longer justify the length of his stay in Washington, or convince himself that his presence had not "jinxed" the bill somehow. On the night of December 17, in a mood of deep depression, he cut short his visit and flew home to Seattle.

4.

On Friday, December 18, neither Gorman nor I had the stamina to sit through another day of tension and frustration in the House gallery, so we stayed away completely. Gorman had another task anyway: he was hosting a farewell party for Senator Yarborough in the hearing room of Yarborough's Committee. Anne, my fiancée, had come down from New York for the weekend, and in the late afternoon —having heard no news from the House—we walked over to shake hands and share a drink with the departing Senator and his admirers. Yarborough and his wife greeted the guests at the door, smiling broadly and tacitly insisting that nothing mournful would be allowed; Gorman, with his immigrant Irish roots, had instinctively planned a wake.

The short receiving line terminated in the center of the crowded hearing room, which I hadn't seen since the hearing on August 28. The room had been less raucous then, the atmosphere more charged. Yarborough had been on the dais instead of at the door, holding a gavel instead of a succession of hands. I wondered if August 28 had been a happier day for Yarborough, even without the tributes; certainly (I thought with a grimace) it had been a more exciting day for the NHSC. But many of the same faces were here again—Lee Goldman, Bob Barclay, Noble Swearingen, Bill Lucca, Jay Cutler, Carey Parker—all men whom I'd met while working on S. 4106. To a lesser extent, and for different reasons, the moment was poignant for me as well as for Yarborough.

Gorman had vanished early, after agreeing that he would join Anne and me for dinner downtown at 6:30. He reappeared an hour or so later, all smiles, with unexpected news: the House had just passed the alcoholism bill, and "Your bill is up *right now!*"

Anne and I ran virtually all the way to the House. I still could not believe Gorman's words, and sensed that we would arrive in the gallery only to find the House discussing another conference report and H. R. Gross standing alertly at the microphone. But my instincts were wrong. Only two men stood at the microphones: Harley Staggers and Paul Rogers.

Staggers had already begun his speech on H.R. 19860, the EHPA; Jim Menger and Ed Williamson sat dutifully beside him. When Staggers finished, he graciously answered questions from Congressman Bingham (who sought assurances that urban as well as rural areas would receive doctors), then yielded the Floor to Rogers. Rogers adeptly handled the long, technical questions of Missouri's Durward Hall, a Republican and a doctor, then assuaged what appeared to be substantial misgivings on the part of Congressman Clarence Brown of Ohio.

Fascinated, we watched as the Floor amendments began. Staggers himself offered the first, an amendment to provide malpractice insurance for all PHS doctors (not just those in the new program). Surgeon General Steinfeld had drafted the amendment and persuaded Staggers to offer it; he argued that since every Administration had desired malpractice coverage for PHS doctors, this one amendment might prevent a veto of the bill. Apparently, however, Steinfeld had neglected to tell Staggers that HEW had not authorized his action, and Staggers blandly announced to the House that the Surgeon General had requested the amendment.

No one on the House Floor seemed to notice this revelation, and the amendment was duly accepted, but I squirmed uneasily in the knowledge that Staggers' innocent disclosure would inevitably create even greater difficulties for Steinfeld.

Brock Adams proposed the next amendment, at the request of the American Optometrical Association, to ensure that the government consulted other health professionals as well as physicians in selecting communities for assistance under the new program. The House accepted Adams' amendment readily enough, but when Bingham tried to delete organized medicine's "veto power" (the result of Carter's amendment in Committee), his proposal was quickly defeated on a voice vote.

All of this had taken some time, and when I glanced at my watch, I found to my surprise that the House had consumed much of the two hours allotted for debate even as we watched—apparently nothing sinister had motivated the Rules Committee after all. I also noticed that it was late; we couldn't possibly meet Gorman for dinner by 6:30. Reluctantly, I left the gallery to find a phone, hurriedly trying to reach Gorman and postpone our dinner. Of course there were no pay phones to be found, and in my eagerness not to miss any of the debate, I finally just picked up one of the telephones reserved for Congressmen. As I was talking to Gorman, explaining mundanely that we would have to eat later, a Congressman reputed to have underworld connections walked up quickly to use the telephone next to mine on the lacquered table. He reached for the receiver, then checked himself; glowering at me, he angrily slammed the phone down and rushed away. My imagination fastened on this incongruous incident, and as I walked back into the House gallery, Anne informed me excitedly, "They passed it!" After a week of waiting, I had managed to miss the Great Event.

I had also missed one significant speech.* Congressman John Schmitz of California, a member of the John Birch Society, had attacked the bill bitterly, employing publicly for the first time in the entire legislative history of the NHSC the argument we had once feared might defeat it:

> Mr. Chairman [sic], I am strongly opposed to H.R. 19860, the Emergency Health Personnel Act, and urge that it be wholly rejected by the House.
>
> The full significance of [the bill] has not yet been brought out in our debate.
>
> The Public Health Service was never intended to provide medical services in competition with private physicians— whether or not some bureaucrat thinks that their services in a given area are "inadequate." The Public Health Service is supposed to deal in public health, not private care—in disease prevention, not in the treatment of patients. To bring the PHS into direct medical care is to take another long step toward socialized medicine—the last thing we need, considering the rate at which we are already plunging into it. Enthusiasts for programs of this kind should be reminded over and over again that socialized medicine has been a colossal failure in every country that has tried it—and, to their sorrow, there have been many. We can still block it in the United States. Defeat of this bill would be a good place to start.

(That the House ignored Schmitz—and that more of his colleagues did not voice similar objections—is very significant, for the explanation does not lie solely, or even primarily, in the speciousness of his argument. Many members of the House, and even the Senate, are still ready to denounce "socialized medicine," but except for Schmitz, none of them ever expressed public opposition to the NHSC in

---

* In fact, the speech may have been submitted in writing rather than delivered. The *Congressional Record* does not differentiate between written and oral addresses, and Anne, who was present at the time, does not remember hearing this one.

any of its many forms. Why? Because (at the risk of over-simplifying a bit) the type of Congressman who still fulminates against "socialized medicine" does not come from an urban area—urban Congressmen are mostly liberal Democrats—or from Suburbia—suburban Congressmen of either party are above all *respectable*; moderates, not fervent ideologues. A Congressman who attacks "socialized medicine" publicly almost certainly has a rural constituency, for only rural areas still produce very conservative Congressmen consistently. But rural areas have another salient feature: most of them have great difficulty finding, keeping, or replacing doctors. With an Orange County constituency, Schmitz himself stood as an ironic exception to this rule, for what happened to the NHSC in Congress—and to Schmitz's argument—is symbolized by the reaction of Representative Tim Lee Carter of Kentucky: on July 20 he excoriated the bill as "socialized medicine" during the Health Subcommittee meeting, and on November 24 he cosponsored it.)

The International Coffee Agreement, that would-be displacer of the EHPA and the alcoholism bill, was finally under consideration as Anne and I left the House Gallery. Outside, we unexpectedly encountered Jim Menger. Thanking him as humbly as I could, I realized belatedly that he too was no villain, but rather one of the architects of the victory we (or at least Anne) had just witnessed. Menger smiled warmly, generously, and didn't reprove me for the hasty judgments I had formed earlier. "I told you we could handle it," he said simply, and for the moment I was only too happy to forget some of the other things he had once told me. For the first time, I began to appreciate Menger's true Capitol Hill professionalism, his ability to work unremittingly in behalf of a bill simply because Staggers approved it—regardless of his personal views. When I thought of Menger in contrast to Dr. Egeberg's subordinates, I felt a novel respect for him, and a tenuous bond. I realized suddenly how little I really knew of Menger's role in the bill's legislative progress, and I realized, too, that the NHSC story might be told in a wholly different fashion by Menger or someone else who had worked on the bill from the House side.

(One thing I didn't realize—although it soon became clear—was how narrowly the bill had escaped disaster. Had it not passed when it did, it would have been put off until the following week and lost irretrievably in the last-minute inundation of conference reports. Except for those conference reports and some emergency legislation, the EHPA was the last new bill the House passed in the 91st Congress —just as it had been the last new bill passed in the Health Subcommittee, the House Commerce Committee, and the Rules Committee.)

On the way back to the Senate through the Capitol's subterranean passageways, Anne and I had another unexpected encounter, this time with Senator Magnuson. He had just come from another frustrating day of the SST filibuster, and he was so tired and discouraged that the news of the House passage did not cheer him perceptibly. "I've just been fighting Proxmire all afternoon," he explained glumly, and invited us to join him on the Senate subway for the brief ride to the Old Senate Office Building. I cursed the SST silently, angry that the filibuster had deprived Magnuson of the satisfaction of seeing his health bill passed even as it had made that passage possible. (The next morning, however, he paused to savor the victory briefly—and to "apologize" for having been uncommunicative in front of my fiancée!—before resuming his lonely stand on the Senate Floor).

At the office, with Magnuson sitting exhausted in his private room, I called Bergman to tell him the good news. Bergman said very little—he too was exhausted. Only later did I learn from his wife that he had hung up the phone and, in relief, begun to cry.

5.

Mike Gorman, however, was in a mood to celebrate when Anne and I joined him for our delayed dinner. With both health bills safely passed, the weeks of tension were dispelled, and in addition, we now believed the President would have no opportunity to pocket-veto the legislation. Thanks to the SST filibuster, Congress would almost certainly remain in session until January 2, and we had made very elaborate preparations to ensure that Nixon received the bills by Saturday night, December 19. The President's constitutionally allotted ten days for considering them would thus expire on the night of December 31 (since Sundays don't count); with Congress still in session, he could veto the bills, or sign them, or allow them to become law automatically without his signature—but he couldn't pocket-veto them, allowing them to die unsigned. In the event of an outright veto (still a possibility, we admitted), Congress could override the President's action with a two-thirds vote of both Houses—a majority we considered eminently feasible, since both bills had passed almost unanimously in the House as well as the Senate.

Of course, our scenario hinged on having the bills reach the President promptly, and this explained our painstaking preparations. In normal circumstances, the alcoholism bill and the EHPA might not have arrived at the White House for many days, perhaps even weeks. Under standard parliamentary practices, an official messenger would have transmitted the House-passed bills to the Senate (this alone might take two days or more), and then Yarborough's Committee would have scrutinized them both. It might take Yarborough several days to assemble a quorum, and if his Committee did not approve the House amendments, another few days would be lost appointing a House-Senate conference committee and arranging a meeting. The conference committee might take some time to reach agreement on a single version of each bill, and then the House and Senate would have to vote on the conference reports. Even if Yarborough's Committee simply accepted the House versions, the bills would still have to be reported out, placed on the Senate calendar, and brought to a vote. The Senate Enrolling Clerk would then spend at least a day preparing official copies of the bills, which the Speaker of the House and the President pro tem of the Senate would each have to sign before another messenger took the legislation to the President. Even without unexpected delays, in other words, the bills might not reach the President until the eve of adjournment, and under such circumstances, Nixon might not be able to resist the temptation to pocket-veto them.

In cooperation with Congressman Rogers, however, we had completely short-circuited this lengthy process. We had arranged, first of all, for one of Rogers' aides to "hand-carry" accurate copies of the House-passed bills to the Senate and to the Senate Enrolling Clerk within hours of the House vote. Second, we had secured Yarborough's agreement to have the bills held at the desk in the Senate, rather than referring them to his Committee. In effect, the Committee had thus agreed in advance to any changes the House might make, obviating the need for a conference, and the House had obliged us in turn by amending the bills immediately before passage so that they reassumed their original Senate numbers (i.e., H.R. 19860 had become S. 4106 again). The Senate would thus have to do nothing more than agree, by a voice vote, to accept the bills in their present form. The Senate Enrolling Clerk, meanwhile, would already have transcribed the House-passed bills into their final, official form, and the necessary signatures could be obtained immediately after the perfunctory Senate vote. A messenger would be standing by to rush the bills to the White House, and they would reach the President within twenty-four hours of the House vote—i.e., on the night of December 19.

Feeling somewhat proud of ourselves for this ingenuity, Gorman and I finally relaxed (fortunately, Proxmire had relaxed his filibuster too, permitting the Senate to act on any legislation that did not pertain to the SST). Gorman flew off the next day to a long-delayed Christmas and New Year's holiday in the Caribbean, and I took a weekend off from work, after checking and double-checking that every link in our scheme was sound and that the bills would indeed reach the President on Saturday night.

When I returned to work on Monday morning, however, I received some sickening news. Far from having reached the President as planned, the two bills were still sitting at the desk in the Senate, not having been considered and not having been passed. Senator Dominick, I learned, had objected to the hasty action planned for both bills, and since Dominick was the ranking Republican on the Health Subcommittee, Yarborough had had to accede to his wishes. I never found out Dominick's specific complaint about the alcoholism bill, but we should have anticipated his displeasure with the House-passed version of S. 4106. For Dominick had offered the amendment in committee that deleted the National Advisory Council provision from the original bill, and yet Rogers had restored the Council in the EHPA. Dominick's legislative assistant told me firmly when I called that his employer would never agree to the Council, and that he would demand a conference so that it could be stricken from the legislation again.

Alone, with Gorman thousands of miles away and incommunicado, I had no idea how to overcome this newest and unanticipated obstacle; Magnuson and his other aides, who might have instructed me, were by now wholly preoccupied with the SST filibuster. It suddenly seemed as if S. 4106 would fail to become law after all, and for the most ridiculous and insignificant of reasons. To save the bill, I knew Magnuson and Rogers would willingly agree to delete the National Advisory Council provision as Dominick insisted; the Council mattered, but not that much. Unfortunately, however, only a conference committee could change the bill now, and a conference would almost certainly doom the entire legislation (indeed, the President could pocket-veto S. 4106 and the alcoholism bill if they reached him any later than *today*, December 21).

We simply could not afford a conference, but if I explained this candidly to Dominick's assistant, I might jeopardize the bill even further. For he probably did not know that the Administration opposed S. 4106: Glen Wegner's lobbying efforts and Steinfeld's negative testimony had been confined to the House. If he now learned the bill had problems "downtown," his partisan loyalties might lead him to make the pocket veto easier—rather than more difficult—for President Nixon.

Under the circumstances, I first tried to see if the Senate could not pass the bills in spite of Dominick. I hastily called Gene Godley, Yarborough's Administrative Assistant, who had taken over all Committee business now that Forsythe and Goldman had both left Capitol Hill. Godley said we were powerless; Dominick had the privilege of holding the bills at the desk in the Senate for another twenty-four hours. If he chose to do so, the bills could not reach the President until the night of December 22, which meant the ten-day period would expire on the night of January 2—hours after the 91st Congress adjourned. But Godley did provide one useful piece of information: Dominick, he said, had fractured his spine in a skiing accident over the weekend, and was confined to a hospital far from Washington. So it seemed highly unlikely that Dominick himself felt concerned about the Council provision of the House-passed bill; probably his assistant had intervened on his own initiative, although in the Senator's name.

Hoping we had correctly deduced our real obstacle, Bob Maher and I quickly concocted a small plot. He agreed to tell Dominick's aide, if he called, that Rogers would not accept the elimination of the Council under any circumstances, even in a conference. Then I called the aide again. Rogers, I told him, would insist on the Council provision, and consequently a conference could accomplish nothing— except to make it difficult for S. 4106 to reach the White House at all. I urged him to call Bob Maher if he didn't believe me. Instead of losing the bill altogether in the "adjournment crush," I argued, why not have Dominick negotiate personally with Magnuson later? Perhaps Dominick could persuade Magnuson to specify in the appropriations bill that no funds could be used for setting up the Council; it could exist in writing, but not in fact. "Dominick managed this bill on the Floor," I insisted; "The most important thing now is that it become law; after that, Dominick can talk with Magnuson about how the law should be funded."

At last Dominick's assistant relented. He called Godley and told him Dominick no longer objected to either bill. Godley quickly told the Majority Leader's office, and the Senate immediately approved both bills in consecutive voice votes. I called the Enrolling Clerk, who said the official copies of the bills had been ready since Saturday ("I thought there was a rush on these bills," he added, puzzled). Now the Speaker of the House and the President pro tem of the Senate could sign the Enrolled Bills, and the messenger could finally take them to the White House. Relieved, knowing the bills would still reach the President in time to preclude a pocket veto, I relaxed again.

But I relaxed too soon. On Tuesday, December 22, I searched the *Congressional Record* in vain for confirmation that the bills had been sent to the President the night before. Panicked, I called the Majority Leader's office for an explanation.

"You're not going to believe this," the Majority Leader's aide began cautiously, "but the bills are still sitting at the desk in the Senate. They have to be signed by the Speaker and by the President of the Senate, you know, before we can send them to the White House. The Speaker signed them all right, yesterday afternoon, and we would have had them signed over here like we normally do, by the President pro tem—whoever happens to be the Presiding officer at the time the bills are ready to go. But this time we got a call from Vice President Agnew's office. He insisted on signing the bills personally, in his Constitutional role as President of the Senate. I've never seen this happen before, but apparently it's all legal. If he wants to exercise his right to sign the bills, then we have to hold them for him until he comes up here to do it. And so far he hasn't shown up, even though his office called us about this yesterday."

We had just been the victims, as Bergman would have said, of a tackle at the goal line. I felt more as if I'd been slugged in the solar plexus with a large, clenched fist. By insisting on the Vice President's formal role as an officer of the Senate, the Administration had made it impossible for the bills to reach the President in time to prevent a pocket veto. Obviously Agnew had nothing to do with it personally; either it was a neat trick Nixon's advisers had thought up to create more pocket-veto "options" for the President (there were several other bills in the same position), or else it was the clever work of Glen Wegner. Whatever the explanation, the result was the same: the Executive Branch had frustrated the efforts of the Legislative Branch—and through a *legislative* maneuver.

I had dutifully memorized, in college, an observation of Professor Neustadt's: the distinguishing feature of American government is not (as the textbooks inanely repeat) "separation of powers," but rather separate institutions sharing powers. I had never really learned the lesson until now. The Vice President is the President of the Senate, yes; but he is also the obvious henchman of the President of the United States. As such, he had changed the entire legislative situation confronting our bill—to the benefit of the President and to the detriment of the body over which he (occasionally) presides. He'd only been performing his Constitutional function, the Administration could say, and—unfortunately for us—the Constitution granted the Senate no means to retaliate. So we could do nothing, except fume. But if someone had walked into Magnuson's office just then singing the praises of the Founding Fathers, I would have throttled him.

As it turned out, Vice President Agnew visited Capitol Hill late on the afternoon of December 22, signed S. 4106 and the other bills he had compelled to languish in the Senate, and then departed. His belated action did not help us: a delay of twenty-four hours had been achieved, and that was all Nixon needed. S. 4106 and its companions reached the White House at 10 P.M. on December 22. Congress would adjourn on the afternoon of January 2. And at 10 P.M. on January 2, unless President Nixon had signed it, S. 4106 would fail to become law. We had tried for weeks to make a pocket veto impossible, and we had lost by hours.

XII

A NEW YEAR'S RESOLUTION

1.

Washington Report on Medicine and Health has a limited subject matter—health politics—and consequently a limited circulation, but on the other hand, its subscribers read it very closely each week. Its uniqueness does not lie in its compilation of Congressional and Executive actions in the health field (information readily available elsewhere), but rather in the zeal with which its editor, Jerry Brazda, covers the gossip and personalities behind those actions. The subtitle of *Medicine and Health,* in fact, is "Backstage Talk in the Capital," very little of which fails to reach Brazda's ears. Talk is talk, of course, and talk is often misleading or erroneous, but even Brazda's critics will concede that they seldom leave the *Medicine and Health* mailing envelope unopened on their desks.

I read the final issue of *Medicine and Health* for 1970 a few days after S. 4106 had finally reached the White House, and found it full of items bearing indirectly on our bill.

One story, for example, kept readers current on developments in the "Egeberg Affair" (as Brazda called it); it intimated that Health and Welfare Secretary Richardson was trying to kick Dr. Egeberg not out, but gently upstairs. Discussion of the impending "shake-up" at HEW included speculation about the Surgeon General. "Steinfeld lost points recently," Brazda wrote, "when he went to Rep. Harley O. Staggers (D.-W.Va.) to do some unauthorized negotiating on the Emergency Health Personnel Act. Steinfeld has consistently aroused the wrath of intra-departmental enemies of the PHS Commissioned Corps." Further along, Senator Magnuson's name appeared. Magnuson had decided, *Medicine and Health* said, to remain as Chairman of the HEW Appropriations Subcommittee in the 92nd Congress rather than change to a different subcommittee. President Nixon, on the other hand, was reported to be considering a veto of the HEW Appropriation bill Magnuson had just steered through the SST filibuster—the White House apparently felt Magnuson had not learned his lesson from the last veto, for the funds he had provided HEW again exceeded the President's budget request by several hundred million dollars.

None of these tidbits interested me as much as the lead article on the front page, however:

> A Presidential veto threat hangs over several health measures sent to the White House during the pre-Christmas Congressional rush. Two measures believed in particular danger are the Emergency Health Personnel Act and the Alcoholism Bill, considered by the White House to be too expensive and not in keeping with Administration health plans. . . . Suspicion that the Emergency Health Personnel Act and the alcoholism measure are in trouble was heightened when Vice President Agnew delayed signing the measures long enough to make them, and several others, subject to a pocket veto after Congress concludes its session . . .

Nothing in this item came as news to us; only its tone and prominent position on the front page were disturbing. We had already begun trying to avert the pocket veto, and fortunately, we had worked on the same problem earlier in the month; only in the hours after the House passed the bill had we assumed, blissfully, that we had made a pocket veto impossible. Now we were back to our glum position at the beginning of December, before the SST filibuster: we had to persuade the President to sign the bill.

In previous weeks, we had already started our new lobbying effort. Magnuson had written Secretary Richardson about the bill regularly since the end of November, and he had made it clear in writing that he would hold Richardson personally responsible for the Administration's ultimate decision on the bill. More important, Magnuson had called Richardson on the morning of December 18 (hours before the House passed the bill), and he had obtained a useful if qualified promise from the HEW head: Richardson would not recommend a veto of either S. 4106 or the alcoholism bill, but he would not necessarily recommend that the President sign them, either—nor would he accept responsibility if Nixon vetoed the bills on someone else's advice.

Richardson's pledge encouraged us very little, but at least he had reversed the Department's outright opposition to the bill, expressed only a few weeks earlier at Rogers' hearings. More important, he had shortened our list of targets: if HEW would not recommend a veto, only the White House staff and the OMB still might. Even before the bill had passed, therefore, we had begun to explain to a number of people at the other end of Pennsylvania Avenue why the President should sign it.

Bergman first visited the White House in between our torturous waiting sessions in the House gallery. He had failed to persuade Governor Evans to write Presidential adviser John Ehrlichman about the bill (although he had induced a faculty colleague who knew another adviser, Daniel Patrick Moynihan, to write *him*), but at least he had a letter of introduction to Ehrlichman from some

Washington State Republicans who claimed to be good friends with the former Seattle lawyer. The letter got Bergman precisely as far as Ehrlichman's staff, no farther. But he reasoned with the young staff man at length anyway, knowing that S. 4106's proponents would probably never obtain a higher audience at the White House. The staff man knew about the bill, for he had read one of Glen Wegner's memoranda, and Bergman quickly found that Wegner had left several major misconceptions behind him. Speaking as a "private citizen" and a "concerned physician," rather than as Magnuson's representative, Bergman did not succeed in wholly overcoming the staff man's skepticism about the bill, but he found the discussion mildly encouraging and the time away from the House gallery well spent.

Next Bergman visited the OMB, a block away. The OMB provides the President with a recommendation on each bill that reaches him, and often the OMB's advice appears to count more heavily than that of the relevant Department and even the White House staff. Bergman discovered the man who would write the OMB's recommendation in the Office's Human Resources Division, and this official seemed happy to talk about the bill (although he modestly warned that in this case, Nixon's staff might have the decisive voice). The OMB official had also read Wegner's memoranda, and appeared surprised when Bergman described the bill in wholly different terms. Wegner had apparently portrayed S. 4106 as an ill-conceived panacea for the nation's health problems, but Bergman stressed the marginal and experimental nature of the proposed program.

After Bergman had flown home to Seattle, I spoke with the OMB official myself. "Tell me the 'pros,'" he said; "HEW only gave me the 'cons.'" We spent a full hour discussing S. 4106 in detail, and the OMB official surprised me with his insightful grasp of the bill. I had always thought of OMB personnel as indifferent little trolls, anonymously wrecking someone else's legislation in a dimly lit basement near the White House. But this official showed an understanding of the bill far more precise and sophisticated than any I'd encountered elsewhere in the Administration, even among the "health experts" at HEW (many of whom appear to feel that their M.D. degrees entitle them to pronounce on health legislation even without studying it).

At the end of our talk, I felt that I'd had a fair hearing, and the OMB official said candidly he favored the bill more than he had a few hours before. But he concluded with some blunt advice. "I'll tell you," he warned, "what I write may be less important to the President than political considerations. Don't forget that the alcoholism bill, unlike yours, at least had some support from HEW and the AMA at one time or another. Yet even the alcoholism bill is in deep trouble now. Your bill, I would say, is a very likely candidate for a veto of some sort regardless of what I recommend. If I were you, I'd keep looking for ways to convince the people at the White House."

The advice made obvious sense. HEW wouldn't recommend a veto (the Secretary had promised), and it sounded now as if the OMB wouldn't either. Unless the President simply acted perversely, therefore, he would veto the bill only on the advice of his politically sensitive advisers at the White House. We had to convince them that the President would be wise to sign the bill, or foolish to let it die.

We first tried to generate more pressure from the Senate. Before Bergman had left, in fact, he and I had attempted to persuade Senator Jackson to call the President about the bill. Jackson enjoyed extremely cordial relations with Nixon, for he had been the President's first choice for Secretary of Defense and subsequently his key Senate ally on military policy. Unlike Magnuson, who rarely supported the President on military issues (and whom, in turn, the

President had already made "the most-vetoed Senator of the Nixon Administration"), Jackson could place a call to Nixon and be certain of receiving a reply. Like Magnuson, however, Jackson had become deeply involved in defending the SST, and since both Senators desperately needed help from the White House to save the embattled aircraft, Jackson considered it an inopportune moment to ask Nixon for a favor on a wholly separate issue. With profuse apologies and some suggestions for alternative tactics, Jackson had therefore declined to call the President about S. 4106.

Other Senators, fortunately, were not similarly constrained. Senator Randolph, for example, repeatedly called Nixon's staff to make it very clear that he hoped and *expected* the President to sign the bill, and Randolph—as Chairman of the Public Works Committee—had a rather weighty voice. Senator Dominick too was soon on record at the White House urging Nixon to sign the bill; his assistant made amends for his recent behavior by calling in the name of his recuperating employer and pointing out to Nixon's aides that the Senate Floor Manager of S. 4106 naturally wanted the bill to become law. Congressmen Rogers and Staggers must have been similarly active, for when Magnuson called the White House staff himself he learned that a number of Congressmen, as well as Senators, had asked that their support of the bill be conveyed to the President. As an added measure, we mailed directly to the White House a copy of our press release on the bill's passage—a release whose phraseology we had aimed more at Nixon's staff than at the Capitol press corps.

Not all of our efforts were carried on at the official level, nor did we hesitate to use slightly unorthodox tactics when the opportunity arose. Shortly after S. 4106 passed the House, for example, I received a call from SAMA's Jeff Harris in Los Angeles. One of his medical-school classmates, Harris told me, was coming to Washington, D.C., to spend Christmas with his girlfriend and her family. The young lady, whatever her charms for Harris' friend, interested Harris and me solely for the accident of her parentage: her father happened to be one of Nixon's very closest advisers at the White House. Harris had suggested to his friend that if the girl's father seemed in genuine holiday spirits, a worthy topic of conversation for a guest to initiate at the dinner table might be S. 4106, the Emergency Health Personnel Act. Who better to broach the subject than a young medical student? And what better audience than a man who had the President's ear daily? Harris' friend proved receptive to the suggestion; a few days before Christmas, he sat in our office while I briefed him on the bill.

Humorous (and perhaps efficacious) as such a ploy might be, it symbolized how amorphous and unfocused our strategy had become once HEW and the OMB were "neutralized" and the White House remained as our sole target. We had, in fact, no real strategy at all; all we had were tactics, and while the tactics were eclectic and perhaps imaginative, nothing underlay them or bound them together except simple desperation. All we were doing was applying pressure from every conceivable source, trying to reach some imaginary "critical mass." We had not altered the expectation on Capitol Hill and among the medical press that the President would pocket-veto the bill now that he had a chance to do so. A pocket veto would thus provoke only disappointment, not shock or even surprise, and this very predictability of the reaction to the pocket veto only increased the likelihood that Nixon would resort to it. Somehow, and within a very few days, we had to create a political environment in which a pocket veto of S. 4106 would be an *outrage*. But how?

Unfortunately, we never had an opportunity to devise the strategy we needed. As they had so often in the past, events simply overtook us, and forced us onto the defensive. In football and war, the best defense is said to be a strong offense. Our problem was somewhat different. We had ten

days to determine whether or not, in legislative politics, a
strong defense might be a sufficient offense.

2.

On the morning of December 22, the national press revealed that the Nixon Administration was about to close
the entire Public Health Service hospital and outpatient-
clinic system.* The allegedly imminent action—which
friends of the PHS had long feared, but hardly expected so
soon—would be justified to the public as an "economy"
measure, the reports said. The Administration would contend that the PHS facilities were "underutilized" and "inefficient," and that the patient groups they served could
receive adequate care from private practitioners (perhaps
under contract with the government) or from the Veterans
Administration. The closures would harm no one, and save
money for the government—or so the Administration would
argue.

Neither the press nor Congress accepted this innocent
explanation of the Administration's motives or the consequences of the planned closures. Observers recognized that
if the closures took place, the PHS would be as good as
dead. And S. 4106, a bill to set up a new PHS program,
would be dead too.

Congressional reaction to the leaked story of the impending closures was consequently angry and instantaneous.
Congressman Rogers fired off a vociferous telegram to the
President, warning him not to proceed with any closures
without prior approval from Congress—approval that Rogers and Nixon both knew would never be forthcoming.

---

* The PHS system, although no longer vast, still included eight
hospitals and thirty clinics in some twenty-six states, serving approximately 600,000 people.

Congressman Edward Garmatz of Maryland, the Chairman of the House Merchant Marine Committee, announced that he would hold hearings on the matter the very next day, December 23, and he advised HEW pointedly that Secretary Richardson had better plan to testify about the Administration's plans (Richardson didn't appear, so Garmatz rescheduled the hearings for December 28). Whoever had disclosed the story to the press was obviously in for serious trouble if Nixon's "hatchet men" could discover his identity.

Congressional protests did not emanate solely from the House, either. Magnuson and Yarborough both wanted to register their opposition to the alleged plan, so Gene Godley (Yarborough's aide) and I immediately drafted a joint letter for the two Senators. To add emphasis, Godley obtained additional signatures from all the available members of Yarborough's Committee, and I then took the letter to other members of the Appropriations Committee (under whose imposing letterhead we had typed the protest). Alarm over the closure plan was so great that we even secured the signature of Georgia's Richard Russell, the Senate's most senior member and the Chairman of the Appropriations Committee itself. Russell's name had special significance, not only because of his position and his known reluctance to sign such joint appeals under ordinary circumstances, but also because (as the White House knew) he was on his deathbed in a nearby hospital. We acquired another important signature purely by chance: hurrying between offices with the letter in my hand, I ran into Senator Jackson in the hallway. Happy to forget the SST filibuster for a moment, Jackson unhesitatingly took out a pen and signed his name across the bottom of the page.

In all, thirteen Senators signed the letter during a hectic two-hour period. We could have found dozens more had not the logistical problems of running the letter from office to office been so time-consuming. As it was, the signers included many prominent Senators, and a number of Republicans on whom the Administration would ordinarily have relied for support. The Senators themselves might have settled for a letter that merely protested the planned closures, but since the fate of S. 4106 was so clearly tied to that of the hospitals and clinics, Godley and I had included a final, blunt paragraph:

> Congress has repeatedly stressed the need to keep the Public Health Service alive and vital, and to adopt it to new roles. Only yesterday,* Congress passed and sent to you an act that would expand the role of the Public Health Service in providing adequate medical care to this nation. This act reflects the overwhelming, bi-partisan sentiment of Congress that the Public Health Service should not only continue its present functions, but should be utilized in bold new programs as well. Any decision to close the existing facilities of the Public Health Service would, therefore, not only have tragic consequences in terms of health care in the United States, but would also be contrary to the expressed intent of Congress . . .

A special courier carried the letter to the White House. He arrived in the afternoon, on December 22—several hours before the official copy of S. 4106 that the Vice President had delayed so successfully.

3.

After our courier had left for the White House, another courier arrived at Senator Magnuson's office from HEW.

---

* "Only yesterday . . ." In fact, S. 4106 had not yet reached the President, but we did not know this, or learn of Agnew's intervention, until after writing the letter. As the reader will have noticed, some events in Chapters XII and XIII have not been presented in strict chronological order, but rather in a sequence designed to make them clearer. December 22, for example, was a particularly busy day; not only did we learn of the proposed PHS closures and the Vice President's action, but on the same day the events described in the next section (3) took place.

He brought with him a letter from Secretary Richardson. I signed for it, and tore open the envelope immediately. I found inside the single most disconcerting piece of correspondence in the history of S. 4106:

Dear Senator Magnuson:

Thank you for your letter of November 30th [!], which reviewed for me the current status of S. 4106, a bill to establish a National Health Service Corps and related bills pending in the Congress that would attempt to improve the distribution of health manpower resources within the country.

The problem of assuring that adequate medical care is made available to all Americans is one which is of deep concern to this Administration. As Dr. Steinfeld noted in his testimony, a copy of which is enclosed, this Department is currently engaged in a full-scale review of health policy options for the President's consideration.

We feel that it is imperative that any National Health Service Corps proposal, or other proposal for improving the delivery of health care, be considered within a total framework of current programs and planned initiatives in health care. Therefore, until our review of health policy options is completed and the President's recommendations on health are transmitted to the Congress, we recommend that the consideration of these bills be deferred.

With best regards,

Sincerely,
Elliot L. Richardson,
Secretary

The most remarkable thing about this letter was not what it reflected about the bureaucratic mind—responding three weeks late, by courier, with a jargon-filled distillation of Steinfeld's testimony, and recommending blandly that action which Congress had already completed be "deferred." The important thing was that Richardson had not written it—or, probably, even had it written for him. This suggested strongly that Magnuson's November 30 letter had not reached the Secretary himself: perhaps it had been routinely shuttled to the Congressional liaison office (Glen Wegner's province) or intercepted by some other official who imagined that *he* was "in charge" of S. 4106. That the Chairman of the HEW Appropriations Subcommittee could not be certain that his letters reached the Health and Welfare Secretary was irritating enough. But something else worried us more: Richardson himself apparently did not control Departmental policy on S. 4106. The letter, after all, was dated December 21, and three days earlier Magnuson and Richardson had discussed S. 4106 by phone; neither the content nor the tone of the letter could be reconciled with the phone call (nor would Richardson have referred to the November 30 letter instead of to the phone conversation itself).

Having received the letter, we could now understand why the White House staff and the OMB had continued to receive Wegner's "briefing memoranda" despite Richardson's promise not to recommend a veto of the bill (for this is precisely what Wegner *had* recommended). And if Richardson was not handling S. 4106 personally—if Departmental policy on the bill was being set below the Secretarial level—was it not entirely conceivable that HEW would "officially" recommend a veto after all?

We did not have to wait long to confirm these new fears. On the same afternoon, one of our most reliable "spies" called with disturbing news: HEW had drafted and sent to the White House "veto messages" for both S. 4106 and the alcoholism bill.

Magnuson and his top aides were still on the Senate Floor, inaccessible and completely preoccupied with the SST; I decided at once to call Mike Gorman, even though he was in the Caribbean and the story of the day's events would ruin his holiday. The call took an hour to go through, and Gorman sounded irritated and terribly dis-

tant when he finally came on the line. He was furious when
I told him how Agnew had wrecked our careful plans, for
he had left Washington thinking that we had absolutely
precluded the possibility of a pocket veto. News of the
"veto messages," however, caused him more puzzlement
than alarm; he didn't know how to interpret them exactly.
They might not mean HEW had recommended vetoes, he
pointed out: perhaps the normal procedure was to have
such messages on hand in case the President decided independently to veto a bill. Yet even if HEW had prepared
them innocently, he admitted, the fact that veto messages
were lying around at the White House might encourage
Nixon to use them. The really disconcerting thing was that
veto messages do not normally accompany pocket vetoes;
only outright vetoes require an explanation, since the President must send such bills back to Congress. If someone in
the White House had *requested* HEW to draft the veto
messages, we might be in even more serious trouble than we
thought.

Still, Gorman remained calm, and admonished me not to
panic. "The trouble with you amateurs is that you're all
such damned alarmists," he said. He decided that we should
determine first whether HEW had actually prepared the
veto messages, or whether our "spy" had simply heard a
rumor. Gorman gave me the name of one of his own friends
at HEW, a man he said would know—or at least be able to
find out—what had really happened. "Please relax," Gorman advised, and then added with mock gruffness, "and
Redman—whatever you do, just don't bother me again,
okay?" The tone of his voice indicated that he wanted me
to bother him again immediately if necessary.

I quickly called Gorman's friend, and realized at once
that whoever he was, he didn't trust the people in his office,
or even his secretary. He spoke with the forced nonchalance
of a man whose mistress has phoned during a family dinner.
"Yes . . . I see . . . well, things here are just about the same

. . . your project certainly has possibilities . . . I'm glad you called . . . yes, I'll certainly keep you informed . . . see you later." Not knowing what to expect, I concluded the one-sided conversation and simply waited.

Hours later, Gorman's friend called back. "I'm at home now," he said, "so we can talk freely." He told me that our information had been correct: HEW had prepared veto messages on both bills. Moreover, he said that HEW had definitely recommended a veto of the alcoholism bill—notwithstanding Richardson's promise to Magnuson. "I couldn't find out what the Department recommended on S. 4106," he said apologetically. "Plenty of people seem to know, but no one will talk about it." He concluded with a gratuitous remark: "Something funny is going on around here, you can be sure of that."

4.

On Saturday, December 26, the White House announced that President Nixon had pocket-vetoed the Family Practice Act, the bill Yarborough had written with Dr. Amos Johnson to train more family doctors. Congress had begun a Christmas recess on December 23, after staying in session continuously since early November, and no one had guessed that the recess would have consequences other than a brief respite from the SST filibuster. But Nixon had surprised us. I read the news the morning after the announcement, on the front page of *The New York Times;* I had gone to New York to spend Christmas with relatives, and the pocket-veto story abruptly ruined my holiday cheer.*

The Administration had never supported the Family Practice Act, but no spokesman had ever suggested that the

---

* Officially, the pocket veto "occurred" on December 24, the first day of the recess. The White House did not announce it until the 26th.

President might veto it. Congress had passed the bill nearly unanimously, and could easily have overridden an outright veto; with the pocket veto, of course, the President had denied Congress that opportunity: a pocket-vetoed bill is never returned to Congress.

I first reacted to the news with anger at Nixon and with sympathy for Senator Yarborough. The Family Practice Act had been Yarborough's final legislative effort, the small triumph with which he had concluded his Senate career. Now, in his last week on Capitol Hill, his victory had been wrested from him without warning. I could imagine his fury and dejection—and the gloating of some petty politicians within the Administration. My second reaction, more considered, might have been explained by an observation of Thomas Hobbes's: we humans are so self-centered, he wrote, that even sympathy and mourning are not sincere or altruistic emotions, but rather the lachrymose sentiments engendered by the thought of similar misfortunes befalling ourselves. For what disturbed me most about the pocket veto, I soon admitted to myself, was not what it meant for the Family Practice Act, but what it *might* mean for S. 4106.

The two bills, after all, had much in common. If Nixon was punishing Senators who had opposed him on key issues, or if he was simply pocket-vetoing Democratic health legislation when he could, then Magnuson's bill would certainly die over New Year's as Yarborough's had died over Christmas. The justification Nixon had offered—that Yarborough's bill would have further complicated "the almost unmanageable current structure of Federal government health efforts"—was as versatile as it was specious, and sounded suspiciously as if it had been prepared with January 2 specifically in mind. One thing was certain: the pocket veto of the Family Practice Act meant trouble ahead for S. 4106.

Only as I rode the Metroliner back to Washington that

night did I suddenly realize something more significant about Nixon's pocket veto: it might be unconstitutional. All at once, with the cold December landscape rushing by, I forgot about the politics and the personalities of the pocket veto and tried to remember what I had learned about the pocket veto itself earlier in the month, when I had asked Hugh Evans in the Legislative Counsel's office to explain it to me. At that point, before the interminable delays on the House Floor, we had thought S. 4106 might reach Nixon exactly ten days before Christmas—a day when Congress would certainly not be in session—and I had asked Evans whether this would give the President an opportunity to pocket-veto it. Evans couldn't give me a definitive answer, but he had referred me to the Constitution, two Supreme Court decisions, and the collected opinions of the Attorneys General. "I don't know what political problems you might encounter trying to stop a pocket veto," Evans had told me when he gave me the reference books, "but you certainly should take time to acquaint yourself with the legal problems—the pocket veto is a very complex issue."

On the Metroliner, I struggled to remember what I had read; I bitterly regretted having studied the problem so cursorily. Fortunately, I had been customarily tardy in returning the books, and they were still on my desk at the office, two blocks from the train station; I could read them thoroughly when we arrived in Washington. Even without the books, I could recall the most surprising thing they had shown me: despite what I'd been taught in junior high school, the "pocket veto" is *not* a "power of the President." It's not a power at all, in fact, but simply a name for the situation in which the President cannot return to Congress a bill to which he objects—*cannot* return, because Congress has adjourned. But Congress had not adjourned: it had taken a short Christmas recess. Did the recess *prevent* Nixon from returning the bill? I wondered. Why couldn't he have vetoed the bill outright and returned it, with Congress voting on overriding the veto when it came back on

Monday? I couldn't hope to resolve these questions on the Metroliner; I had to see those books again.

By the following morning, December 28, a hasty review of the sources Evans had recommended convinced me that the President had indeed acted unconstitutionally. More important, many lawyers on Senate staffs—including Hugh Evans, Gene Godley, and Carey Parker—had reached the same conclusion independently. True, the Constitution was decidedly ambiguous; the Supreme Court had never clarified the matter fully; and since the nineteenth century, the President had often asserted the "right" to use the pocket-veto "power" whenever Congress was not in session. But from the same sources—the Constitution, the Supreme Court decisions, and the opinions of the Attorneys General—we could easily make a case for the proposition that the pocket veto was wholly inapplicable during a brief recess in the midst of a Congressional session.

Although the arguments on each side of the issue were technical and extremely complicated,* we knew Congress

---

* The relevant section of the Constitution (Article I, Section 7) reads:

> . . . if any bill shall not be returned by the President within ten days (Sundays excepted) after it shall have been presented to him, the same shall become law, in like manner as if he had signed it, unless the Congress by their adjournment prevent its return, in which case it shall not be a law.

The key issues are a) what constitutes an "adjournment" under this section, and b) when does an adjournment "prevent" a bill's return? The Constitution unfortunately does not distinguish between different types of adjournment, but clearly an adjournment *sine die* (i.e., at the end of a Congress) is not equivalent to a "recess" or to the adjournment at the close of each working day. Similarly, the fact that the House and Senate are not physically in session does not "prevent" the President from returning legislation. Such a rule of construction, the Supreme Court said (in *Wright v. United States*, 1938), "would also require the man who is President personally to return such bills . . ." In the same decision, the Court also said:

> To say that the President cannot return a bill . . . in a recess during a session of Congress, and thus afford an opportunity for

would be justified in attacking Nixon for claiming to have pocket-vetoed the Family Practice Act—and we knew the President or his spokesmen would have to respond. The Administration would have great difficulty making a convincing legal case to justify its position, and the press would certainly give the debate prominent attention: the 91st Congress, in its efforts to halt the Vietnam War, had already made the Constitutional division of power between the President and Congress a major issue. For Parker and Godley, a protest against the "illegal" use of the pocket veto would serve two purposes: to prevent a further Presidential encroachment on the powers of Congress, and to resurrect, if possible, the Family Practice Act. For Magnuson's office, the protest also had a third motive: to create such a controversy over Nixon's pocket veto of one health bill that he would be exceedingly reluctant to pocket-veto another only a few days later, even though in the second case there could be no question of his Constitutional right to do so.

A Congressional outcry that would jolt the White House and command the attention of the news media would best serve all of these purposes. The protest began on the first day after the recess, December 28, with vociferous Senate speeches by Yarborough and Senator Kennedy. We devoted the remainder of the day to more extensive research, and the following morning I gave Carey Parker a long memorandum on the subject. The protest quickly gathered force. Parker drafted for Kennedy an incisive letter to Attorney General John Mitchell, setting forth the Constitutional objections and demanding that the Administration justify the President's action. Then Parker conferred with the staff of

---

the passing of the bill over the President's objections, is to ignore the plainest practical considerations and . . . to erect a barrier to the exercise of a constitutional right.

For a full discussion of both sides of the issue, see Senator Kennedy's remarks of December 31, 1970 (*Congressional Record*, January 2, 1971, S21817).

Senator Sam Ervin of North Carolina, the acknowledged Senate expert on Constitutional issues and the tenacious guardian of Constitutional purity in government. Parker also sent Ervin a copy of the memorandum, although undoubtedly the imposing North Carolinian had already performed his own, exhaustive research.

On Wednesday, December 30, the storm these preliminary efforts had signaled broke with full force. At a press conference, Senator Ervin quickly tutored a bewildered but nonetheless eager group of reporters in the Constitutional complexities of the issue, then declared flatly that far from being pocket-vetoed, the Family Practice Act had actually become law without the President's signature. Dr. Amos Johnson, a constituent of Ervin's who had flown in from Garland, North Carolina, informed the press at the same time that the American Academy of General Practice intended to bring suit against the Administration in order "to give the Supreme Court an opportunity to settle this issue between the President and Congress." The assembled reporters may not have understood the issue in detail, but they sensed a conflict developing and obligingly made the story Page One news across the country.

By Thursday, December 31, the arbiters of political controversy—the news media—began to demonstrate that the Congressional viewpoint on the pocket-veto issue impressed them. Newspapers editorialized about the "questionable legality" of the President's move, and pointed out that Nixon had already vetoed a surprising number of health bills during his two years in office. On the same day, Senator Kennedy received the Justice Department's reply to his December 29 letter and, to our delight, the justification the Administration offered for the pocket veto was even more tenuous and tortuously reasoned than we'd expected. The letter was signed by Assistant Attorney General William H. Rehnquist, putatively the Administration's top Constitutional scholar, and the press soon reported (on the basis of a "leak") that Rehnquist had in fact recommended to

Nixon, when asked for advice before Christmas, that he *not* pocket-veto the Family Practice Act. According to the "leak," Rehnquist had warned Nixon that a pocket veto might be unconstitutional, and that an outright veto would be a safer legal course. The press noted the discrepancy between Rehnquist's letter to Kennedy and his supposed advice to Nixon, and speculated that the advice had been rejected because the White House knew Congress would override an outright veto. (In fact, of course, the Administration also had matters of Constitutional precedent to consider, and a formal veto—unless made on a day when Congress was in session—would have been a major concession in the Executive-vs.-Legislative power struggle.)

These efforts did not exhaust our assault on the pocket veto; Hugh Evans, for example, drafted us a Constitutional amendment to clarify the issue once and for all, and we carefully let word slip to the Administration that the amendment would be introduced at the beginning of the 92nd Congress. Yet we doubted the pocket-veto issue would ever be resolved. Even if a proper suit could be brought, the Supreme Court might decline to hear it; the Court is cautious nowadays about intervening in conflicts between the President and Congress. Our "Constitutional amendment" was even more quixotic, a mere tactic in our psychological war with the White House; the issue was simply too arcane and technical to induce thirty-eight state legislatures to act, and who would be willing to devote the necessary years to such a crusade? Even if the Family Practice Act had become law without Nixon's signature—as Senator Ervin contended—the issue remained largely academic, for Congress has never mustered the Constitutional power to force the President to administer such a law if he chooses to ignore it. In a sense, then, the only tangible result we could expect from The Great Pocket Veto Controversy would be a meaty law-review article by some aspiring Constitutional scholar.

In another sense, though, the attack on the President's

"misuse" of the pocket veto had been highly successful.
Until the controversy had arisen, Nixon could have pocket-
vetoed S. 4106 and the alcoholism bill with perfect impunity. He could still pocket-veto them if he wished, and
on unimpeachable Constitutional grounds (for the 91st
Congress would have adjourned for the final time on January 2), but not without infuriating Congress and the Washington press corps. For a full week, lawmakers and editori-
alists had been castigating Nixon for pocket-vetoing a
health bill; if he now pocket-vetoed two more health bills
within forty-eight hours of peak criticism for the first, the
fact that he had acted constitutionally would not prevent
the controversy from re-erupting. The vetoes would pin an
"anti-health" label on Nixon and his Administration, and
the news media would carry the message to every home in
America. However uncomplicated a pocket veto of S. 4106
might have seemed to the White House a week before, by
New Year's Eve the consequences of such a step had become
a little more somber. And the President now had only two
days left in which to make his decision.

5.

If we'd known how great the pocket-veto furor would
become, or if we'd felt more confident that the threat of
further controversy would dissuade Nixon from pocket-
vetoing another health bill, we might simply have waited
until January 2 to see what would become of S. 4106. Already there were hopeful signs. Secretary Richardson, for
example, had testified at Congressman Garmatz' hearing on
December 28 that the Administration had reached no final
decision on the fate of the PHS hospitals and clinics; the
press unanimously opined that the Congressional protest of
the previous week had forced the reprieve. Perhaps the
same pressures, combined with the pocket-veto outcry,

would be enough to persuade Nixon to sign the two health bills remaining on his desk—or so we hoped.

But at the beginning of the week, we hadn't foreseen how fully the PHS and pocket-veto incidents would develop, and we had still had time for one last, desperate ploy. If only we could convince Nixon that he wouldn't have a chance to pocket-veto the bills after all, we might force him into taking some form of positive action: an outright veto, with its attendant bad publicity and the risk of being overridden, or a reluctant signing of the bills. But as matters stood, Congress could deny Nixon the opportunity to pocket-veto the bills only if it held its final session on Sunday, January 3, instead of Saturday, January 2.

The problem, of course, was that a January 3 session appeared virtually impossible to arrange. Not only does Congress rarely meet on Sundays, but the 91st Congress expired by law at noon on that day (since it had first convened at noon on January 3, 1969, and the life of a Congress may not exceed two years). The Sunday session would be too brief to have a legislative function, and few Congressmen or Senators could possibly be persuaded to attend. More important, the SST filibuster would definitely end on the afternoon of January 2—for Senator Proxmire had so agreed after wringing the concessions he wanted from a reluctant Senate Leadership—and with the passage of the DOT Appropriation, the 91st Congress would have no further business, no reason to come back into session Sunday morning. Even if, for some unforeseen reason, the filibuster failed to end, the President had warned that he would summon the 92nd Congress on Monday morning, January 4, to pass emergency legislation to keep the nation's transportation systems in operation until Congress resolved the SST issue. No one, therefore, had any incentive to attend a futile Sunday-morning session on January 3. No one, that is, except a Senator whose legislation would otherwise be vulnerable to a pocket veto.

Magnuson was such a Senator. And harried as he was by the SST filibuster, he was determined not to let S. 4106 die. He called me into his office on December 28 and pointed out that the Senate could perhaps meet in a pro forma session on January 3; all that was needed was one Senator to sit in the Chair and call the Senate to order, and a second Senator to move that the Senate adjourn. Such pro forma sessions were not unheard of, he added, although they had never been used for such a purpose, and in fact there existed a record for brevity of a pro forma session: six seconds.* "Senator Hughes sponsored the alcoholism bill," Magnuson reasoned, "so he should be willing to sit in the Chair for six seconds, and I'll move that we adjourn." And as it turned out, Senator Hughes was indeed amenable to such a scheme.

The pro forma session would have its limitations, of course. It could only make a pocket veto of S. 4106 and the alcoholism bill technically impossible, and if Nixon chose to veto either bill outright, Congress—with only two Senators in the Chamber—would be powerless to override the veto on Sunday morning, before the 91st Congress expired at noon. Still, an outright veto meant political problems for the President, for it would force him to issue a public veto message; the bills would die, but not quietly. So despite its shortcomings, the pro forma session seemed worth an attempt.

Almost immediately, however, our plans for the Sunday session encountered difficulties. The Majority Leader's staff pointed out that the House as well as the Senate would have to meet on Sunday, since a final adjournment of *either* House on January 2 would enable Nixon to pocket-veto the

---

* In mid-1970, before an interim recess, two Senators had made a determined effort to break this record, but the Senator voicing the adjournment motion had misspoken himself, and by the time he had phrased the motion properly, twelve seconds had elapsed.

bills (because the House, by its adjournment, would have prevented the return of the vetoed bills). More important, by custom the final session of Congress requires a set ritual, and the Leadership of both Houses must attend. "If Maggie can get the House Leadership to agree to a Sunday session," the Majority Leader's aides said, "we might be able to do it. Otherwise, we'll have the adjournment ceremonies on Saturday, the way we planned."

As it turned out, the weary Leadership of neither House would agree to stage the traditional adjournment ceremony on Sunday morning. In each House, however, we at least enlisted the Leadership's staff in a minor conspiracy to make the Administration *believe* a Sunday session might take place. If the President waited until the last minute, calling our bluff, he would still be able to pocket-veto the bills, but if, by chance, he reacted in advance to what he thought would be a Sunday session, he might take positive action of one form or another—and we knew an outright veto would not appeal to his political instincts. So although the possibility of fooling the White House was almost infinitesimal, we nonetheless made practically as much commotion about the "impending" Sunday session as we did about the pocket veto of the Family Practice Act during the week before New Year's. And, with a few selected phone calls, we made certain that people at the White House "discovered" our plans.

Now, at last, we literally could do nothing except wait, and hope.

6.

On New Year's Eve, Magnuson's Press Secretary, Duayne Trecker, drove Anne and me to a party on the outskirts of Washington, D.C. As soon as he arrived to pick us up, he burst into a broad grin. "Nixon just signed the bill!" he said jubilantly. "The White House called to tell us right before I left the office." At first, I didn't believe him. "Damn it, Trecker, did he really sign it?" Trecker insisted that he had; the bill had become law.

A snowstorm had hit Washington, and Trecker had to drive attentively over the treacherous streets. I just put my head back against the seat and laughed. I still couldn't believe that the struggle had finally ended, and that we'd really won.

We arrived at the party safely, and Trecker let us out of the car. As he did so, he took me by the shoulder and said apologetically, "I'm sorry, Ric. The President didn't really sign the bill. I was only pulling your leg. I couldn't let you leave without telling you the truth. But have a Happy New Year anyway."

Happy New Year. The phrase sounded sick.

7.

On Friday, January 1, Congress took a one-day recess for New Year's. The President, we were told, had gone to Camp David on New Year's Eve, taking with him all the bills on his desk. The White House would say nothing more. I wondered ruefully whether or not, had our bill reached the President one day earlier, he would have claimed it had been pocket-vetoed on January 1; Congress, after all, was not in session. But it didn't matter. Congress wouldn't be in session at 10 P.M. on January 2 either—the hour at which our bill would die, unless Nixon signed it.

On Saturday, January 2, the Senate came back into session for the final, cathartic time in the 91st Congress. On the Floor, Senator Proxmire extracted his final promises from his exasperated colleagues: the SST, it was agreed, would be voted "up or down" no later than March 31, and meanwhile the DOT would get its funds.

In Senator Magnuson's office, alone while the entire staff went to the Senate Chamber to watch the end of the filibuster and the 91st Congress, I took a deep breath and dialed the White House switchboard. Had the President signed the two health bills? I asked.

Minutes passed while my call was transferred and retransferred. Finally I was connected with an anonymous clerk who kept records of the President's official actions. The clerk kept me waiting while he scanned the lists in front of him. "The President just signed eighteen bills," came the matter-of-fact voice. "Let's see now, one of them was the alcoholism bill." Another pause. Then, "Oh yes, and one was S. 4106."

Numbly, trembling in a manner I wished I could control, I half-ran, half-stumbled to the Senate Floor to tell Senator Magnuson his National Health Service Corps bill had become law. The 91st Congress adjourned for the final time just as I arrived. The only Congress I had ever seen— the Congress whose birth I had witnessed two years before— was over. The dance of legislation was complete.

EPILOGUE

The law is flexible enough that a sound administrator could do a lot of good with it, but on the other hand, someone who didn't want to implement it could find loopholes in it . . .

—Jack Forsythe,
quoted in *National Journal*,
February 27, 1971

It is true that the Secretary of HEW may be reluctant to exercise his powers, that the necessary funds have to be appropriated by the next Congress, that numerous difficulties may arise in implementation, and that all may be subsumed in President Nixon's New Health Deal, once it comes. Even so we now have an embryo national health service supported by Federal funds: an AMA nightmare has materialized.

—*The Lancet*
(British medical journal),
January 16, 1971

A complete account of S. 4106 after it became Public Law 91–623 would require a book in itself, but it would be a book concerned primarily with public administration and bureaucracy, not the legislative process. The bill became a law less than six months after Magnuson introduced it; the law itself, thanks to the Nixon Administration, had no real impact until the summer of 1972, a full year and a half later. The events of the intervening months are worth recounting, if only briefly, for they illustrate that the dance of legislation never really ends, and that a law may intensify rather than terminate the perpetual struggle over policy.

Political considerations had forced Nixon to sign S. 4106 despite the veto recommendations of his top aides, but the Administration evidently hoped to ignore the new law. In a clumsy attempt to keep the public and the press ignorant, the White House made no announcement of S. 4106's fate— alone of all the bills on Nixon's desk—and in fact it took us nearly a week just to learn the Public Law number. This "silent treatment" kept the new law out of the news for a full week after Nixon signed it (on December 31, it turned out), but then it backfired completely. If the White House had announced the signing of S. 4106, the bill might have received a routine paragraph or two in the *New York Times* article that summarized health legislation passed in the 91st Congress. As it was, the *Times* learned of the new law only after that summary had been printed—and consequently at a time when the health correspondent had nothing else to write about. The result was a front-page article on January 6, with a two-column headline: LAW LETS U.S. PAY PHYSICIANS WHO ENLIST TO SERVE IN SLUMS. The *Times* article was reprinted all across the country, and it changed everything. Overnight, the requests for doctors poured in; Chicago alone wanted ninety. The HEW staff worked nights and weekends just to open all the mail. On February 18, Nixon went on nationwide television to say that he would ask Congress for $10 million for a new program, which he called the "National Health Service Corps." The "identifiable administrative unit" had been identified, if not established (later, when it *was* established, its explanatory brochure said the NHSC had first been proposed by Nixon).

In fact, Nixon waited several more months before asking Congress for the $10 million, and by that time Magnuson had already provided $3 million in a supplementary appropriation. When Nixon finally did ask for the $10 million, Magnuson's subcommittee voted $15 million (cut to $12.5 million in conference), so by midsummer of 1971, the NHSC had almost $16 million available—an amount, by Nixon's own calculations, that should have provided 960 doctors. But there were no doctors, not yet. There was an "interim" Director of the NHSC, a black Jamaican PHS career officer named H. McDonald Rimple, and there was someone to answer the telephone, "National Health Service Corps; may I help you?" Other than that, there were only delays.

The delays took several rather perverse forms. First, the Administration claimed that the Selective Service status of NHSC doctors was unclear; the program might not satisfy a doctor's military obligation after all. This misconception took a surprisingly long time—many months—to clear up. Then the Administration had difficulty selecting a National Advisory Council; on April 20, Secretary Richardson had announced that the Council would be named within a few weeks, but in fact it was not named until late November. The Council eventually included Dr. Nolan of West Virginia, but not Dr. Bergman, who was named as a "consultant"—and then never consulted. One proposed member of the Council was a woman who had signed a report saying the PHS should be abolished; she died before HEW got around to appointing her. The Administration's treatment of Council appointments had some other bizarre aspects, such as the following letter that William Hall, a Seattle health worker, received from the Republican State Central Committee of Washington State:

Dear Mr. Hale [*sic*]:

The Nixon Administration has requested political clearance
for your appointment as a member of the Health Service
Corps Advisory Committee [*sic*] of the U.S. Department of
Health, Education & Welfare, from this State's political
screening committee consisting of National Committee-
woman Mrs. Harlan J. Anderson, National Committeeman
Kenneth R. Nuckolls and the undersigned.

I am happy to inform you that you have been cleared by our
office and am confident that you will hear soon from Washington D.C., regarding this appointment.

> Sincerely,
> Earl J. Davenport,
> State Chairman

Despite Mr. Hall's "political clearance," he never heard
from Washington, D.C., at all. The Council, of which he
never became a member, met for the first time in December
1971—a year after S. 4106 had become law.

The Administration had promised to have NHSC doctors
"in the field" by October 1, 1971, and yet it missed that self-
imposed deadline. Later, Secretary Richardson promised to
announce the first assignments at a December 14 press conference; the press conference was cancelled. Despite con-
tinual pressure from Magnuson and Rogers, the anniver-
sary of S. 4106's signing passed without a single NHSC
assignment having been made. In January 1972, the first
two communities were selected—Jackman, Maine, and Im-
mokalee, Florida. In February, sixteen more areas received
NHSC doctors. A year after Nixon's nationwide television
announcement, in other words, eighteen communities had
NHSC doctors—despite the President's promise of 600
physicians and despite the growing backlog of funds already
appropriated for the program. In his 1972 "Health Message," Nixon again termed the NHSC part of "my new
health strategy," and promised that by "midsummer, more

than 100 communities around the nation will be benefiting from these [NHSC] teams." Yet the President requested only $8.4 million for the program for Fiscal Year 1973—less than he had requested the year before, and $4 million less than Congress had given him. As *Washington Report on Medicine and Health* noted, the Administration "virtually ignored" the NHSC in its explanation of the HEW budget. When, in May, the Administration finally announced that 152 NHSC doctors would be assigned to 122 communities in 39 states, the law was already up for renewal; the *New York Post* commented editorially that "perhaps the belated development is a kind of side effect of Potomac fever, brought on by the 1972 Presidential race." Senator George McGovern—who had declined to cosponsor S. 4106—said in a Senate speech in June that his Administration would greatly expand the NHSC; the Nixon Administration, on the other hand, testified against renewal of the law at Senate hearings later in the summer—an odd position to take on a program the President had claimed as part of his "new health strategy."

In short, the Nixon Administration's initial response to the NHSC was disheartening to those who had worked on S. 4106, and perhaps we may be forgiven for having asked ourselves, more than once, whether the man who took an oath to faithfully uphold and execute the laws had faithfully upheld and executed Public Law 91-623. Some details of the NHSC's early administration simply baffled us. The OMB, for example, promptly insisted that the NHSC "pay its own way" within a few years with fees collected from patients, although the law itself contained no such requirement. HEW, on the other hand, spent nearly $1 million of the first NHSC appropriations on "studies" by private consulting firms, despite a restriction in Public Health Service law that limits such expenditures to 1 percent of total program funds. And in one particularly noteworthy fiasco, the Department sent an NHSC doctor to the Seattle Free Clinic, then canceled the assignment while the doctor was actually on his way to Seattle.* (Later, after extended negotiations, the assignment was again authorized on a "temporary" basis.) Because of these and many similar incidents, a frustrated member of the National Advisory Council concluded in 1972 that the Administration's NHSC policy was one of "delay, distortion, dilution and discrimination." Strong language from someone whom a Republican "political screening committee" had evidently approved.

But just as publicity about the new law had immediately brought a flood of requests from needy communities, the operations of the NHSC itself, even at its limited level, immediately created adherents—and even converts. As *American Medical News*, the weekly AMA paper, reported:

> Public response to the program has been enthusiastic, and, in some cases, heartwarming. Leading citizens of Glenville, West Virginia, have spent thousands of borrowed dollars remodeling an abandoned church so their NHSC-assigned health care team might have a clinic to work in.
>
> In South Bronx, New York, two Corps physicians are helping the Montefiore-Morrisania Child Care Project to reach 11,000 residents of a large ghetto tenement district— adults as well as children—many of whom had never before received primary care.
>
> And in isolated Jackman, Maine, a Corps physician and his wife, a Swiss-born RN, work as a team delivering medical and nursing care—and some occasional veterinary services as well—to the French-American population of an area which had seen 14 MDs come and go over a period of seven years.

---

* The Administration has also spent nearly $1,000,000 of NHSC funds on "planning and study" contracts with three profit-making firms in Washington, D.C., despite a provision of Public Health Service law limiting such expenditures to one percent of the total program budget. Using Nixon's figures, the $1,000,000 could have put sixty doctors in the field.

In the face of these "unconventional success stories," as *American Medical News* called them, the AMA testified in favor of renewing the NHSC law at the same Senate hearings where the Administration announced its opposition. And the AMA went one step further. Recognizing that NHSC doctors need time off occasionally for continuing education, conferences and vacations, the AMA has organized "Project USA," a volunteer program of private doctors who will fill in for NHSC physicians on a short-term basis.

The AMA's endorsement of the NHSC may have been partially responsible for a switch in Administration policy in early 1973, at the beginning of Nixon's second term. In announcing its health plans, the Administration promised that the NHSC would be greatly expanded. At the same time, however, virtually every other health program in HEW has been slated for drastic cutbacks or outright termination. Needless to say, the NHSC is too limited a program to compensate for the wholesale disestablishment of Federal health efforts, which is what the Administration apparently contemplates. No doubt the NHSC's small size, and its ability to offset costs with fee collection, has had something to do with the program's sudden popularity at the White House. Perhaps, too, the President feels the need to move ahead with one highly visible and popular health program while attempting to dismantle so many others. But the notion of a vast NHSC in the context of an atrophied national health policy is too ugly to applaud.

The simple fact is that health spending has become, after foreign policy, the major battleground on which the impending struggle between Congress and the President will be fought. Nixon has signaled his intentions clearly, first by vetoing the HEW appropriation for the third time in four years, then by replacing Secretary Richardson with former OMB head Caspar W. ("Cap the Knife") Weinberger. If Congress makes a stand, streamlining its own appropriations process and resisting the President's grasp for complete control of yet another policy area, the struggle over health will become the showdown of the seventies. Although the outcome remains uncertain, a bitter fight is inevitable.

Against this unsettled backdrop, it is pointless to predict the NHSC's future. The program may indeed expand, as the President promises, or it may perish in the general melee. Regardless of the outcome, however, the NHSC has not failed. Even under its limited use thus far, the program has provided health care to thousands of Americans. The results, as the AMA has said, have been heartwarming. More important, perhaps, a permanent change in American health policy has probably taken place: government-paid doctors are caring for the poor and the needy, and the government itself has recognized, for the first time, its direct responsibility for health care. The dance of legislation, the struggling through mazes to a breathless end, has paid off.

What has become of the characters who played a role in the legislative history of S. 4106? Elliot Richardson has become Secretary of Defense. Dr. Vernon Wilson and Surgeon General Jesse Steinfeld resigned their HEW posts at the beginning of Nixon's second term. Dr. Egeberg has been replaced (although he remains a special assistant for health); John Zapp has been transferred to another post; Glen Wegner left his job at HEW, spent a brief time on the White House staff, then left Washington in a quixotic attempt to obtain the Republican nomination for the U.S. Senate in Idaho. William Rehnquist, who "justified" Nixon's pocket veto of the Family Practice Act, now sits on the U.S. Supreme Court; at the time of his nomination, Senator Kennedy said, "he did not see his role in the Department of Justice as assuring that its activities were either just or Constitutional; his only concern was that a reasonable advocate could make a tenable argument to support a given action, no matter how close to the edge of a Constitutional precipice." Kennedy, who has become Chairman of the Senate Health Subcommittee, has also filed suit against the Administration for its "illegal" pocket veto; the author of the victimized bill, Senator Yarborough, was defeated in the 1972 Texas primary in his attempt to gain a new nomination to the Senate. Lee Goldman is once again a member of the Health Subcommittee staff; Jim Menger, on the other hand, has retired and begun raising organic vegetables near San Diego. Congressman Schmitz, who attacked the NHSC as socialized medicine on the House Floor, became briefly a member of the House Health Subcommittee, then lost his bid for renomination to his House seat; in the summer of 1972, following the shooting of George Wallace, Schmitz became the Presidential nominee of the American Independent Party.

Congressman Rogers is now the Chairman of the House Health Subcommittee in name as well as in fact, and like Kennedy, he has shown himself to be a particularly active Chairman and a vigorous advocate of new health legislation. Senator Jackson made a determined attempt to win the Democratic Presidential nomination in 1972, and although some critics denounced him as a conservative or even a reactionary, the *Milwaukee Journal* pointed out during the Wisconsin primary that "his liberalism expresses itself in measures like the Emergency Health Personnel Act, which established a corps to improve health services in areas of urban and rural poverty." Senator Magnuson, on the other hand, seems happy to continue his work in the Senate, and he has added to his NHSC success with several other major health bills, including a dental-care program for children and his own national-health-insurance proposals. Now the third-ranking Democrat in the Senate, with nearly forty years of Congressional service behind him, he appears likely to remain a power on Capitol Hill for some years to come.

Mike Gorman remains the nation's leading health lobbyist, and official Washington has finally acknowledged his role publicly: in January 1972, a great appreciation banquet was held in his honor, and the guest list included virtually every living public official involved in health affairs. Characteristically, Gorman made light of the whole evening and promptly got back to work.

Abe Bergman continues to work on a variety of health projects at both the local and national levels, and in the summer of 1971 he provided me with a job at his hospital in Seattle, giving me an opportunity to see how health care looks at the basic level, remote from the politicians. In midsummer, we flew to Washington, D.C., briefly to see how the National Health Service Corps was coming along, and at that time, naturally, it was a disappointing trip. At the end of our visit, as we left Washington for the airport and our flight home, the cab turned off Constitution Avenue and we passed the Simón Bolívar monument, my favorite among the city's many equestrian statues. In the midst of our discouragement about the delays and inaction of the NHSC program, I looked at Bolívar and remembered, somehow, the only statement of his I had ever heard, the discouraged pronouncement that "he who serves the revolution plows the sea." I wondered, ruefully, if the same were not true of those who serve reform and the legislative process, but that gloomy thought was not the reason I felt sad. I felt sad because the cab was taking us to the airport instead of to Capitol Hill.

APPENDIX

Public Law 91-623
91st Congress, S. 4106
December 31, 1970

An Act

84 STAT. 1868

To amend the Public Health Service Act to authorize the assignment of commissioned officers of the Public Health Service to areas with critical medical manpower shortages, to encourage health personnel to practice in areas where shortages of such personnel exist, and for other purposes.

Be it enacted by the Senate and House of Representatives of the United States of America in Congress assembled, That this Act may be cited as the "Emergency Health Personnel Act of 1970".

SEC. 2. Part C of title III of the Public Health Service Act is amended by adding after section 328 the following new section:

Emergency
Health
Personnel Act
of 1970.
58 Stat. 695;
81 Stat. 539.
42 USC 248.

"ASSIGNMENT OF MEDICAL AND OTHER HEALTH PERSONNEL TO CRITICAL NEED AREAS

"SEC. 329. (a) It shall be the function of an identifiable administrative unit within the Service to improve the delivery of health services to persons living in communities and areas of the United States where health personnel and services are inadequate to meet the health needs of the residents of such communities and areas.

"(b) Upon request of a State or local health agency or other public or nonprofit private health organization, in an area designated by the Secretary as an area with a critical health manpower shortage, to have health personnel of the Service assigned to such area, and upon certification to the Secretary by the State and the district medical societies (or dental societies, or other appropriate health societies as the case may be) for that area, and by the local government for that area, that such health personnel are needed for that area, the Secretary is authorized, whenever he deems such action appropriate, to assign commissioned officers and other personnel of the Service to provide, under regulations prescribed by the Secretary, health care and services for persons residing in such areas. Such care and services shall be provided in connection with (1) direct health care programs carried out by the Service; (2) any direct health care program carried out in whole or in part with Federal financial assistance; or (3) any other health care activity which is in furtherance of the purposes of this section. Any person who receives a service provided under this section shall be charged for such service at a rate established by the Secretary, pursuant to regulations, to recover the reasonable cost of providing such service; except that if such person is determined under regulations of the Secretary to be unable to pay such charge, the Secretary may provide for the furnishing of such service at a reduced rate or without charge. If a Federal agency or a State or local government agency or other third party would be responsible for all or part of the cost of the service provided under this section if such service had not been provided under this section, the Secretary shall collect from such agency or third party the portion of such cost for which it would be so responsible. Any funds collected by the Secretary under this subsection shall be deposited in the Treasury as miscellaneous receipts.

"(c) Commissioned officers and other personnel of the Service assigned to areas designated under subsection (b) shall not be included in determining whether any limitation on the number of personnel which may be employed by the Department of Health, Education, and Welfare has been exceeded.

"(d) Notwithstanding any other provision of law, the Secretary, to the extent feasible, may make such arrangements as he determines necessary to enable officers and other personnel of the Service in providing care and services under subsection (b) to utilize the health facilities of the area to be served. If there are no such facilities in such area, the Secretary may arrange to have such care and services provided in the nearest health facilities of the Service or the Secretary may lease or otherwise provide facilities in such area for the provision of such care and services.

National
Advisory
Council on
Health Man-
power Shortage
Areas.
Establishment
Membership.

"(e)(1) There is established a council to be known as the National Advisory Council on Health Manpower Shortage Areas (hereinafter in this section referred to as the 'Council'). The Council shall be composed of fifteen members appointed by the Secretary as follows:

"(A) Four members shall be appointed from the general public, representing the consumers of health care.

"(B) Three members shall be appointed from the medical, dental, and other health professions and health teaching professions.

"(C) Three members shall be appointed from State health or health planning agencies.

"(D) Three members shall be appointed from the Service, at least two of whom shall be commissioned officers of the Service.

"(E) One member shall be appointed from the National Advisory Council on Comprehensive Health Planning.

"(F) One member shall be appointed from the National Advisory Council on Regional Medical Programs.

The Council shall consult with, advise, and make recommendations to, the Secretary with respect to his responsibilities in carrying out this section.

Term.

"(2) Members of the Council shall be appointed for a term of three years and shall not be removed, except for cause. Members may be reappointed to the Council.

Compensation.

"(3) Appointed members of the Council, while attending meetings or conferences thereof or otherwise serving on the business of the Council, shall be entitled to receive compensation at rates fixed by the Secretary, but not exceeding $100 per day, including traveltime, and while so serving away from their homes or regular places of business they may be allowed travel expenses, including per diem in lieu of subsistence, as authorized by section 5703(b) of title 5 of the United States Code for persons in the Government service employed intermittently.

80 Stat. 499;
83 Stat. 190.

"(f) It shall be the function of the Secretary—

"(1) to establish guidelines with respect to how the Service shall be utilized in areas designated under this section;

"(2) to select commissioned officers of the Service and other personnel for assignment to the areas designated under this section; and

"(3) to determine which communities or areas may receive assistance under this section taking into consideration—

"(A) the need of the community or area for health services provided under this section;

"(B) the willingness of the community or area and the appropriate governmental agencies therein to assist and cooperate with the Service in providing effective health services to residents of the community or area;

"(C) the recommendations of any agency or organization which may be responsible for the development, under section 314(b), of a comprehensive plan covering all or any part of the area or community involved; and

"(D) recommendations from the State medical, dental, and other health associations and from other medical personnel of the community or area considered for assistance under this section.

84 STAT. 1870

"(g) To carry out the purposes of this section, there are authorized to be appropriated $10,000,000 for the fiscal year ending June 30, 1971; $20,000,000 for the fiscal year ending June 30, 1972; and $30,000,000 for the fiscal year ending June 30, 1973."

SEC. 4. Title II of the Public Health Service Act is amended by adding after section 223 the following new section:

Appropriation.

58 Stat. 683;
81 Stat. 539.
42 USC 202.

"DEFENSE OF CERTAIN MALPRACTICE AND NEGLIGENCE SUITS

"SEC. 223. (a) The remedy against the United States provided by sections 1346(b) and 2672 of title 28, or by alternative benefits provided by the United States where the availability of such benefits precludes a remedy under section 1346(b) of title 28, for damage for personal injury, including death, resulting from the performance of medical, surgical, dental, or related functions, including the conduct of clinical studies or investigation, by any commissioned officer or employee of the Public Health Service while acting within the scope of his office or employment, shall be exclusive of any other civil action or proceeding by reason of the same subject-matter against the officer or employee (or his estate) whose act or omission gave rise to the claim.

62 Stat. 933,
983; 80 Stat.
306.

"(b) The Attorney General shall defend any civil action or proceeding brought in any court against any person referred to in subsection (a) of this section (or his estate) for any such damage or injury. Any such person against whom such civil action or proceeding is brought shall deliver within such time after date of service or knowledge of service as determined by the Attorney General, all process served upon him or an attested true copy thereof to his immediate superior or to whomever was designated by the Secretary to receive such papers and such person shall promptly furnish copies of the pleading and process therein to the United States attorney for the district embracing the place wherein the proceeding is brought, to the Attorney General, and to the Secretary.

"(c) Upon a certification by the Attorney General that the defendant was acting in the scope of his employment at the time of the incident out of which the suit arose, any such civil action or proceeding commenced in a State court shall be removed without bond at any time before trial by the Attorney General to the district court of the United States of the district and division embracing the place wherein it is pending and the proceeding deemed a tort action brought against the United States under the provisions of title 28 and all references thereto. Should a United States district court determine on a hearing on a motion to remand held before a trial on the merit that the case so removed is one in which a remedy by suit within the meaning of subsection (a) of this section is not available against the United States, the case shall be remanded to the State Court: *Provided*, That where such a remedy is precluded because of the availability of a remedy through proceedings for compensation or other benefits from the United States as provided by any other law, the case shall be dismissed, but in the event the running of any limitation of time for commencing, or filing an application or claim in, such proceedings for compensation or other benefits shall be deemed to have been suspended during the pendency of the civil action or proceeding under this section.

62 Stat. 869.
28 USC 1.

"(d) The Attorney General may compromise or settle any claim asserted in such civil action or proceeding in the manner provided in section 2677 of title 28 and with the same effect.

80 Stat. 307.

"(e) For purposes of this section, the provisions of section 2680(h)

62 Stat. 985.

Liability
insurance.

of title 28 shall not apply to assault or battery arising out of negligence in the performance of medical, surgical, dental, or related functions, including the conduct of clinical studies or investigations.

"(f) The Secretary or his designee may, to the extent that he deems appropriate, hold harmless or provide liability insurance for any officer or employee of the Public Health Service for damage for personal injury, including death, negligently caused by such officer or employee while acting within the scope of his office or employment and as a result of the performance of medical, surgical, dental, or related functions, including the conduct of clinical studies or investigations, if such employee is assigned to a foreign country or detailed to a State or political subdivision thereof or to a non-profit institution, and if the circumstances are such as are likely to preclude the remedies of third persons against the United States described in section 2679(b)

80 Stat. 307.

of title 28, for such damage or injury."

Approved December 31, 1970.

LEGISLATIVE HISTORY:

HOUSE REPORT No. 91-1662 accompanying H.R. 19860 (Comm. on
                Interstate and Foreign Commerce).
SENATE REPORT No. 91-1194 (Comm. on Labor and Public Welfare).
CONGRESSIONAL RECORD, Vol. 116 (1970):
    Sept.21, considered and passed Senate.
    Dec. 18, considered and passed House, amended, in lieu of
                H.R. 19860.
    Dec. 21, Senate concurred in House amendments.

91st CONGRESS
2d SESSION   **S. 4106**

IN THE SENATE OF THE UNITED STATES

July 21, 1970

Mr. Magnuson (for himself, Mr. Jackson, Mr. Cranston, Mr. Hughes, Mr. Kennedy, Mr. Nelson, Mr. Randolph, and Mr. Williams of New Jersey) introduced the following bill; which was read twice and referred to the Committee on Labor and Public Welfare

---

A BILL

To amend the Public Health Service Act in order to provide for the establishment of a National Health Service Corps.

1   *Be it enacted by the Senate and House of Representa-*

2   *tives of the United States of America in Congress assembled,*

3   That this Act may be cited as the "National Health Service

4   Corps Act of 1970".

5   Sec. 2. Title III of the Public Health Service Act is

6   amended by adding at the end thereof a new part as follows:

1   "PART J—NATIONAL HEALTH SERVICE CORPS

2   "ESTABLISHMENT OF NATIONAL HEALTH SERVICE CORPS;

3   FUNCTIONS

4   "SEC. 399h. (a) There is established in the Service a

5   National Health Service Corps (hereinafter in this part re-

6   ferred to as the 'Corps') which shall be under the direction

7   and supervision of the Surgeon General.

8   "(b) It shall be the function of the Corps to improve

9   the delivery of health services to persons living in com-

10   munities and areas of the United States where health per-

11   sonnel, facilities, and services are inadequate to meet the

12   health needs of the residents of such communities and areas.

13   Priority under this part shall be given to those urban and

14   rural areas of the United States where poverty conditions

15   exist and the health facilities are inadequate to meet the

16   needs of the persons living in such areas.

17   "STAFFING; TERM OF SERVICE

18   "SEC. 399i. (a) The Surgeon General shall assign

19   selected commissioned officers of the Service and such other

20   personnel as may be necessary to staff the Corps and to

21   carry out the functions of the Corps under this part.

22   "(b) Commissioned officers of the Service in the Corps

23   and other Corps personnel shall be detailed for service in

24   the Corps for a period of twenty-five months. An individual

25   detailed to the Corps may voluntarily extend his service ·in

1   the Corps for a period not to exceed an additional twenty-

2   five months. An individual shall have the right to petition

3   the Director (appointed pursuant to section 399j of this

4   part) for early release from service in the Corps at the end
5   of twenty-four months of service therein.
6   "DIRECTOR OF THE NATIONAL HEALTH SERVICE CORPS
7   "SEC. 399j. The Corps shall be headed by a Director
8   who shall be appointed by the President, by and with the
9   advice and consent of the Senate. It shall be the responsibil-
10 ity of the Director to direct the operations of the Corps, sub-
11 ject to the supervision and control of the Surgeon General.
12   "AUTHORITY OF SECRETARY TO UTILIZE CORPS
13   PERSONAL
14   "SEC. 399k. The Secretary is authorized, whenever he
15 deems such action appropriate, to utilize commissioned
16 officers of the Service and other personnel detailed to duty
17 with the Corps to—
18   "(1) perform services in connection with direct
19   health care programs carried out by the Service;
20   "(2) perform services in connection with any direct
21   health care program carried out in whole or in part
22   with the Department of Health, Education, and Wel-
23   fare funds or the funds of any other department or
24   agency of the Federal Government; or
25   "(3) perform services in connection with any other
1   health care activity, in furtherance of the purposes of
2   this Act. Should services provided under this subsection
3   require the establishment of health care programs not
4   otherwise authorized by law, the Secretary is author-
5   ized and directed to establish mechanisms whereby
6   recipients of such services shall pay, to the extent
7   practicable, for services received. Any funds collected

8   in this manner shall be used to defray in part the oper-
9   ating expenses of the Corps.

10   "NATIONAL HEALTH CORPS ADVISORY COUNCIL

11   "SEC. 3991. (a) There is established a council to be
12   known as the National Health Corps Advisory Council
13   (hereinafter in this section referred to as the 'Council'). The
14   Council shall be composed of twelve members appointed as
15   follows:

16   "(1) three members from the Department of
17   Health, Education, and Welfare, serving outside the
18   Corps, to be appointed by the Secretary;

19   "(2) three members appointed by the Secretary
20   from private life;

21   "(3) three members detailed to duty with the
22   Corps, at least two of whom shall be commissioned offi-
23   cers of the Service, to be appointed by the Secretary;
24   and

25   "(4) three persons who have received more than
1   minimal health care services from the Corps, to be ap-
2   pointed by the Secretary after the Corps has been in
3   operation for a period of at least one hundred and
4   twenty days and to be appointed from geographically
5   dispersed areas to the extent practicable.

6   "(b) Members of the Council shall be appointed for a
7   term of three years and shall not be removed, except for
8   cause. Members may be reappointed to the Council.

9   "(c) It shall be the function of the Council—
10   "(1) to establish guidelines with respect to how the
11   Corps shall be utilized and to consult with and advise the

12   Director generally regarding the operation of the Corps;

13   "(2) to assist the Surgeon General, at his request,

14 in the selection of commissioned officers of the Service

15 and other personnel for assignment to the Corps, and to

16 approve all assignments of Corps members;

17   "(3) to establish criteria for determining which

18 communities or areas will receive assistance from the

19 Corps, taking into consideration—

20   "(A) the need of any community or area for

21 health services provided under this part;

22   "(B) the willingness of the community or area

23 and the appropriate governmental agencies therein

24 to assist and cooperate with the Corps in providing

1 effective health services to residents of the com-

2 munity or area;

3   "(C) the prospects of the community or area

4 for utilizing Corps personnel after their tour of duty

5 with the Corps;

6   "(D) the recommendations of any agency or

7 organization which may be responsible for the de-

8 velopment, under section 314(b), of a comprehen-

9 sive plan covering all or any part of the area or

10 community involved; and

11   "(E) recommendations from the medical, den-

12 tal, and other medical personnel of any community

13 or area considered for assistance under this part.

14   "MANPOWER LIMITATIONS SUSPENSION

15   "SEC. 399m. (a) Commissioned officers of the Service

16 detailed to service with the Corps and other personnel em-

17 ployed in the Corps shall not be included in determining
18 any limitation on the number of personnel which may be
19 employed by the Department of Health, Education, and
20 Welfare.

21   "(b) Notwithstanding any other provision of law,
22 the Corps may, to the extent the Secretary determines
23 such action to be feasible, utilize the facilities and personnel
24 of hospitals and other health care facilities of the Service in
25 providing health care to individuals as authorized under this
1 part, and to lease or purchase such other facilities as may
2 be required to carry out the purposes of this Act.

3   "AUTHORIZATION FOR APPROPRIATIONS

4   "SEC. 399n. There is authorized to be appropriated
5 the sum of $5,000,000 annually to carry out the provisions
6 of this part; for the fiscal years of 1971, 1972, and 1973."

LIST OF ABBREVIATIONS

AAMC	Association of American Medical Colleges
ABM	Anti–ballistic missile
ACA	Americans for Constitutional Action
ADA	Americans for Democratic Action
AFL-CIO	American Federation of Labor–Congress of Industrial Organizations
AMA	American Medical Association
APHA	American Public Health Association
COA	Commissioned Officers Association (of the U.S. Public Health Service)
DOT	U.S. Department of Transportation
EHPA	Emergency Health Personnel Act
GAO	General Accounting Office
HEW	U.S. Department of Health, Education and Welfare
HSMHA	Health Services and Mental Health Administration (of HEW)

HUD	U.S. Department of Housing and Urban Development
NASA	National Aeronautics and Space Administration
NHSC	National Health Service Corps
NIH	National Institutes of Health
OMB	Office of Management and Budget
PHS	U.S. Public Health Service
SAMA	Student American Medical Association
SNMA	Student National Medical Association
SOB	Senate Office Building
SST	Supersonic transport
UAW	United Auto Workers
UCLA	University of California at Los Angeles
UPI	United Press International

INDEX

Adams, Brock
  as cosponsor of NHSC, 92–93,
    96, 148, 221–22, 249
  introduction of NHSC bill and,
    103–6
Agnew, Spiro, 156, 165, 217
  getting NHSC bill to Nixon and,
    258–59, 261, 269n, 272
Airport-Airways Development Act
    (1970), 196
Albert, Carl, 246, 247
Alcoholism bill (1970), 241, 242,
    245–48, 255, 256, 261, 264, 270–
    73, 280, 282
American Academy of General
    Practice, 278
American Independent Party, 294
American Medical Association
    (AMA), 47, 60, 62, 130–31
  alcoholism bill and, 264
  Knowles opposed by, 42

NHSC and, 39, 135, 152–54, 181,
    291–92
  1967 draft law and, 65
American Optometrical Association,
    249
American Public Health Associa-
    tion (APHA), 127–29, 134
Americans for Constitutional Ac-
    tion (ACA), 204
Americans for Democratic Action
    (ADA), 204
Anderson, Harlan J., 289
Anti–ballistic missile (ABM)
  scientists opposed to, 18n
  Senatorial opposition to, 56, 85,
    201, 203–4
Appropriations Committee (Sen-
    ate), 29, 45
Armed Services Committees (House
    and Senate), 33, 40, 83

311

Association of American Medical Colleges (AAMC), 113
Aviation Subcommittee (Senate), 196

Barclay, Robert
NHSC and, 128, 129, 134, 147, 184–85, 248
Barer, Stan, 29–30, 36, 37, 54, 86, 95, 107, 112, 166
Bergman, Abraham B., 142, 164, 169–71, 176
  as aide to Magnuson, 27–29
  AMA meeting on NHSC and, 152–54
  in averting pocket veto, 235, 236
  briefing on PHS by, 63
  characteristics of, 27–28, 54–55, 295
  correspondence with, 215, 217, 218, 231–32
  enlisting Johnson's aid, 148
  in floor-amendment strategy, 61, 65–67, 72
  HEW cooperation and, 43–50
  House passage of NHSC and, 243–45, 247, 252–53
  lobbying activity of, 219–22, 262–64
  national health insurance and, 184
  Nelson's NHSC bill and, 80, 81
  NHSC Advisory Council and, 288
  in NHSC House hearings, 222–24
  in NHSC Senate hearings, 114–15, 124–27, 134
  outlines NHSC, 30–38
  Rogers and, 89, 102
  Wegner on, 161–62
Bergman, Judy, 134, 169, 171
Bingham, Jonathan, 222–23, 248, 249
Boggs, J. Caleb, 160
Bolívar, Simón, 295
Bone, Homer T., 190–93
Brazda, Jerry, 74, 134, 153, 260, 261
Brown, Clarence, 248
Brundage, Avery, 206
Bryan, William Jennings, 26
Budget Bureau, abolition of PHS and, 64

Bullitt, Stimson, 19
Byrd, Robert C., 180, 207
Byrd Resolution, 207

Cambodia, invasion of, 55–58, 84, 172, 217
Carswell, G. Harrold, 56
Carter, Tim Lee, 99, 221, 223, 249, 251
Christensen, Richard, 194
Church-Cooper Amendment, 56, 57, 85, 217
Churchill, Winston, 208
Cloture Rule, 237
Commerce Committee (House; Committee on Interstate and Foreign Commerce), 106, 218, 221–31
Commerce Committee (Senate), 28, 106–7, 195
Commissioned Officers Association (COA), 129, 134
Committee reports, 140
Comprehensive Health Planning and Public Health Service Amendments of 1966 (Public Law 89–749), 51–52
Congress, 16–20, 41
  HEW relations with, 42–43
  1970 appropriations bills and, 216–17
  See also House of Representatives; Senate; and specific committees
Congressional staffs, see Senatorial staffs
Constitution, pocket veto and, 276n
Cooper, John Sherman, 157–59
Cotton, Norris, 177
Cranston, Alan, 104, 156, 303
Cromwell, Oliver, 189
Cutler, Jay, 139, 148, 149, 156–60, 248

Davenport, Earl J., 289
Democratic Party, 25, 201–3
Department of Transportation Appropriations Subcommittee, 178–80, 236–38, 281, 285
Dicks, Norm, 36, 37, 185

Dirks, Harley, 57, 75, 87, 109, 110,
111, 147, 169, 182, 234
career of, 44–46, 112, 179
enlisting support of Egeberg, 176,
177
in floor amendment strategy, 69,
70
forming NHSC without legislation, 43–49
getting Yarborough's support, 107
on HEW, 71–72, 88
lobbying effort directed at HEW
by, 174–75
"Doctor corps," 72, 75
Doctor shortage, 31–36
Doctors
government employment and
salaries of, 62
NHSC bill and, 100, 130–34, 224,
288; see also American Medical
Association
use PHS to satisfy draft, 64, 65
yearly number of graduates, 34
Dominick, Peter
amendment proposed by, 149,
151, 157, 158, 225
as Floor Manager of NHSC, 156–
61, 165
funding for NHSC and, 150–51
in getting NHSC bill to Nixon,
255–57, 265
Draft Law
NHSC House hearings and, 22–23
1967 amendment to, 64–65
PHS doctors and, 64, 65
SAMA proposal and, 132–33
Draft status of NHSC doctors, 288

Eagle, Miss, 110
Egeberg, Roger O., 65, 236
appraisal of, 48–49, 181–83
on "doctor corps," 72, 75
on executive concern for health
care, 41–42
in floor-amendment strategy, 61,
67–72
forming NHSC and cooperation
of, 44–49, 176–81
internal opposition to, 62, 252
NHSC Senate hearings and, 118,
120
Nixon inaccessible to, 46–47

replacement, 218, 261, 293
Wilson compared with, 142
Ehrlichman, John, 46–47, 236, 262–
63
Eisenhower, Dwight D., 25, 42n,
63, 128
Eisenhower, Edgar, 194
Emergency Health Personnel Act of
1970 (EHPA; House bill: HR
19246), 225; see also National
Health Service Corps
Ervin, Sam, 277–78
Evans, Dan, 236, 262
Evans, Hugh E.
forming NHSC without legisla-
tion and, 50–52, 54
NHSC draft bill and, 77
pocket veto and, 275, 276, 279
Executive Branch
Congressional directives and, 41
in legislative process, 16–19
Executive Reorganization Plan
(1968), 64

Family Practice Act (S. 3418), 126
273–80, 283, 293
Finch, Robert, 49
Fish and Wildlife Service, 27
Fogarty, John, 89, 146
Forsythe, Jack, 91–92, 110–11, 136,
139, 155, 256
coauthorship of NHSC bill and,
87–88
on flexibility of law, 286
in getting Yarborough's support,
100–2, 107–9
Frankel, Harley, 68, 74–75, 118, 132
Fulbright, J. William, 192
Furfari, Marguerite, 168, 174

Garmatz, Edward, 268
General Accounting Office (GAO),
204
Godley, Gene, 256, 257, 268, 269,
276, 277
Goldman, Lee, 111–15, 128, 130, 136,
139, 140–41, 149, 225, 248, 256,
294
Goldwater, Barry, 193–94
Gorman, Mike
aid asked by, 183–85
celebration dinner with, 253

Gorman, Mike (*cont.*)
enlisting help of, 147, 167
in getting NHSC to Nixon, 255
House-bill passage and, 241, 242, 244–48
idea of enlisting Woodcock suggested by, 173
recognition of, as health lobbyist, 294–95
on Staggers, 218
supports NHSC, 145–47
veto of NHSC and, 271–72
Graham, Billy, 194n
Grinstein, Jerry, 26–29, 195, 203–4
Gross, H. R., 243–48

Haddock, Hoyt, 147
Hall, Durward, 248
Hall, William, 288–89
Hammerskjöld, Dag, 206
Harris, Jeff, 131–32, 217, 222
Hart, Philip, 238
Hayden, Carl, 199
Haynsworth, Clement, 56
Health, Education and Welfare, Department of (HEW)
abolition of PHS and, 62, 63, 141, 142
alcoholism bill and, 264
cooperation of, in forming NHSC, 40–52
cutback of health plans of, (1973), 292
effort to overcome resistance of, 174–83
factions of, 61–62
feuding with White House over health care, 41–42
floor-amendment strategy and aid from, 61, 66–70, 74, 75, 76
forming NHSC and budget of, 28, 29, 40–43, 112–13, 261, 290
NHSC House hearings and opposition of, 226–31
NHSC Senate hearings and, 118–20, 135
public health and, 35
Surgeon General and, 141
veto of NHSC proposed by, 218, 262, 270–72

Health, Education and Welfare Appropriations Subcommittee (Senate), 75, 87, 178–80
"Health Message" (Nixon; 1972), 289–90
Health Package (Nixon Administration), 156
Health Security Act (1970), 183, 184
Health Services and Mental Health Administration (HSMHA)
doctors in federal service and, 64
in floor-amendment strategy, 66, 67, 70, 71
NHSC concept and cooperation of, 43–44, 47, 48, 50, 61, 178
in NHSC Senate hearings, 117–18
Health Subcommittee (House), 55, 99–100, 106, 294
Health Subcommittee (Senate), 55, 149–52, 294; *see also* Labor and Public Welfare Committee
Hickel, Walter J., 75n
Hill, Lister, 89, 129, 146
Hill-Burton hospital-construction funds, 235
Hobbes, Thomas, 274
House of Representatives
control of health legislation in, 89
invasion of Cambodia and silence of, 56
self-image of, 168–69
See also specific committees
Housing and Urban Development, Department of (HUD), 45
Huff, Sam, 20
Hughes, Harold, 79, 104, 156, 159, 282, 303
Humphrey, Hubert H., 202

Internal Security Committee (House), 243

Jackson, Henry M. "Scoop," 195, 202, 203, 238, 268, 294
support of, for NHSC, 79–85, 93–96, 104–5, 120–22, 155–57, 264–65, 303
Jarman, John, 89, 222, 223
Javits, Jacob K., 121, 139
John Birch Society, 250

Johnson, Amos, 278
  enlisting aid of, 148
  Family Practice Act and, 273
  in NHSC House hearings, 231
  in NHSC Senate hearings, 125–27
Johnson, Lyndon B., 64, 146, 159, 192, 195
Judiciary Committee (Senate), 78

Kennedy, Edward M., 104, 139, 156, 199, 294
  getting support of, for NHSC, 95–96, 98, 303
  national-health-insurance bill of, 142, 183–85
  pocket veto of NHSC and, 277–79
  on Rehnquist, 293–94
Kennedy, John F., 208
Kennedy, Robert F., 96
Kent State, 56, 84
Kimmey, James R., 127–29, 222
Knowles, John M., 42

Labor and Public Welfare Committee (Senate), 40, 53, 57, 79, 80
  changing Chairmen of, 164–65
  hearings of, 112–37
  meeting of, 148–52
  NHSC report, 140–41
Laird, Melvin R., 83
Langlie, Arthur B., 192
Lasker, Mary, 145, 146
Lewis, Flora, 217, 218, 226
Lindsay, John V., 96
Loan forgiveness, 150, 220, 224, 225, 229
Long, Huey, 33
Lucca, William, 129, 134, 184–85, 222, 248

McCarthy, Eugene, 195
McCarthy, Joseph, 193–94
McCormack, John, 103, 245
McGance, Phil, 173
McGovern, George, 290
McGovern-Hatfield Amendment (Amendment to End the War), 85, 201
McKinley, William, 26
Magnuson, Don, 194
Magnuson, Jermaine Elliott, 195

Magnuson, Warren G.
  ABM opposed by, 85, 201, 203–4
  antiwar amendments supported by, 85
  biography of, 26, 189–209
  consumer-protection legislation introduced by, 28, 195
  dental-care-program legislation introduced by, 294
  ecology and transportation legislation introduced by, 30
  on Finch, 49
  gun-control legislation and, 195–96, 201
  HEW appropriations (1970) and, 28, 29, 40–43, 112–13, 261, 290
  health-field legislation of, 29
  Jackson's relationships with, 83–86, 195
  as legislator, 80–82
  liberalism of, 201–3
  national health insurance supported by, 183–85, 294
  in nerve-gas issue, 85
  PHS closure opposed by, 268
  plans to switch chairmanships, 178–80
  pro forma session of Senate and, 282, 283
  unemployment-compensation legislation introduced by, 190–91
  voting patterns of, 202–5
  Yarborough and, 107–9
  See also National Health Service Corps; SST
Maher, Bob, 167, 169–71, 182
  assurances of passage of NHSC given by, 185–86
  in getting NHSC to Nixon, 257
  NHSC favored by, 89–91, 95
  NHSC House bill and, 219, 225, 226
  Rogers' opposition to bill and, 99–103
Mail
  answering, in Senate, 54
  invasion of Cambodia and, Senate, 57
Malek, Frederick V., 74–75
March on Washington (1970), 57
Maritime Council of AFL-CIO, 129

Medicaid, 62
Medicare, 62, 154
Medicine, opposition from organized, 37, 39, 223, 249; *see also* American Medical Association
Menger, Jim, 219, 245, 248, 251, 252, 294
Merchant Marine Committee (House), 268
Merchant seamen, 35, 129, 147
Metcalf, Jack, 26
Military, the, need to reassure, 83; *see also* Draft law
Miller, Jack, 193–94
Miller, William, 158, 159
Mills, Wilbur D., 206
Mitchell, John, 277
Morse, Wayne, 192
Moynihan, Daniel Patrick, 262
Murphy, George, 150
Murphy bill (1970), 220
Muskie, Edmund S., 202, 205

Nader, Ralph, 195
National Aeronautics and Space Administration (NASA), 45, 196, 197
National Cancer Institute Act (1937), 29, 78, 194
National health insurance, 32, 183–85, 294
National Health Service Corps (NHSC; Public Law 91–623; previously: Senate bill S. 4106 and—as Emergency Health Personnel Act of 1970—House bill HR 19246)
  amendment in committee, strategy for forming, 54, 57–58
  assignment criteria for, 151–52, 157–59
  averting veto of, 235–36, 243, 261–83
  commitment to, 75–77
  cosponsorship function and, 77–80
  creating, without legislation, 40–52
  draft bill to establish, 72, 77
  floor amendment, strategy for forming, 58–61, 73–75, 87
  future of, 293
  getting bill to Nixon, 253–55, 257–59
  in Health Subcommittee meeting, 148–52
  in House, 166–78, 180, 181, 185–86, 216–32, 238–52
  implementing, 287–93
  introducing bill for, 95–106
  limiting scale of, 39–40
  National Advisory Council for, 149, 151, 225, 255, 256, 288–90
  Nelson's bill and, 80–82
  Nixon administration opposes renewal of (1973), 290, 292
  outline of, 30–38
  as proposed by Nixon, 287–88
  publicity for bill proposing, 93–97
  returns to Senate, 253–55
  Senate hearings over, 112–37
  Senate voting on, 155–63
  studies involving, 290–91
  text of bill, 303–8
  as vehicle for book, 20–21
National Institutes of Health (NIH), 63, 64, 146
National Product Safety Commission, 28
National Science Foundation, 29, 194
National Transportation Act (1970; proposed), 29–30, 54, 179, 189, 208
Naval Affairs Committee (House), 192
Nelsen, Ancher, 221
Nelson, Gaylord, 103, 156
  getting support from, 79–82, 95–96, 98, 131, 303
  SST filibuster and, 237, 238
Neustadt, Richard, 11–14, 37, 258–59
NHSC, *see* National Health Service Corps
Nixon, Richard M.
  abolishing PHS as aim of, 63, 64, 128–29, 165–66, 267–69
  abolishing Surgeon General position and, 141
  Bergman lobbies aides of, 243
  delays implementing NHSC, 287–93

Nixon, Richard M. (*cont.*)
floor amendment and opposition
expected from, 61, 62
getting NHSC bill to, 253–55,
257–59
HEW appropriations vetoed by,
113
House Rules Committee and,
239–41
as inaccessible to Egeberg, 46–47
invasion of Cambodia decided by,
55–56, 172
on Magnuson's 1962 campaign,
194*n*
national health insurance opposed by, 142, 183, 184
NHSC as bill "proposed" by, 287–
88
NHSC opposed by administration
of, 118, 177, 178, 218
nerve-gas issue and, 207
1970 appropriations and, 216–17
pocket-vetoes Family Practice Act,
253, 258, 259, 273–80, 283
problem of veto of NHSC by,
235–36, 243, 261–83
public health care and, 42, 62,
128, 181, 229
Republican majority in Senate
and, 165
signs NHSC into law, 283–85
welfare reform and, 180
Yarborough's challenge to, 117,
123
Nolan, Robert L., 232
hearings on NHSC and, 130, 222
223
lobbying efforts of, 147–48, 167,
172–74
on NHSC Advisory Council, 288

Occupational Health and Safety
bill (1970), 137
Office of Education, 75
Office of Management and Budget
(OMB; former Budget Bureau),
41
NHSC and, 230, 243, 262–64,
290
Nixon Administration health
policy and, 62
PHS and, 65

O'Neal, Dan, 140

Palmer, Craig, 93–96, 99, 102, 217,
221
Parker, Carey, 139, 148, 248
national health insurance and,
184
pocket veto of NHSC and, 276–
78
Peace Corps, 34
Penn Central Railroad collapse,
245–46
Pepper, Claude, 242
Peralta, Jermaine Elliott (Mrs. Mag-
nuson), 195
PHS, *see* Public Health Service
Platt, Laurence, 34, 80, 92
NHSC project as viewed by, 68,
69, 71
NHSC Senate hearings and, 118
Platt amendment, 65
Platt proposal, 34–36
Pocket veto
constitutional issue of, 275–77
NHSC and, 235–36, 243, 261–83
suit against Nixon's use of, 294
Poison Prevention Packaging Act
(1970), 107
Pompidou, Georges, 206
President's Commission on Rural
Poverty, 33
Presidents, growth of power of, 16–
17; *see also* Executive Branch
and specific Presidents
Project USA (AMA project), 292
Prouty, Winston, 157
Proxmire, William, 252
SST and, 236–37, 255, 281
Public Health Service (PHS)
abolishing, 63–66, 128–29, 165–66,
267–69, 280, 281
creating NHSC without legislation and, 44, 47, 50, 51
as divisive issue in HEW, 62, 63,
141, 142
duties of, 35
Frankel's plans for, 68, 74–75
limited scale of NHSC and, 39–
40
NHSC House bill and, 224–25,
250
NHSC Senate hearings and, 125–35

Public Health Service (*cont.*)
  NHSC use of doctors in, 34–36
  1970 amendments for, 55
  1967 draft law and, 64–65
  private health care as outside
    scope of, 35
  removing, from NHSC bill, 142–
    44
  system of, 267*n*
  Yarborough and, 122–27
Public Health Service Amendments
  of 1970, 55, 57, 58, 90–91

Randolph, Jennings, 173, 174, 265,
  303
Rehnquist, William H., 278–79,
  293–94
Reuther, Walter, 173–74
Richardson, Elliot, 176, 180
  Egeberg and, 261
  new post of, 293
  NHSC and, 227, 236, 262, 270–
    72, 288, 289
  PHS closure and, 268, 280
  as a "progressive," 76
  replaced at HEW, 292
Rimple, H. McDonald, 288
Robison, Howard, 223
Rogers, Paul
  as chairman of House Health
    Subcommittee, 294
  forming NHSC and, 55
  in getting NHSC bill to Nixon,
    254, 256
  getting support from, 89–94, 96
  NHSC House bill passage and,
    235, 238, 242, 243, 245, 248
  in NHSC House hearings, 221–31
  opposition encountered by, 99–
    100, 107, 109, 119, 124, 133
  reaction of, to PHS closure, 267–
    68
  reenlisting aid of, 102–6, 110, 145,
    166, 167, 178, 185
  veto of NHSC and, 265
Roosevelt, Franklin D., 192, 197,
  208
Rules Committee (House), 239–43
Russell, Richard B., 87, 268

Saxbe, William B., 151

Schmitz, John, 250, 251, 294
Selective Service Act, 33, 36; *see also*
  Draft law
Senate
  academic literature on, 15–19
  cosponsorship function in, 77–80
  invasion of Cambodia and, 55–
    57, 84, 172, 217
  legislative function of, 15–19
Senate committees
  floor amendments and preroga-
    tives of, 58–59
  invasion of Cambodia and, 57
  See also specific committees
Senatorial staffs
  growth of (post–World War II),
    17
  legislative function and, 17–18
  qualities of, 90, 116
  workings of, 202–3, 209–15
Senators, types of, 199–201, 214
Shannon, Robert, 130–31, 153–54,
  222–25
Shultz, George, 47
Sisk, Bernie (B. F.), 242
Socialized medicine
  as divisive issue in HEW, 62–63
  source of opposition to, 250, 251
  to strengthen private practice,
    37–39, 60
Sorensen, Theodore, 204
Springer, William, 242
SST (supersonic transport), 36–37,
  122, 179, 196, 206
  filibuster over, 236–37, 243, 245,
    252–56, 268, 281–85
  Nixon and, 265
Staats, Elmer, 204, 205
Staggers, Harley O.
  getting support from, 105–10,
    145–48, 221
  hearings held by, 166–68, 171–75,
    178, 180, 181, 185–86, 218, 221–
    22
  introduction of NHSC by, 105–7,
    152
  NHSC House bill passage and,
    234, 235, 238–42, 245–48
  NHSC Senate hearings and, 130
  staff of, 169
  Steinfeld and, 261
  veto of NHSC and, 265

Steinfeld, Jesse, 67, 248, 249
  in disfavor, 261
  in NHSC House hearings, 226–
    31, 256, 270, 271
  NHSC Senate hearings and, 118
  resigns, 293
  support from, 120, 175, 176
Stennis, John, 122
Stevenson, Adlai, 25
Student American Medical Associa-
  tion (SAMA), 130–34, 224
Student National Medical Associa-
  tion (SNMA), 134n
Supersonic transport, see SST
Supreme Court, pocket veto and,
  276n–77n
Surgeon General
  compromise over use of, 143–45
  evolution of office of, 63, 64
  NHSC and, 120, 141–42, 225, 248,
    249
  Wilson and office of, 142–44
Swearingen, Noble, 128, 129, 134,
  248

Thurmond, Strom, 79, 116
Trecker, Duayne, 96, 283–84
Truman, Harry S., 146

United Auto Workers (UAW), 173,
  174

Van Ness, Bill, 86, 95, 105
Vietnam war, 55–58, 84, 195, 198,
  217

Wallace, George, 202, 294
Wegner, Glen, 135, 236, 256, 293
  as HEW lobbyist, 118–19, 175
  House Rules Committee and,
    240
  NHSC House bill and, 234, 235,
    238

NHSC Senate bill and, 161–62
  veto of NHSC and, 258, 263, 271
Weinberger, Caspar W., 292
Wilbur, Richard, 153
Williams, Harrison, 104–5, 303
Williams, John, 159
Williamson, W. E., 168, 169, 219,
  245, 248
Wilson, Vernon, 143–45, 175–76,
  225, 293
Wilson, Woodrow, 15
Women's Rights Amendment to
  the Constitution, 78
Woodcock, Leonard, 173–74, 231
World Environment Institute Reso-
  lution (1970), 29, 30, 54, 189
Wright Brothers Award, 196
Wright v. United States (1938), 276

Yarborough, Ralph, 164, 173, 294
  farewell party for, 247–48
  floor-amendment strategy and co-
    operation of, 59
  getting support from, 80, 82, 89–
    96, 100–2, 107–12
  in Health Subcommittee meeting,
    149–52
  hearings held by, 112–37, 178,
    224, 230
  HEW appropriations and, 112–13
  Magnuson and, 107–9
  national health insurance and,
    183, 184
  NHSC House bill and, 253–54
  NHSC passage and, 161, 239
  NHSC Senate bill on floor and
    absence of, 155, 157
  pocket veto of Family Practice
    Act and, 273, 274, 277
  PHS closure opposed by, 268
  quorum problem of, 136–39, 148

Zapp, John, 67, 69–71, 176, 293
Zionchek, Marion, 191